NATIONAL UNIVERSITY
LIBRARY   SAN DIEGO

STRONG ARTS,
STRONG SCHOOLS

D0465390

STRONG ARTS, STRONG SCHOOLS

*The Promising Potential
and Shortsighted Disregard
of the Arts in American Schooling*

CHARLES FOWLER

OXFORD
UNIVERSITY PRESS

OXFORD

UNIVERSITY PRESS

Oxford   New York

Athens Auckland Bangkok Bogotá Buenos Aires
Cape Town Chennai Dar es Salaam Delhi Florence Hong Kong Istanbul
Karachi Kolkata Kuala Lumpur Madrid Melbourne Mexico City Mumbai
Nairobi Paris São Paulo Shanghai Singapore Taipei Tokyo Toronto Warsaw

and associated companies in

Berlin   Ibadan

Copyright © 1996 by Charles Fowler

First published in 1996 by Oxford University Press, Inc.

First issued as an Oxford University Press paperback, 2001
198 Madison Avenue, New York, New York 10016

Oxford is a registered trademark of Oxford University Press

All rights reserved. No part of this publication may be reproduced,
stored in a retrieval system, or transmitted, in any form or by any means,
electronic, mechanical, photocopying, recording, or otherwise,
without the prior permission of Oxford University Press.

Library of Congress Cataloging-in-Publication Data
Fowler, Charles B.
Strong arts, strong schools: the promising potential and shortsighted
disregard of the arts in American schooling / Charles Fowler.
p. cm. Includes index.
ISBN 0-19-510089-1 (Cloth)
ISBN 0-19-514833-9 (Pbk.)
1. Arts—Study and teaching—United States.   I Title.
LB1591.5.U57F68   1996
372.5'044—dc20   95-23834

1 3 5 7 9 10 8 6 4 2
Printed in the United States of America
on acid-free paper

⸺ FOREWORD ⸺

C harles Fowler's writings have always borne a freshness of outlook that
stands the test of time. In fact, he often seemed ahead of his time, perhaps because he sensed from the beginning that arts education needed to be justified constantly in educational systems. He pushed the edge, urging arts educators to meet the challenge of changing conditions and not to
claim a free ride in the curriculum based on tradition alone. He advocated
that students guided to discovery of inner resources through the arts provide
the best justification for the continuation of arts programs in the schools.

Charles Fowler knew he was writing his last book when he wrote *Strong
Arts, Strong Schools*. The title encapsulates not only the focus of his book but
also the principal belief that provided a foundation for his life's work in arts
education. He was singular in his commitment to reach outward to those in
the community who ultimately decide on the inclusion of the arts in public
education. His gift of articulating and communicating the value of the arts in
education was unsurpassed. Based on this extraordinary ability and his experience with communities throughout the nation, he offers in this book rea-
soned arguments for why the arts have value for individual students and why
systemic inclusion of the arts in education makes for strong schools. In the
end, his metaphor of strength—strong arts programs in the schools will yield
strong schools—is an apt message for Americans, whose respect for brawn is
cultural bedrock.

Significantly, Charles Fowler, who could sound the alarm with the best
critics of education, here chooses optimism. Had he surveyed his more than
forty years in arts education with regret, this book would have been quite

different. Instead he makes it clear that arts professionals must always direct their message to the public. The arts are good for students. They provide something for individuals that nothing else can. They engage potential in students in ways unlike anything else. They provide an essential part of a complete education. Children and youth are therefore harmed, bereft of the opportunity for full development, to the extent that schools do not provide opportunities to learn the arts. That is the simple message Fowler puts into the hands of his readers. It synthesizes the best thought on the subject.

Strong Arts, Strong Schools was Charles's final published contribution to the ongoing quest to move the arts from their peripheral status in the school curriculum to a position where they play a central role in the general education of all students. Readers of this book may also wish to know that Charles Fowler left a financial legacy in support of arts education, specifically to support innovation through discourse, dialogue, and publication. A significant part of his estate and royalties from his publications support the Charles Fowler Fund for Innovation in Arts Education at the University of Maryland, where biennial colloquia, now named in his honor, began in 1993. The first probed social and moral values as a curriculum component in music education. The second (1995) examined the theoretical underpinnings of multicultural music education. The third (1997) explored the philosophical constructs of music education as praxis, hosting a gathering of the May Day Group. The fourth colloquium (in 1999) embraced all the arts in its consideration of the role of research in arts advocacy. The fifth (announced for 2001 as this foreword goes to press) continues the inclusion of all the arts as it addresses how elements of the community most effectively collaborate in formal partnerships to enhance school arts programs. Information about the Charles Fowler Colloquia at the University of Maryland can be found at the website of the Charles Fowler Papers in the Performing Arts Library:

<www.lib.umd.edu/PAL/fowler.html>.

If nothing else, *Strong Arts, Strong Schools* and the University of Maryland colloquia demonstrate Charles Fowler's understanding that the last word has never been and will never be spoken or written in defense of arts education. The best defense evolves from dialogue that continually extends our understanding of the arts experience into the public arena.

Marie McCarthy and Bruce D. Wilson
University of Maryland, College Park
August 2001

⚊ PREFACE ⚊

This is a book I have wanted to write for a long time. Like
many other professionals, artists and educators have been
quite content with communicating among themselves.
They tend to be insular and isolated, detached from the larger
world in which they operate. They seldom reach out to the decision makers—school-board members, school administrators,
teachers, and parents—and this isolation has cost them dearly in
terms of establishing broad public understanding and support.
One result is that naive attitudes continue to prevail, for example, the belief that the arts are extracurricular, that they are vocational education rather than a mainline part of the general
education program, and that they are strictly for the talented.

In recent years, arts and education professionals have tried to
make sure that the arts are regarded as basic, like social studies
and mathematics, but they have not been altogether persuasive.
To help put the arts on an equal footing, they have determined
that arts instruction be evaluated in the same way as other major
subjects are. And they have established content standards for the
various arts curricula—dance, music, theater, and the visual
arts—in keeping with the passage of the Goals 2000: Educate
American Act, passed by Congress in 1994. This act acknowledges that the arts are a core subject, as important to education as
English, mathematics, history, civics and government, science,
and foreign languages. Important progress is being made.

This book explores and summarizes what I have learned from my more than forty years in arts education. It expresses the frustrations I have felt during the past three decades watching the arts in schools expunged in order to give more time to "important" subjects. Never a truly flourishing enterprise, the arts in American schools have become increasingly downtrodden, slighted, and compromised, and there is little excuse for how they have been mishandled and ignored at the expense of American youth and American education. But their circumstances appear to be changing for the better.

There are very good reasons that we should try to make a better case for the arts, and my intent is that this book supply them. Certainly the main one is to improve the basic education of American youth. Students genuinely love their involvement with the arts. They like the challenge of striving to meet a high standard, being actively involved, and exploring their own inner resources. But not all students have adequate access to arts instruction, and this book is a cry of alarm with respect to the attenuated lives of these children.

The book is addressed to the public and to those who already have an interest in the arts but perhaps not a full-blown perspective on them. The intent is to provide insight into and understanding of the possible educational value of the arts and how they can and should complement learning in general and education in particular.

No one person knows enough about all the arts to write a book like this. I have therefore relied on a broad array of professionals: Rebecca Hutton, executive director of the National Dance Association; Barbara Wills, executive secretary of the American Alliance for Theatre and Education; and Nancy Larson Shapiro, executive director of the Teachers and Writers Collaborative. Judith Burton, professor and coordinator of arts and arts education, Teachers College, Columbia University, was especially helpful, supplying articles and information that provided great insight. I leaned on her expertise.

Eleanor Dougherty, education program specialist for educational research and improvement of the U.S. Department of Education, supplied important studies and information. David O'Fallon provided invaluable insight into and perspective on the current educational reform movement, and I have incorporated a number of his ideas. I want to thank Allan Alson, superintendent of the Evanston (Illinois) Township High School, for supplying information about that school system's arts programs.

Heading my research team was Aleta Margolis, an adjunct faculty member in the School of Education at American University. She and her staff of graduate students—Danielle Jones, Sandrine Krasnopolski, Enrique S. Pumar, and Katherine MacDiarmid—did a superb job of obtaining copyright permissions and compiling an accurate list of state high school graduation requirements in the arts. Gail Crum, a researcher at the Music Educators National Conference, compiled a list of these requirements, thereby facilitating our work. I could never have written this book without the intelligence and the effort this team brought to these efforts.

I also want to mention the enthusiasm and the encouragement of Maribeth Anderson Payne, executive editor for music at Oxford University Press, and the extraordinary professionalism of the editors and staff there.

I owe them all an enormous thanks.

C.F.

⌣CONTENTS⌣

STRONG ARTS, STRONG SCHOOLS

part one

CONDITIONS

T he arts in the schools do not, cannot, and should not exist in isolation. They necessarily must operate in the framework of general education. When they are part of the curriculum of American schools—and this cannot be taken for granted—inevitably they are there because they give students an indispensable educational dimension. Indeed, the relationship of the arts to general education is crucial to establishing their educational value and legitimacy and developing a vital and essential curriculum.

Just as important is the relationship of the arts to society and to American culture. The schools are a conduit for inducting youth into the established civilization, and the arts are a distinctive, profound, and pervasive part of that civilization. Schools are negligent if they do not take that responsibility seriously and make that interrelationship clear. The arts, like other subjects in the curriculum of American schools, are affiliated with the schools' important responsibility to pass on the civilization—in this case, our rich and rewarding cultural heritage—to the next generation. The connection of the arts to the basic educational curriculum is crucial, but this relationship needs to be made explicit, convincing, even pivotal.

What impediments prevent the arts from being thought of as basic to the schools' general education curriculum? The public does not always value the arts in the same way that they do science, mathematics, even history. Diminishing budgets cause boards of education to make choices, and where the arts are only marginally valued, they often take the brunt of cutbacks. In such schools the arts exist in an indifferent, even hostile, environment. Their educational importance is viewed as expendable.

Generally, people do not see any relationship between the arts and American influence and affluence. They may acknowledge that the arts can lead to a more satisfying life, but their connection to what are truly important—jobs and livelihood, the global economy, and our ability to compete in world markets—may escape them. That relationship needs to be made explicit, not a simple task.

Classroom teachers, pressured to teach the traditional basics and to make certain that their students excel on standardized tests, sometimes view the arts as frivolous, distracting students from the real and important learning that is the main and required business of education. They often do not recognize the substance of arts study or the breadth it can add to vision and comprehension.

In the arts, as in the sciences, we do not have to operate unilaterally. Just as biology, chemistry, and physics operate under the broad banner of the sciences, the arts—creative writing, dance, music, theater, and visual arts (including the media)—are a universe of separate but related areas of human insight. No single art can fully escape its relationship to the other arts, nor should it try. The arts provide multiple ways to experience, understand, and express the world and our relationship to it. They are one of the fundamental repositories of human wisdom. They educate the imagination and develop originality. They represent significant ways for students to discern, express, communicate, figure out, and understand the human universe. The national standards for arts education, developed by a consortium of national arts education associations and published in 1994, specify this interrelationship of the arts in several ways: first, by making a strong case for the arts as a whole; second, by establishing standards for all the arts; and third, by recommending interdisciplinary curricula.

Understanding and respecting these connections between

the arts and general education, as well as among the various arts, are essential to the development and presentation of all the arts in the schools. Without that perspective, art will be disconnected from the larger world in which it operates. Consequently, it will become narrower in scope and a less valued part of a comprehensive curriculum of general education.

Interlocking the arts with American society, with our economic influence and affluence, and with education as a whole is an illuminating idea. Understanding the context of the arts and their possibilities will lead to an informed and broadened perception of them and will place the arts in the mainstream of the human struggle for a better and more humane tomorrow. The chapters in Part I explore the state and the promise of arts education; the important, though seldom understood, relationship of the arts to the economy; and the way the arts and education, functioning dynamically, can be improved.

_ chapter one _

ONE NATION, UNDERCULTURED
AND UNDERQUALIFIED

The arts have enormous educational potential, presenting a multitude of
learning and teaching opportunities. Students who are involved in the
arts are more motivated, more engaged, more sensitive, and more focused,
creative, and responsible. They perform better in all aspects of school,
including academic achievement. The SPECTRA (Schools, Parents, Educators, Children, Teachers Rediscover the Arts) program, for example, is a
four-year model program in arts education conducted in two elementary
schools, Hamilton and Fairfield, in southwestern Ohio.[1] The program
infuses the arts throughout the curriculum. In order to raise the arts to curricular significance, an hour a day for each student is dedicated to art, music,
dance, drama, or the media arts. A thorough evaluation of this program
reveals that it has improved attendance and reduced discipline problems. To
establish the validity of the program, SPECTRA students were compared with
two control schools that did not alter their curricula. All together, more than
600 students at three grade levels in four schools participated in the study.
The SPECTRA group scored considerably higher in math comprehension and
demonstrated a significantly higher degree of improvement on total reading
scores, reading vocabulary, reading comprehension, and math comprehension than students in the control schools did. As might be expected, SPECTRA
students made significantly more improvement in total arts appreciation than
did either of the control groups. The report concluded that after only one
year of the program, "sufficient evidence exists to support the idea that arts
in schools is a significant contributor to the academic achievement and affective well-being of children." These are not idle claims but the result of an
empirical evaluation of the program in 1992/1993.

Even though the SPECTRA program shows the educational potential of

7

the arts, the arts have not prospered in American schools. Indeed, as I observed in an earlier book,

> The possible significance of the arts in the education of American youth is largely unrecognized, often ignored, generally underrated. For the past decade, perhaps longer, arts programs in many American schools have been systematically dismantled. Access to the vast treasury of American and world culture is denied to many American children with the result that their education is incomplete, their minds less enlightened, their lives less enlivened.[2]

A recent report on the arts in education found that the arts are being pushed to the curricular periphery.[3] *Toward Civilization*, a report on arts education conducted by the National Endowment for the Arts in 1988, gives further evidence of the paucity of support for the arts in public education. This report states that "the artistic heritage that is ours and the opportunities to contribute significantly to its evolution are being lost to our young people."[4] One nation, undercultured and underqualified. Is this the best we can do?

THE STATUS OF THE ARTS

The unrelenting pressure on schools to serve corporate and commercial needs has established an elite core of subjects in American schools that are labeled *the basics*, the subjects that every student must master. But the arts are seldom admitted to this club, a shutout that has angered those who recognize their enormous educational potential. Why can't the arts command anything more than marginal status in the public educational system?

In 1985 the Getty Center for Education in the Arts launched a nation-wide effort to make art education more academic, with the thought that increased rigor and a broader curriculum encompassing aesthetics, art history, and art criticism as well as the development of the skills of production would alter perceptions of art education and establish it as a basic part of the curriculum. The center believes that if we want art education to be a basic subject, we must make it look and act like one. That is what gains respect for a subject.[5] These efforts are still under way. Clearly, finding the way to become basic is the central galvanizing issue in the field of arts education today.

What has kept the arts on the fringes of educational respectability? What keeps them from being basic? Is it that our educational and corporate leaders do not equate the arts with mentation? Is it that they do not associate the arts with the particular utilitarian abilities that they expect education to impart? The fundamental purpose of American schooling today, whether or not you agree with it, is preparation for work. We have been advised to hold out against the tidal wave of the economic imperative,[6] but are our economic problems a temporary malady? We must remember that schools have been serving the nation's economic agenda for at least thirty years. As educational priorities have shifted to serve the needs of commerce and international competition, the arts appear more and more frivolous, totally superfluous to these controlling purposes. This is the reality we face in the arts.

Arts electives are being replaced by computer science, more math, more English, more history, exactly what economic interests dictate. Many of our school systems have accepted the concepts explored in *A Nation at Risk: The Imperative for Educational Reform*,[7] and this is why making study of the arts more serious and sequential or focused on the acquisition of knowledge, as the National Endowment for the Arts advocates,[8] is not enough. Please note that I did not say it is wrong; it is just not enough. Being more intellectual and demanding about the way we teach the arts will not alone succeed in winning them basic status, because the arts were not excluded for only those reasons. Rather, they were excluded because in light of the main purpose of education, they appear expendable, extraneous, and nonessential.

The goal of attaining the status of a basic subject by teaching the arts as rigorous disciplines is somewhat misguided. I say "somewhat" because enriching the art curriculum has, by and large, been good in and of itself. But to be basic, the arts will have to show the corporate world that what they are asking of education is too limited for their own good. We will have to point them and the schools to a larger universe. We will have to show them that the arts can serve our country and our youth in incredibly important ways— ways that will enhance education, enhance life, and, yes, enhance the ability of people to be productive citizens. We must win the schools *and* industry. If we choose not to, the status of the arts will continue to remain marginal or even decline further. After all, we have a responsibility to make certain that the talents and human potential of our children are realized, not squandered.

The heartening news is that the arts already do connect with this larger educational agenda in rather startling ways. In spite of the deeply ingrained "arts-for-arts'-sake" attitude that prevails among those who teach the arts, education in the arts actually does impart some very practical habits of thought. I want to suggest five areas in which I think the arts make natural and unique connections with the deeper purposes of education. All relate directly to mentation in every art form and, at the same time, develop abilities that are generally not acquired from other subjects.

Thinking Receptively

Perhaps the thing that the arts do best, at their best, is open the doors to learning. They open our eyes, our ears, our feelings, our minds. They make us more sensitive and aware. Encounters with music, for example, invite us to explore worlds of meaning that lie right next to the curtain that the old Persian proverb says has never been drawn aside. They help us break through the linguistic, logical/mathematical restrictions and devotions of public education. The arts awaken our curiosity about the mysteries of the intuitive and imaginative worlds beyond the obvious, the crass, the commercial, and the simplistic black-and-white views that prevail in so many American classrooms. They invite us to join in adventures that quicken our senses and our minds, that enliven us by exciting our exploratory nature. As Maxine Greene, holder of the William F. Russell Chair in the Foundations of Education at Teachers College, Columbia University, stated, "The more the listener can hear, the greater the likelihood of unconcealment. We pour our energies into a work to bring it alive ... to go beyond the confinement of a single reality."[9] Through such encounters, children learn to be open to experience, and they discover that the arts illuminate life in all its mystery, misery, delight, pity, and wonder.

Thinking Aesthetically

Success in American manufacturing means creating reliable, well-made products. That means that all along the line, people must *care* about what they are doing. The arts teach that kind of caring. Study of any of the arts can furnish people with a crucial aesthetic metaphor of what life at its best might be. The arts can transform the way we think and operate. They can provide an aesthetic value orientation. Ideally, the aesthetics of the arts become the aesthetics of life. Through the arts we appreciate how all the elements—the details—make the expressive whole and how important those details are. And in the process, we learn how to handle frustration and failure in pursuit of our goals.

The aesthetic awareness we learn through study of the arts becomes a way we relate to the world. Our aesthetic view becomes a natural and important part of our encounter with life. It is the way we bring our sensual and rational beings together to come to terms with the world around us. The arts are a celebration of excellence. They are the way we learn to release our positive energies toward an aesthetic result.

The important point here is the possible transfer of our aesthetic frame of reference from the arts to other realms of life, something that educators have tended to overlook. The ability to think aesthetically, applied across the board, can make a substantial difference in the quality of life. That is why the arts are *not* the domain of the privileged, the rich, or the talented but belong to us all. It is in the best interests of business—their self-interest—to see that all their employees have a substantial education in the arts.

Thinking Creatively

If there is a fourth R that needs to be added to the traditional three, it is Reasoning.[10] Many Americans cannot think straight, and American business is suffering for it. Here the arts can make another unique contribution. Particularly in their creative aspects, the arts require abstract reasoning. Among all the subjects in the curriculum, the arts are unique in that there are fewer absolutely right or wrong answers. It is precisely the ambiguities of these forms of symbolic expression that require us to exercise a higher order of thought processes. When is a poem, a painting, or a musical composition finished? When is the interpretation of music perfected? What makes choreography and music meld? When is a painting fully understood? What gestures best express a particular character? What is appropriate? These are the kinds of complex problems, as Elliot Eisner reminds us, that we deal with in our personal relations with others at home and in the workplace.[11] Two plus two equals four is not relevant to the kinds of difficult thinking and decision making we are so often required to make in the adult world. The arts can provide opportunities for this higher form of reasoning if we choose to teach them so that they do.

Art is an invitation to exercise the same intellectual skills as the artist does, to envision, to set goals, to determine technique and exercise it, to figure out, to evaluate, to revise, to continue to imagine and solve problems—in a word, to *create*. In this act there is enormous self-discipline. American enterprise is looking for creative problem solvers, people who can think a situation through to find an innovative solution.[12] Oddly enough, many corporate executives have not made the connection between their need for employees who possess such problem-solving skills and the capacity of the arts to develop those skills. They fail to understand that the organic and spontaneous nature of the arts is not at odds with, but rather is a complement to, their own penchant for mechanization and systemization.

Problem solving in the context of the arts does not have to be academic in the usual definition of that term. The danger of trying to be like the academic subjects is that the arts will relinquish one of their strongest cards, that they are refreshingly different in the way they are taught and learned. In adopting an academic approach, therefore, we must be careful that we do not make the arts just as dull as many of the other subjects, just as left brained. For example, some people actually recommend that students in band classes keep notebooks.[13]

We cannot keep young people in school by giving them more drudgery. In fact, the action, delight, and personal challenge that the arts induce can help prevent students from leaving school. The arts, like athletics, can make school enjoyable to students who cannot find joy anywhere else. They can touch the spirit of students whose spirit is denied in every other quarter. I do not think we should apologize because the arts are user friendly; we should capitalize on it. The arts can help reduce the high dropout rate that is such a concern to us all.

Thinking Communicatively

No commercial enterprise can be successful without effective communication. In an information society, if you cannot communicate, you are seriously handicapped. No wonder American business is worried about our high school graduates: They have difficulty communicating because they have not been introduced to many of the tools of communication. Even though the emphasis in arts education has been largely on expression, all art forms are also means of communication. Each of the arts functions as an important and unique communication system, and education in the arts is primarily a search for meaning.

The arts are forms of thought every bit as potent in what they convey as mathematical and scientific symbols are. They are the ways we human beings "talk" to ourselves and to one another. They are the languages of civilization through which we recount and relay the stories of our lives. The arts are modes of communication that give us access to the stored wisdom of the ages. Most important, they are the ways we conceptualize our ideas and imagination so that they can be shared with others.

When we educate our artistic possibilities, we awaken our perceptions and levels of awareness. We put more of our mind to work. We develop our capacity to view the world from different perspectives and to absorb from it more broadly. We immediately open windows to understanding. As Eisner pointed out, when we deny children access to a major expressive mode such as music, we deprive them of "the meanings that the making of music makes possible."[14] The same could be said of depriving children access to the expressive modes of art, dance, poetry, and theater. We deprive them of the meanings that these arts provide. We impoverish their minds. And we restrict our capacity to express and to communicate.

Furthermore, when we turn off these important parts of what human beings are—shut down some of the engines of life—we create an underclass of uncultured citizens. One of the problems of American education is that it produces too many people who operate in very limited modes. A part of them is forever frustrated and denied. As workers, such people do not make good businesspeople, good plumbers, good salespeople, or good mayors. Can we afford another generation of lost youth?

There are many indications that the failure of schools to cultivate and refine the sensibilities has had adverse affects on the younger generation. My observations in schools are that drugs, crime, hostility, indifference, and insensitivity tend to run rampant in schools that deprive students of instruction in the arts. In the process of overselling science, mathematics, and technology as the panaceas of commerce, schools have denied students something precious: access to their expressive/communicative being and their participation in creating their own world. In inner-city schools that do not offer instruction in the arts, the students have little pride and less enthusiasm, and such deprivation saps their lives of vitality and potential.

Thinking Culturally

The other area that is unique to the arts is what they teach us about ourselves and other people. The arts can establish a basic relationship between the individual and the cultural heritage of the human family. As advancing systems for travel and communication bring the peoples of this world closer, understanding human differences becomes increasingly important. The foundations for peace between peoples depends on intracultural connection and exchange. Recognizing our interdependence as peoples is the backbone of commerce in today's world. How can we have real teamwork any other way?

The greatest gift one people can give to another is to share their culture. One of the most revealing ways that we do this is through the arts. Cultural artifacts breath their origin. They tell us who *we* are and who *they* are. If we are not to be a country of many separate peoples, we must establish commonalities of culture as well as some understanding of our many different artistic legacies. If we do not find common ground, we shall create cultural separatism. To share artistic creations across cultures is to share our deepest values. Recognizing our similarities and understanding our differences establish the base for cultural cohesiveness and respect, two vitally important values in a shrinking world in which technology seems to deny our humanness. Science and mathematics do not provide this kind of insight.

IN CONCLUSION

We do not need more and better arts education to develop more and better artists any more than we need mathematics in the core curriculum primarily to develop mathematicians. Rather, we need more and better arts education to produce better-educated human beings, citizens who will value and evolve a worthy American civilization. *Better-educated human beings:* That is the justification for making the arts an essential part of general or basic education. That is why the arts are a common heritage to be shared by all. And that is why the schools have an obligation to pass on that heritage to the next generation. Access to that heritage is a right of citizenship.

Paul E. Burke, a member of the commission on standards for school mathematics (of the National Council of Teachers of Mathematics), pointed out:

To be educated, you need to know various habits of thought. There is a mathematical approach that works in some situations. But kids have been exposed to that for eight years before high school. And it's not the only approach. Art and history also involve certain habits of thought that are worth acquiring.[15]

And, he might have added, so do dance, music, and theater. Citizens who are receptive to experience and want to learn, recognize and respect good craftsmanship, care about detail, are committed to an artistic result, and have the ability to judge their own efforts by the highest standards are essential to an efficient and productive society. We need citizens who can think for themselves, communicate effectively, and understand and appreciate our ethnic diversity. The arts are an excellent educational resource for teaching these competencies. They are fundamental enablers. They can play a vital role in making humans functional.

What I am suggesting is that we must take action to save our arts programs from more cutbacks and our children from more deprivation. We must rescue the arts for America's children by finding the ways to develop an Arts-as-Basic Curriculum, one that will stress the ABCs of the arts for all students, one that will focus on teaching the competencies of the arts that serve the real priorities of the schools. The arts can serve the larger purposes of education naturally because of the thought processes that are indigenous to them, because they can teach habits of thought that are receptive, aesthetic, creative, communicative, and cultural. The arts do not have to be distorted to serve these purposes. When it comes to basic education, the arts can hold their own.

Our business and educational leaders need to be reminded that artistic habits of thought contribute significantly to their interests. Arts education should make these connections obvious. Arts teachers must learn to face their paranoia about utility and realize that they can be true to their own purposes and be useful at the same time. If the arts are to be basic, they must relate to the society in which they exist. As someone said, "The last thing a sea fish discovers is salt water." Society is the salt water of arts education.

What America must realize is that we will not be a nation that is qualified until we are a nation that is cultured. The two go hand in hand. When the arts come to be viewed as forms of human perception that are invaluable to every human being and to the enterprises that sustain us, we all will be required to study the arts. The arts will be basic. But that status is not something we can ask for; it is something we must earn.

_ chapter two _

THE ARTS AND ECONOMICS: OPPORTUNITIES MISSED, MISUNDERSTOOD, AND MINIMALIZED

Amerian culture, from movies and fast food to popular music and blue jeans, is being assimilated around the world. We are the dominant creators and distributors of a mass culture that is a global phenomenon. Yet for most Americans, the economic enormity of our cultural exports is invisible and easily ignored.

AMERICAN INFLUENCE

The globalization of markets, including those in the arts industry, is an economic fact of life today. Competitiveness in the world marketplace is a major concern of American industry, and the arts are an important contributing factor to our success in winning this economic competition with other nations. Why the arts? American exports in television, film, popular music, video, and print media dominate the world's entertainment markets. But in his study "The American Arts Industry," Harry Hillman Chartrand, chief economist of Kultural Econometrics International, reminds us that this is not their only or main contribution to American global success. In addition, the applied arts—including advertising, architecture, the crafts, jewelry, and fashion as well as product and interior design—marry aesthetics to utilitarian values, and it is this amalgamation that makes products marketable: "From buildings to urban planning; from product design to effective advertising; from corporate 'imaging' to designer fashion: the applied arts have the most pervasive and significant economic implications of any sector of the arts industry."[1] But affluence is not the only important contribution of the American culture to American prominence in the world. The arts also are part of the lifestyle we export. The entire world, for better or worse, is becoming Americanized.

David Rieff, a senior fellow at the World Policy Institute, points out that "American mass culture is everywhere triumphant."[2] There is a tidal pull toward similarity in the realms of capitalism, commerce, materialism, food, architecture, visual imaging, and music. According to Rieff, "One can now travel the entire world and never be very far from a Coke, a Big Mac, or the sound of some American entertainer. There are video rental stores in villages in India where most dwellings still have no electricity." He notes that "American consumer culture is corrosive of all traditions and established truths."[3]

There is no denying that American influence has prospered just about everywhere, but has it obliterated or been injurious to traditional cultures? Orlando Patterson, John Cowles Professor of Sociology at Harvard University, believes that those who argue that Americanization results in the homogenization of the world ignore "the increased vitality of local cultures and ethnicities in recent times." As the Third World reacts to the diffusion of Western culture, particularly American popular music, the effect of the global exchange process has been "the revitalization and generation of new musical forms." That is, the international consumership for centrally produced and distributed popular music has been a stimulus, not an impairment, to the development of the local culture. Even though America is at the helm of creating the world's first truly global culture, local and indigenous traditions continue to flourish, sometimes because of this influence: "The semi- and non-literate masses of the Third World invariably react to Western cultural influence in a nonpassive manner, reinterpreting what they receive in the light of their own cultures and experience."[4] Musicologist Peter Manuel commented that local cultures "adapt these foreign elements in distinctly idiosyncratic ways that alter their function, context and meaning."[5]

The global culture, now and in the foreseeable future, is quintessentially American, "because only America has already, to a very large extent, accommodated these new realities." As long as customers keep buying, the question of quality will remain relatively unimportant. The simplicity of the arts, their vernacular directness and instant appeal, and their capacity to accommodate every possible taste provide "American culture with its unique global reach and seductiveness."[6]

AMERICAN AFFLUENCE

America's arts industry is enormous and lucrative, creating thousands of jobs and contributing to our economic prosperity in significant, if almost unrivaled ways. Commercial (for-profit) and nonprofit performing arts represent a major American economic enterprise that far surpasses and outshines sports. Although the American public tends to underrate the arts industry as minuscule and insignificant, in reality it is one of the primary engines of the economy (Table 2.1).

The American artistic workforce is formidable and pervasive. But many parents persist in discouraging their offspring from taking up an artistic profession because they believe that the arts provide little monetary reward and lack stability and prestige. These perceptions are not altogether accurate, particularly the economic reality. True, perceptions of the financial plight of artists are generally correct. If a person decides to be a dancer, choreographer, painter, sculptor, musician, composer, actor, writer, or poet, making a living can be difficult, but literally thousands of jobs in the arts industry do pay very well. Although there is no way to calculate precisely the total

TABLE 2.1 *Components of the Arts Industry*

Recreation	*Entertainment*
Performing arts	Motion pictures
Motion pictures	Television/radio broadcasts
Spectator events	Video production
Entertainment	Records/tapes
	Musical composition
	Live performing arts
Copyright	*Occupation*
Book publishing	Actors
Music publishing	Directors
Radio/television	Announcers
Motion pictures	Architects
Video production	Authors
Theatrical production	Dancers
Band/orchestra	Designers
	Musicians
	Composers
	Painters
	Sculptors
	Craftspeople
	Photographers
	Teachers

Source: Based on Bruce Seaman, *A Perspective on the Arts Industry and the Economy* (Washington, D.C.: Research Division, National Endowment for the Arts, October 1993), p. 9.

TABLE 2.2   *The American Arts Industry*

Enterprise	Industrial Output in U.S. $Billions (1989)	Percent of GNP
Arts industry	$ 314.5	6.0
Literary arts	$ 145.6	2.8
Media arts	$ 147.2	2.8
Performing arts	$ 14.3	0.3
Visual arts	$ 7.4	0.1

Source: Adapted from Harry Hillman Chartrand, "The American Arts Industry: Size and Significance" (unpublished study, Research Division, National Endowment for the Arts, 1992), p. 14.

economic activity of goods and services produced by the arts industry, the estimates in Table 2.2, based on data obtained from the Bureau of Economic Analysis of the U.S. Department of Commerce, reveal the enormity of the arts output.

The net output of the arts industry in 1989 was nearly $315 billion, or 6 percent of the U.S. gross national product. That is for the mainline arts; if we count "marginal" arts industries, the gross figure was $443 billion, or 8.5 percent of GNP.[7] In terms of global influence and economic competitiveness, the arts industry is, surprisingly, the United States' second largest net export, after defense products. The arts are indeed a significant and substantial contributor to our financial well-being.

THE COMPLEMENTARITY OF ARTS AND SCIENCES

Unfortunately, the arts are not appreciated for their economic strength. In the public mind, they pale in comparison to the importance accorded to the sciences. As Chartrand reminds us,

> Once upon a time our forebears spoke of "the Arts and the Sciences" in a single breath. Today, however, science threatens to become everything; art to become nothing but a frill on the fringe of the economy. . . . Science generates the technology of the "head" while art generates the technology of the "heart." This "technology of the heart" is most evident in advertising, consumer research, politics and product design where it is the manipulation of images, sounds, and words, i.e. applied art, that sways the consumer.[8]

Chartrand sees two dynamos generating economic competitiveness: the arts and the sciences. "In America," he says, "they are wildly out-of-sync." His advice? "America must re-learn, as have Japan and Europe, what our fore-bears knew: an appropriate balance between art and science is essential for competitiveness, particularly in an increasingly global and polycultural mar-ketplace."[9] But science has not always played fairly in the struggle for domi-nance and for federal dollars.

In 1992, for example, a congressional subcommittee in Washington was informed that the country's impending shortage of scientists and engineers was based on a seriously flawed National Science Foundation (NSF) study. In truth, we have a surfeit of scientists and engineers. But between 1987 and 1990, Erich Block, the former head of the NSF, gave at least fifty-five speeches based on this study and repeated this warning so often that people came to believe it. Consequently, the shortage was blamed for our declining competitiveness, and the NSF won higher federal appropriations.[10]

The arts are competing intensely, but at great disadvantage, for limited and diminishing funds. If education in the arts is to attract more resources, a more effective case will have to be made about how the arts contribute to the prevailing priorities, whether they be competitiveness, our economic future, our workforce, or school reform. If we are going to continue to com-pete advantageously in world markets, we must increase our investment in the development of creativity and the ability to solve problems.

The arts complement the sciences. The development of human imagina-tion is critical to both. Without imagination and the ability to create, we are stuck with life as it is, and not as it might or could be. That is why the arts are a critical, if neglected, component of America's growing problem of competitiveness. "Since the Great Depression of the 1930s," Chartrand tells us, "the contribution of art education to national income has, in effect, been forgotten in America."[11] Innovation lies at the center of industrial success, and creativity may well be America's ultimate economic resource:

> It is the creative act that generates the new knowledge that fuels the information economy. At the core of this new economy is the buying and selling of new ideas, inventions, styles and techniques. . . . Only creativity can conjure up a substitute which turns lead into gold, sand into silicon chips or a first novel into billions in book, movie, T-shirts, toys, records, tapes and other ancillary sales and royalties.[12]

It is paradoxical that at the same time that corporate America has sounded the alarm to educate a creative workforce, it does not connect the arts to this goal. Our chief competitors, Japan and Germany, do not make this mistake. In secondary schools, Japan requires five credit hours of arts education, and Germany requires seven to nine hours. The United States requires zero to two hours.

The arts in America are big business. The explosion of American arts ex-ports to the rest of the world is remarkable. Collectively, the arts—including

movies, television, home videos, and music—have become one of the principal sources of export growth and help give the United States an edge in
international competitiveness.[13]

EDUCATION FOR COMMERCE

The public of the future will attend artistically bankrupt schools. By ignoring the development of creativity and imagination, we are hampering our
effectiveness in competing with nations that do provide their youth with a
background in the arts. The serious decline in the educational status of the
arts started in 1957 with the Soviet Union's launching of its first satellite,
Sputnik. The United States' response was a massive ($1 billion) federal
mobilization of education to meet the pressing demands of national security
and to maintain its competitive edge in math and science. This conscription
of education to serve the nation's political and economic agenda set a prece-
dent. In 1983, the federal report *A Nation at Risk* again tied education
directly to the United States' ability to compete in world markets and to
regain its "once unchallenged preeminence in commerce, industry, science,
and technological innovation."[14]

This same thirty-year period, from roughly 1957 to the present, corre-
sponds to the beginning of the television age and the birth of the technological society. While television saturates us in superficial glitz and vacuous
entertainment, technology demands deeper scientific knowledge and more
highly specialized education. While the former lulls the mind to stupor, the
latter urges it to new levels of literacy. Both these opposing—or comple-
mentary—phenomena have had a serious, and largely deleterious, effect on
arts education in public schools. The public tends to associate education in
the arts with the frivolous world of TV and entertainment, not with the
technological future that has become the serious business of education. The
National Endowment for the Arts' (NEA) study of arts education states that
Americans "generally confuse the arts with entertainment which can be
enjoyed without understanding."[15] That is, it is not the public's fault but,
rather, its lack of background in the arts. Much of this attitude is a reflection
of the way that arts teachers treat the arts, as less than serious and substantive. Consequently, the public tends to underestimate the importance of the
arts and the essential contributions they can make.

Exacerbating the situation is the use of education to serve the interest of
the corporate and business sectors. Hardly a week goes by without some
corporate executive complaining about the quality of our educational system, and usually with good cause. Indeed, AT&T maintains that it spends $6
million a year to educate 14,000 employees in basic reading and math.
American Express claims it spends more than $10 million a year to teach its

employees to do their jobs competently. Other corporations have been forced to become seriously involved in education. Indeed, the total yearly education bill for American businesses and industries may be as much as $210 billion, more than the total cost for elementary and secondary education in the United States. About $250 million of this amount is used for remedial education in basic skills. The rest goes for formal training programs and the cost of instruction on the job. But the question remains: Are schools preparing the kind of prospective employees that American businesses and industries need?

A report by the New York–based Committee for Economic Development, which represents more than 200 major U.S. corporations, states that "our schools stand accused of failing the nation's children and leaving the economy vulnerable to better-educated and more highly trained international competitors." What does business want? The committee's survey of the needs of industry reveals that corporations are looking for young people who, first of all, demonstrate "a sense of responsibility, self-discipline, pride, teamwork, and enthusiasm" and, second, an ability to learn, to solve problems, and to communicate well. Does the committee see any role for the arts in serving these educational interests? Yes, it acknowledges that the arts, which it labels nonacademic extracurricular activities, are worthwhile for "certain students." Even though the committee admits that "music, drama, and art develop an appreciation of aesthetics and cultural awareness and require discipline and teamwork," it suggests that eligibility for participation be based on "a desired level of academic competence."[16]

Given the impact of the arts on America's global influence and the substantial contribution of the arts to the economy, it is difficult to understand why business has relegated the arts to educational oblivion. Corporations continue to demand that schools serve the narrow but very real goal of employability, and the arts continue to fail to connect or command respect, no matter how broad or intellectual their curriculum.

When it comes to the arts, the blindness of some U.S. business executives is endemic in the extreme. Although schools are too often treated as a means to attain economic and technological expertise, there is the matter of the public's acquiescence. Parents often lack sufficient experience with the arts to understand their value. Unknowingly, they exclude the arts because of an overriding concern for the child's economic future. By underestimating the educational potential of the arts, corporate leaders unwittingly relegate the arts to the educational periphery.

I'm not suggesting a conspiracy on the part of big business, especially in light of the ongoing interest of the upper middle class in opera, ballet, theater, and symphony. To be sure, there are individual corporate leaders who do acknowledge the importance of the arts. One example is Winton M.

Blount, chairman of the board and chief executive officer of Blount, Inc., who asserted,

> The "three R's" must be mastered of course, but they are not all there is to the making of a whole person. It is art that stretches the tools of learning through the provinces of the heart and the soul to connect reason to feeling and open within us those capacities that we believe God gave only to human beings.

But such personal acknowledgments tend not to be expressed in policy. They are exceptions, and too few by far.

A report by the secretary of labor declares that "new workers must be creative and responsible problem solvers." It mentions the skills and personal qualities that are needed for solid job performance, including "working on teams," "working well with people from culturally diverse backgrounds," "interpreting and communicating," "monitoring and correcting performance," "seeing things in the mind's eye," and other competencies that can, and often are, taught through the arts. Even though this report states, "We are not calling for a narrow work-focused education," the obvious connections to the arts remain vague.[17]

Many corporate leaders need to be reminded that it will take more than the ability to read, write, and compute to make productive citizens. The schools need to reach beyond mere employability. In fact, what business wants of young people cannot be achieved *without* the arts, and business should want much more than what the traditional basics can provide. But how do we make that case?

WHAT BUSINESS WANTS

Understandably, businesses and industries expect their entry-level employees to be able to read, write, compute, and understand an instruction manual. In their view, these are minimal basic skills that schools should provide, and that view is difficult to dispute. But the intensified influence of business in American education has not always been benign. In serving their own self-interest, corporations have ended up narrowing the curricula and the purposes of education, looking back rather than forward. Since the current educational reform movement began in 1983, schools have been pressured to improve their teaching of basic skills. The result in many elementary schools has been, accordingly, an intensification of academic studies. That is, the technical side of knowledge has been emphasized at the expense of the "soft disciplines in the humanities." The schools established an elite core of learnings labeled the basics, subjects that every student must master. Corporate interests have supported these moves to

cut out the fat: "The barbaric cutting of pounds of flesh dis-cultured education by eliminating the 'fads and frills,' the dispensable arts and electives
in music or dance, for example."[18] Under pressure from American business, many school boards have been all too willing to cut or eliminate the
arts as not essential.

In the 1980s a series of reports by American business declared that students in the United States are both undereducated and miseducated. A 1985
report sponsored by the American Can Company claimed that "business
losses attributable to basic skills deficiencies run into the hundreds of millions of dollars annually because of low productivity, errors and accidents,
and lost management and supervisory time."[19] Another report stated that
"our faith in ourselves as the world's supreme innovators is being shaken.
Japan, West Germany and other relatively new industrial powers have challenged America's position on the leading edge of change and technical
invention." Citing the importance of the nation's capacity to innovate and
use technology creatively as chief components of our economic health, the
report called for broadening the definition of basic skills to include "more of
the skills that will be demanded in tomorrow's technologically-sophisticated
workplace."[20]

Nowhere, however, in any of these reports is there any recognition of
the arts' educational value to the basic education of all students. The
Committee for Economic Development's study clearly indicates just how
marginal a place the arts occupy:

> Although we believe that the development of solid basic and high-
> level academic skills is the primary mission of the schools, we do not
> agree with some recent suggestions that schools should eliminate
> extracurricular activities such as athletics, music, drama, newspapers,
> or student government.... We are convinced that this would unnec-
> essarily penalize certain students for whom these subjects and activi-
> ties form an important part of their education and an incentive for
> staying in school.[21]

In its only acknowledgment of a possible role for the arts, the report com-
ments, "We believe that these *non-academic activities* not only have intrinsic
value but also reinforce scholastic pursuits."[22] Clearly, the arts are viewed
not as basics but as nonacademic extracurricular activities that are worthwhile only for certain students. The possible role of the arts in better educating American youth is largely unrecognized and dismissed.

The committee's report even goes so far as to state, "It may be desirable
and necessary ... to base eligibility for participation on athletic teams or in
other extracurricular pursuits on demonstrated achievement of a desired
level of academic competence." One chief executive officer I talked with put

it this way: "First let's get everybody to read and write, *then* they can learn
the arts." In other words, first you learn to work and then you are permitted
to play. The arts are not perceived as subjects for serious study in American
schools. Ironically, the self-interest of American business is unaware of what
the arts could contribute to the future workforce. If American youth were
sharpened, sensitized, motivated, and made more creative and whole by the
arts, American business would be the ultimate benefactor.

We need more and better arts education to help make young people into
productive and perceptive citizens, people who can understand and appreciate our ethnic diversity, communicate effectively, and think for themselves;
citizens who recognize and respect good craftsmanship and can judge their
own efforts by the highest standards; citizens who are receptive to experience and want to learn. The attributes that the arts teach students are basics;
habits of thought that can help put corporate America back on top. Our
abiding faith in science and technology as the sole answers to our economic
future and our continued global success are fallacious and unrealistic. The
arts are an indispensable resource for sustaining and improving our prosperity both nationally and internationally. Why not take advantage of them?

__ chapter three *__*

SOCIETY AND THE SCHOOLS:
A DYNAMIC RELATIONSHIP

Society and the schools are inextricably linked. The schools reflect society, and society reflects the schools. That linkage contains the dynamics for improving the lot of arts education. How do we determine schools' curricula? Arts education is not only part and parcel of those schools in which it is offered but also of the society that gave it birth. In interacting with society, we alter our culture and, in the process, change our destiny. In fact, becoming cultural engineers may be the only way we can take charge of our own cultural future.

CURRICULUM: ON WHAT BASIS?

Schools are one of the mainstays of the culture. By passing on to the younger generation the knowledge and understanding we have accumulated, we preserve our level of civilization. Here we're talking about something very basic: the survival of life as it has existed. This is the process of enculturation, teaching students how to adapt to the prevailing cultural patterns of their society.

Arts education is part of this process of enculturation, passing along the existing culture to the next generation. The idea of maintaining culture is

Society and the Schools

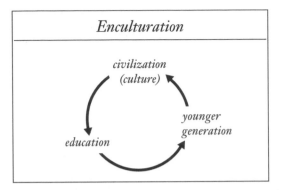

generally the reason for curricula in the arts. Art and music textbooks teach students how to listen, analyze, and interpret; the history of these arts and their various styles, technical aspects, and performance or production. Such curricula concentrate on passing along what exists, on preserving it. It is what Christopher Lasch (author of the *Culture of Narcissism*) called our *custodial* orientation.

Preserving the breadth and richness of our artistic culture is one of the main functions of arts education as a whole. In fact, arts education is the irreplaceable conduit for conveying the artistic heritage of African, Asian, Latino, European, and Native Americans to citizens of the next generation. This alone is an enormous responsibility, a national obligation.

Is this all arts education does? We must ask ourselves, What is the proper role of education? To transmit the culture as it is, or to function as an agent for constructive change? Maintenance is normally the goal we ascribe to education. But schools cannot ignore their influence on the future. What do we want for the arts in tomorrow's American society? Our answer to that question will have an important bearing on how we develop the arts curriculum and how the arts function in the schools.

We all have a hand in creating culture. Everything educators do, everything they believe and value constitutes the culture in which we live. Television, fast food, popular music, and our passion for the automobile are part of the American lifestyle. Commerce and technology can sustain us at the same time that they create an artless world in which humanity takes a

---

Purpose of Education

To transmit culture as it is?
or
To function as an agent for change?

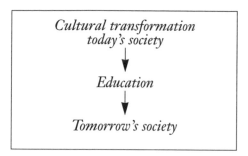

Cultural transformation
today's society

↓

Education

↓

Tomorrow's society

backseat. Elements of our culture can demean the spirit or can resuscitate and illuminate it. The arts are a narrative of life, a reaching out for the meaning of things. Each of us has a hand in creating our culture, in making ourselves.

Even though I am oversimplifying the relationship between the schools and society, it is an interaction that can have either a minimal or a substantial effect. This relationship is an idea that is accepted widely, especially among those who would have the schools serve political and economic agendas. If the schools could not or did not affect the condition of society, why would such energy and effort be put into altering them?

THE APPLICATION TO THE ARTS

Let's look for a moment at how, in general, this relationship between society and education operates and how it can affect arts education. I'm going to suggest several sets of correlates in an attempt to prove my theory. This, I believe, is the beginning of setting up a process for developing a more dynamic arts curriculum.

VALUES

We live in an information-intensive society. We are concerned about maintaining our world lead in electronics and computer science. How does such a society translate these concerns into education? It demands more emphasis on academic subjects. People want information-intensive schools, and so American schools are reorienting themselves to the mind, to the development of cognition.

At the same time, we know that many Americans think of the performing and visual arts as nonintellectual or as essentially emotive in character. To value the mind but to view the arts as mindless means that these subjects are treated as a mere diversion from the more substantive, thought-provoking subjects in the curriculum, as something avocational, a frill. In this kind of value system, the arts are de-emphasized.

Values		
Society	*=*	*Education*
Information intensive		*Information intensive*
Emphasis on mind		*Emphasis on academics*
The arts as mindless		*The arts as unimportant*

What can we do about it? To achieve status and significance in an educational curriculum that stresses the development of cognition, the arts must be presented as they really are: systems that humans have invented to construct and convey meaning.

What meaning do the arts convey? The arts are a set of ways in which people achieve cultural identity and cohesiveness. This is why when we hear a piece of music, we can usually tell its place of origin. Music exudes its culture. This also explains why we celebrate with music. It brings us together. It solidifies the group. Music is also a representation of its time. It is as much an imprint of history as a fossil or a shard. The style of music conveys the character of a people at a particular time. The Charleston evokes America in the 1920s just a surely as a Strauss waltz evokes Vienna in the second half of the nineteenth century.

The arts are ways in which we construct our reality and give representation to our lifestyle and our emotive beings, something that takes considerable thought and knowledge. The arts are a product of the mind. They *are* cognition.

Like any of the other symbolic systems for coding our world—mathematical and scientific symbols, for example—our ability to decode the arts gives us access to meaning. In this way, each art form becomes a device for learning, just as surely as scientific and mathematical symbols do. But this deciphering requires study; it is not something we can take for granted.

Understanding that all the arts were developed because of our human need to formulate, record, share, and store sensory impressions of our world—to see the arts as systems for transmitting knowledge—is to realize their true origins in the human intellect. But most important, it is to begin to realize that the arts are important because humans have used them to express and communicate some of their most brilliant insights. This is why no one can be said to be truly educated without knowledge of the arts.

Approaching each art as a *system of meaning* and *a means of learning* is an important consideration in building a curriculum because it presents the arts as intellectual disciplines. It is a way of operating that ensures that we command a share of the increasingly competitive market for the minds of American youth.

Education	=	*Society*
31 percent have no music		*32 percent have no interest*

We must realize that in using the school program to alter the public notion of the arts as mindless and mystical worlds of pure emotions, we are going beyond mere cultural maintenance. Rather, we are using the schools to instill new values, to change society, in a sense, to transform our culture. We are not content to leave things as they are.

Now let us use our equation (society = education) to look more closely at the problems of music and music education and what the future suggests for curriculum design. To see how this works, I'm going to ask you to consider a few of the problems that exist in classical music today, and then I'll propose some solutions that will have a bearing on what we do in the schools.

ATTITUDES

The National Endowment for the Arts (NEA) has declared that one of its primary challenges is to improve the status of the artist in society.[1] By and large, the American people do not hold artists in very high esteem. Indeed, many Americans believe that artists do not make a decent living and that the arts are not important to our business-oriented culture.

We find a similar problem of attitude in the schools, where the arts exist on the fringes of educational legitimacy. A recent survey of current trends in art education found that art teachers are concerned about the status of art and want art and art education to be accorded recognition and prestige.[2] Instead, however, the arts are regarded as recreational rather than vocational pursuits.

Attitudes		
Society	=	*Education*
Artists have low status		*The arts suffer low academic status*
The arts are not essential		*The arts are unimportant*
61 percent do not participate		*Many people do not grasp the message of the arts or its relevance*

According to John Goodlad, students view music as relatively unimportant and easy, and they don't have much respect for it academically.[3] In fact, many secondary schools don't require them to take music courses at all. A recent survey of sixth and tenth graders by the now-defunct Association for Classical Music found that with few exceptions, students think of classical music as "boring sounds for old, rich people."[4] They don't think classical music has anything to say to them.

It is no accident that the problems identified in society and in schools coincide, so that the problems of the arts in society directly affect the problems of the arts in schools. Similarly, music education in the schools affects music in society. The status of music in society has a great deal to do with the status accorded music in the schools and vice versa.

How can music education improve the lot of musicians and music? One way would be to introduce students to successful musicians. Students need to see that what musicians contribute to society is important. In addition, students need to be shown the importance of music as an expressive vehicle. Music can be taught as a system of meaning, enabling students to discover that classical music does say something to them. By making demands on the students, their thought processes are challenged. In other words, the schools actively work to alter students' attitudes toward music. But in order to raise the value and status of music in American society, we must reach every student.

Again, by assuming this role, music education is taking a responsibility that goes beyond mere cultural maintenance. The schools are actively trying to change community values. They assert some influence over, and take responsibility for, the way our culture is evolving. When we recognize that society determines education and that, in many ways, education determines society, we can interrupt the equation and change the course of the future.

PARTICIPATION

The NEA's survey of public participation in the arts shows us that in 1982, 100 million adult Americans, or 61 percent, never attended a live performance of music, ballet, or jazz. An even more startling finding is that 53 million Americans, or 32 percent of the population, expressed no interest whatsoever in participating in the arts. Data published by the National Center for Education Statistics show that 31 percent of high school students in 1982 did not take even one course in any of the arts.[5] This means that more than 1 million seniors had no instruction at all in the arts during their four years of high school. No wonder we have such a large disinterested public.

Again, notice the coincidence of these figures. (It is important to realize that because of the equals sign, the equations can be transposed: Society = Education, and Education = Society.) The arts curriculum, and certainly music education, is derived from American society and so is directly respon-

Participation	
Society	= *Education*
32 percent of adults show no interest	*31 percent of high school students receive no music education*

sive to it. Arts teachers do not have to maintain the culture as is but can try to develop it. Culture is a dynamic, ongoing process, not something preexisting that we cannot change.

Consider the visual arts, painting, sculpture, design, graphics, and so forth: Education is the means by which we empower people to engage reactively with these systems. In order to encourage more people to seek art experience, we must develop a general curriculum for all students that explores the visual arts as wondrous human inventions, living histories of eras and peoples, and records and revelations of the human spirit. We must demonstrate that the visual arts are languages that speak to all people and that what they say has substance and meaning. At the very least, our arts programs should demonstrate these qualities to all students and the public.

When school boards eliminate or shrink their arts program, they do so on the basis of a hierarchy of subject matters, some of which they believe to be more important than others. Accordingly, they rate the arts as having a low priority in relation to what they believe are a higher order of essentials. Harry S. Broudy, professor emeritus of philosophy of education at the University of Illinois and a longtime spokesman for the arts, noted the shortsightedness of this view:

> The source of meaning and its exfoliation into ideas, theories, values, visions, plans, and inventions is the imagination. It is the matrix and motivator of all that is characteristically human. Dampen image making and image perceiving, and creativity is diminished and intelligence itself is deflated. This is as true in everyday knowing, thinking, feeling, and choosing as it is in the highest reaches of science and art.[6]

When it comes to the arts, then, the schools fulfill a very important role. They not only transfer experience and understanding; they also enable students to interact with the culture. The schools enliven the arts curriculum when they begin to take responsibility for cultural development. They are engaged not just in a process of transmission but in a process of transformation as well. Arts education attempts to alter and improve the arts in American society.

Level of Education		
Society	=	Education
Audiences consist of the better educated		Students are the bright and the talented

LEVEL OF EDUCATION

An NEA survey found that those who attend concerts have attained a higher level of education than those who didn't attend. What is the situation in the schools? Data from the National Center for Education Statistics show that arts offerings are greater in high schools "when over one-third of the students are in an academic program." This survey reveals that "in general, the percentage of schools offering arts courses decreased as the percentage of students in a college preparatory program decreases. . . . [A]nd cultural appreciation courses were offered more frequently in schools when the percent of students expected to go to college exceeded 75 percent."[7]

According to these statistics, the arts excel where the intellect does. Arts programs tend to reach the brighter students, the talented. These statistics coincide with the characteristics of adult audiences of the arts. Apparently, we have a problem of elitism in the arts in American society that is being aided and abetted by the exclusiveness of arts education in the schools.

What can we do? Until all students are given quality learning experiences in the arts, the arts will not enter the mainstream of American life but will remain the domain of the educated elite. So we will want to ensure equality of opportunity to study the arts and make certain our curriculum includes every student. School arts programs must deliberately dispel the notion of elitism. To do so, schools need to offer, at the very least, one or two "grabber" courses designed for all students. The issue is not a matter of a lack of time. The problem is that many students are simply not interested in studying the arts or they do not have a schedule that allows it. Elective courses must attract students.

Music education faces a crucial choice: to continue to reserve music for the few or to begin to offer it to the many, to maintain the status quo or to build a more democratic musical culture.

SUMMARY

The problem in curricular development is that we often follow models for no particular rhyme or reason. High schools mimic colleges and universities. Yet for the most part, college programs teach people to be musicians,

> ### *First Fundamental Goal*
>
> *To establish the arts
> as a vital and valued part
> of American society*

artists, dancers, actors, and writers, or teachers of these disciplines. Many of our high school arts programs attempt to do the same; that is, they confine their educational focus to what is essentially vocational training.

What I hope I've conveyed is a new perspective. I'm suggesting a more anthropological approach to curriculum building, one rooted in the culture. We teach art in order to maintain the level of the civilization at the same time that we realize that education can function as an agent for constructive change. I'm suggesting that curricular applications be broadened.

For example, to the extent that we are dissatisfied with the public's attitudes toward the arts and artists, want larger audiences for the arts, and want the arts to reach a broader public, and the schools attempt to do something about these problems, the schools serve what I call the first fundamental goal of arts education: *To establish the arts as a vital and valued component of American society.*

To the extent that schools serve this first fundamental goal, they will go a long way toward achieving the second: *To establish the arts as a significant force in American schools.* It stands to reason that if the schools begin establishing the arts as systems of meaning for every student, the educational value of the arts will rise.

Using education to solve the problems of the arts in society will make arts education more relevant and more alive. But even more important is curriculum development—thinking of the school arts program as a system of cultural engineering and not just as custodial enculturation—which can rejuvenate the vitality of arts education and its sense of mission.

> ### *Second Fundamental Goal*
>
> *To establish the arts
> as a significant force in
> American education*

— part two —

JUSTIFICATION

I n comparison with other subjects, arts educators have spent a disproportionate amount of time and effort over the years trying to justify the role and value of the arts in schooling. The reason should be obvious: The arts always seem to be on the defensive because their place in general education is tenuous and growing more so.

Not all of this effort has been productive. In many schools, the status of the arts is fragile. When school systems face budget cuts, curtailments of art and music programs are an all-too-common and seemingly easy solution. Reductions often come swiftly and ruthlessly, exacting debilitating losses on faculty and programs. Arts programs are sometimes eliminated by school administrators and boards of education without much anguish or serious debate, as if they are dispensable and unimportant, inconsequential and superfluous. Indeed, the arts are not treated as being in the same educational league as mathematics and science. Whereas they should be viewed as a fundamental part of general education for all students, they are sometimes seen as an expendable luxury the system cannot afford.

Consequently, arts educators have spent an inordinate amount of energy creating arguments to justify the need for arts education. These rationales are designed to persuade the unconvinced, but they usually are only partially effective. Words alone may not be able to convey the real meaning and importance of the arts. If a person has not experienced painting, sculpture, dance, or theater personally, adequately, and effectively, words alone may not be able to explain its value. Rarely do efforts at advocacy compensate for the lack of understanding that could and should have been inculcated in an active study of the arts. In addition, advocacy of one's own subject is often regarded as self-promotional and partisan.

Advocating arts education takes a number of forms, some conflicting. For example, the case for aesthetic education is seemingly at odds with the functional or utilitarian justification for studying the arts. According to the aesthetic philosophy, arts' own intrinsic qualities that make them worthy of inclusion in the education of every person: Art for art's sake. Adherents of this view believe that "beauty is its own excuse for being," echoing Gertrude Stein's "A rose is a rose is a rose."

In contrast, the utilitarian view advances the idea that the arts should be valued because of their practical contributions to human development. Probably the most extreme expression of this view is "A child who blows a horn will never blow a safe." The utilitarian approach attempts to make a convincing case by showing how the arts affect the general education of all students.

The struggle between these two views among arts educators has often reached fever pitch and canceled both sides out. The following are the views of two music educators.

The first educator maintains that "one of the tenets of aesthetic theory is that music is valued for its purposelessness. A facet of the curriculum that believes in its own lack of utility is doomed." In contrast, a second educator opposes claims based on practical values: Practical values "support the study of music for nonaesthetic (nonmusical) reasons. Any profession that seeks justification apart from its subject is on shaky ground."

Art educators go through the same gyrations. One laments, "We do not insist on the educational value of art because its proper role in our lives is a significant end in itself, but because we believe that through art we can promote other outside-of-art behavioral developments." His counterpart adds, "It is an overreliance on the 'art-for-art's sake' arguments that has, regardless of their intrinsic solidity, partially contributed to the sadly consistent relegation of the arts to the curricular caboose."

This kind of bickering over how to justify the arts in education is unfortunate, wasteful, and harmful, and among parents and educators, it has weakened the case for the arts. Is study of the arts a practical necessity? In today's hard-nosed, back-to-basics climate, the need for aesthetic education may be difficult to sell. The aesthetic approach often is viewed as having an elitist ring that can defeat its purpose. Even Bennett Reimer, the foremost exponent of the aesthetic philosophy, questions how philosophical honesty can be balanced with practical efficacy. As schools have adopted increasingly practical approaches to curriculum, aesthetics do not appear to be grounded in human need. Talk to school-board members about the necessity for aesthetic education and they are apt to say, "That's all well and good, but we can't afford it." The utilitarian-versus-aesthetic framework for establishing an arts rationale tends to be counterproductive. We thus need a new and common cause for the arts, a new way to think about the importance of the arts in education.

Today, rationales supporting arts education have shifted to the practical—how the arts can serve the educational and human priorities of the moment. We relate the arts to our prevailing concerns—dropout rates, school reform, cultural diversity, violence—in order to establish their relevance and secure their educational status.

Advocates for arts education must construct a rationale that can convince the uncommitted. It could take many forms, depending on the audience that is being targeted and the circumstances that have to be improved. Several rationales may be more effective than just one. Intrinsic and extrinsic values do not have to clash. Both views can help substantiate the value of the arts in education. Part Two of this book explores a number of different and compelling rationales that support the educational significance of the arts.

_ chapter four _

RECOGNIZING THE ARTS

AS FORMS OF INTELLIGENCE

Among the great movers of the twentieth century, who was the smartest and most important? Physicist Albert Einstein, psychoanalyst Sigmund Freud, social reformer Mohandas Gandhi, modern dance pioneer Martha Graham, Communist revolutionary Vladimir Lenin, painter Pablo Picasso, composer Igor Stravinsky, or writer Virginia Woolf? Harvard University psychologist Howard Gardner remarked that asking who the smartest is probably "isn't a very good question." Collectively, however, these outstanding thinkers created much of our present-day consciousness: the modern mind. We cannot "compare one kind of intelligence with another kind of intelligence," Gardner says. "They are *sui generis*," unique.

MULTIPLE INTELLIGENCES

Gardner's list immediately makes clear that intelligence can take many forms—scientific, political, social, and artistic—and that all are important. This point is the basis of his theory of multiple intelligences and the mistaken notions that people often have about what being "smart" means. Gardner's book *Frames of Mind: The Theory of Multiple Intelligences*[1] poses a serious challenge to those who claim that intelligence is tied just to verbal and mathematical skills, as the Scholastic Assessment Test (SAT), formerly called the Scholastic Aptitude Test, and much of our present-day schooling seem to imply.

Gardner deliberately made a plural of the singular noun *intelligence* because, he explained, "I wanted to challenge the people who believe they own the term 'intelligence,' and that they alone can determine what tests are appropriate and how that word ought to be used in the wider community."[2]

He defines intelligence as "an ability to solve problems or to fashion products to make something of value that is appreciated in at least one culture." In his view, intelligence is related to what a person needs to function as an effective member of a community. His definition challenges the idea that intelligence can be measured with paper-and-pencil tests.

Combining the results of his own work with brain-damaged patients with evidence collected from other sources, Gardner isolated and identified seven autonomous intelligences: linguistic, logical–mathematical, musical, spatial, kinesthetic, and two forms of personal intelligence—interpersonal (understanding other people) and intrapersonal (understanding yourself). The theory provides scientific proof that the arts represent forms of intelligence.

CRYSTALLIZING EXPERIENCES

Gardner believes that even though no intelligence is inherently artistic, "each can be used to create or to understand artistic works, to work with artistic symbol systems, and to create artistic meanings." A person with a high degree of linguistic intelligence, he says, might become a poet, a novelist, or a dramatist or, instead, a lawyer or journalist. A person with a high degree of kinesthetic intelligence might become a dancer or an athlete. "It's an individual choice, a value choice." Artists do not use just one form of intelligence. "In dance, for example, bodily kinesthetic intelligence is important, but so is musical intelligence, spatial intelligence, and probably other intelligences as well." But if you limit intelligence to language and logic, "you are going to miss an awful lot of what is important in the arts."

Why do people seek encounters with the arts, and why is education in the arts essential? Maxine Greene, professor of philosophy and education at Columbia University, thinks the arts provide "inexhaustible insights" that help us understand life's mysteries. They "plunge us into adventures of meaning." They allow us to imagine in new realms and "to break through the boundaries" of linear, logical thinking and go beyond the confines of a single reality. Educating the artistic intelligences nurtures more awareness. "The more the listener can hear, the greater the likelihood of unconcealment." We pour our energies into a work of art to bring it alive. The arts release students, allowing them room for feelings and intuitions that are repressed in every other quarter of life—crowded out, Greene says.

The arts can provide an educational "way through" for many students. Because everybody's mind is different, education should be tailored to the individual. "Kids who have language and logic abilities are going to do fine in school," Gardner points out. "But everyone cannot be smart when you have a single ruler, a single caliber." He suggests that schools "help kids discover areas where they do have some strengths—what I call a crystallizing experience—and to really encourage that." Many children have strengths in one or more of the arts that could give them such experience.

ENCOURAGING DIVERSITY

What do we want from education? According to Elliot W. Eisner, a professor of education and art at Stanford University, the school curriculum is "a mind-altering device." It is a means for changing minds and improving the way people think. "Therefore," Eisner says, "we need to exploit the power of curriculum to optimize whatever potential intelligences individuals possess."

Eisner believes that schools should provide "the conditions through which people become increasingly individuated and optimalized in terms of their particular abilities, the specific kinds of talents they possess." Whereas most schools today aim for a uniform result, the idea of multiple intelligences points to "heterogeneity as an outcome," what Eisner refers to as "productive idiosyncrasy." The end result is "variance in what it is that youngsters are able to do."

In contrast, schools and universities today "really put a corset around the conception of what people can come to understand." The arts show us that there are many more avenues to human understanding than just those through science. Intelligence is knowing. Numerous examples in any of the arts can be used to show how art informs. In Arthur Miller's play *Death of a Salesman*, for example, we see what it can mean to be middle aged and to lose a job. "Almost anybody," says Eisner, "could write about something that is tragic. But to write about it in a way that enables us to feel the experience almost the way in which Willie Loman experienced it is a profound achievement." Playwrights draw on their inter- and intrapersonal and linguistic intelligences.

According to Eisner, the theory of multiple intelligences supports a much larger role for the arts in the curriculum. The various kinds of intelligences point directly to a variety of "ways of knowing." Eisner suggests a balanced curriculum consisting of fields of study that all students should learn, coupled with subjects for which students have particular proclivities and inclinations: "As long as schools operate on an essentially linguistic modality that utilizes a kind of literal, logical, mathematical form of intelligence, it not only delimits what youngsters can know, but also is an impediment to those youngsters whose intelligences are in modalities other than the ones that are emphasized." He offers an analogy: "When you limit the games to basketball, the kids who are three-foot-two are going to be handicapped."

In applying this theory, Eisner theorizes, "teaching would emphasize multiple forms of literacy, not only verbal and written forms, to foster learning." Teachers would encourage students to use their individual strengths. In learning about the Civil War, for example, students would use an array of resources—music, photographs, stories, films, and so on—that offer different kinds of opportunities for youngsters with different capabilities. By broadening the variety of resources, what students absorbed from their study of the Civil War would also be expressed in different forms.

The result of applying the theory to education, according to Eisner, is that schools would no longer operate as assembly lines turning out the same model. "School curricula would become equitable when they provide different strokes for different folks. Equity requires diversity. Sameness is not the same as equity."

WHAT DO WE VALUE?

Gardner reminds us of a truth that we often forget: "Intelligence and creativity are not always used benignly. They are value neutral. You can compose for Hitler. You can paint for Stalin. Einstein's discoveries were used for terrible ends, even as they can be put to uses that are very benign." As important as intelligence is, "character and vision and responsibility are at least as important—probably more important." Moral education determines how you go about using your intelligences.

Harold Taylor, a well-known writer and former president of Sarah Lawrence College, observed

> We have now produced a pluralistic society in which greed, avarice, and selfishness are raised to the level of national ideals. We keep telling ourselves that in order to be mentally healthy we must raise our self-esteem and learn to love ourselves, when what we really need is to do things that command respect and which give ourselves some reason for thinking that we deserve to be loved.

Education, Taylor maintains, should "open up the mind and nourish the sensibilities," and that is what happens when schools cultivate the artistic intelligences.

EDUCATING THE WHOLE PERSON

According to the theory of multiple intelligences, music and the other arts are dimensions of human power. They are major civilizing forces. Although the arts do not necessarily make us more moral, they can help us learn to be empathetic toward others. The arts can teach us to feel and to care. They put us in touch with some of the highest achievements of humankind, inducing us to reach, to live up to something. Encounters with the arts enable us to unlock some of the great stored wisdom of the ages. In other words, the arts are part of what make people well educated. Take them away, and people will be less well educated. There is no replacement. You either acquire the capacity to unlock artistic insights and responses, or you are deprived of these insights and the joys they offer. Children made to live without the arts are inevitably poorer for it. This is why every young person, without exception, should be given access to the study of the arts, not to become artists, but to be better educated.

IMPLICATIONS

If the arts are perceived as noncognitive—as they often are—they will be given short shrift in the schools. American schooling is focused on the development of the ability to think and to figure out. The idea that all human beings have a multiplicity of intelligences and that heretofore schools have limited their concentration to just a few areas, mainly verbal and mathematical intelligence, implies that education should offer broader opportunities that explore these other human potentials.

Gardner's theory shows us the shortcomings of the SAT, which measures a person's potential success in postsecondary education on the basis of two areas only, achievements in verbal and in mathematical ability. This is a prejudicial and narrow definition of human potential and, in a word, unfair. It means that a person who excels in some other area or areas, such as the arts, and whose potentials lie elsewhere than the two tested areas, is at a disadvantage. In a way, such a person's human potential is discounted because the test ignores it.

The educational ramifications of Gardner's theory are both provocative and convincing. If, as he has shown, the human mind has several different cognitive capacities and each person's profile is different, then education should provide opportunities to explore and develop all these capacities. The various arts, commanding as they do various facets of human intelligence, can serve as vehicles to use those human capacities and, in the process, develop them.

The implications for the school curriculum are profound. Gardner is saying that humans have a variety of intellectual potentials that should be recognized and nurtured. Students should be given opportunities to develop these intelligences. Gardner's broadened definition of intelligence means that the curriculum must reach outside its usual confines and open students to their whole mind, rather than just part of it. The arts offer a variety of ways to develop different kinds of cognition. They make demands on the brain that spread thought processes across areas now largely ignored.

APPLICATIONS

Following the Getty Center for Education in the Arts, which maintains that training in artistry should go beyond production and that production alone

will not suffice, the application of multiple intelligences should include discussion and analysis of artworks and some appreciation of the cultural context in which artworks are created.[3]

Gardner offers more detailed instructions: He believes that for younger
children, production activities ought to be central in any art form, since
children learn best when they are actively involved. Perceptual, historical,
critical, and other dimensions of the arts "should be closely related to, and
(whenever possible) emerge from, the child's own productions." Thinking
in the arts medium is crucial to teachers and students. For example, in
visual arts, thinking visually or spatially must occur in the hand and the
eyes. Gardner advises, "Whenever possible, artistic learning should be
organized around meaningful projects, which are carried out over a significant period of time, and allow ample opportunity for feedback, discussion,
and reflection."[4]

In the arts, certain core concepts such as style and expression should be
revisited at various developmental levels in a spiral rather than a sequential
framework. Learning should be assessed in the art form being taught.
("Musical skill must be assessed through musical means.") Artistic learning
goes beyond learning a set of skills or concepts to encompass feelings, their
own and other people's. "It is important for students to understand that the
arts are permeated by issues of taste and value and to encounter individuals
who are willing to defend their values in open discussions. Arts education
needs to be a cooperative enterprise involving artists, teachers, administrators, researchers, and the students themselves."[5]

Gardner believes that "while ideally all students would study all art
forms, this is not a practical option." He would thus rather have a person
well versed in one art rather than having a smattering of knowledge of several arts.

ARTS PROPEL

Proving the accuracy of the theory of multiple intelligences requires new
assessment techniques. Therefore, instead of the usual grading, students
keep "processfolios," accounts of their works in progress. "In their processfolios, students include not just finished works but also original sketches,
interim drafts, critiques by themselves and others, artworks by others that
they admire or dislike and that bear in some way on the current project."[6]

Among the dimensions assessed are students' awareness of their own
strengths and weaknesses, their capacity to reflect accurately, their ability to
build on self-critiques and make use of others' critiques, their sensitivity to
their own developmental milestones, their capacity to find and solve new
problems, their ability to relate current projects to both earlier and future
ones, and their capacity to move comfortably from one aesthetic stance to

another and back again.[7] This approach has been adopted, with considerable success, by a variety of school systems around the country.

> Though the notion of projects and processfolios has a long history in the arts, teachers and curriculum supervisors in domains ranging from history to mathematics have come to appreciate the usefulness of rich and engaging projects and the desirability of that systematic cast of thought involved in reflecting upon one's work and keeping a regular journal. As a long-time arts educator who is used to seeing his field treated as a backwater, I gain special satisfaction from the present circumstance: our ideas and practices may actually provide inspirations to areas of the curriculum that have traditionally been more prestigious.[8]

The theory of multiple intelligences resists the notion of uniform schools instead, basing the school curriculum on the intelligence profile of each student. All people's minds are quite different, and education should maximize each person's own intellectual potential.[9]

_ chapter five _

STRONG ARTS, STRONG SCHOOLS

The best schools have the best arts programs. Excellence in education and excellence in the arts seem to go hand in hand. What is the connection? Why do strong arts programs make better schools? How do the arts enhance general education? This chapter attempts to answer these questions, showing through visual examples why the arts are one of the hallmarks of excellent schooling.

A MORE COMPREHENSIVE EDUCATION

Schools are practical places. The best way to study the world would be, ideally, to experience it firsthand. Thus if you wanted your students to learn about space exploration, you would take them to Cape Canaveral in Florida or to the Jet Propulsion Laboratory in California. But because of the difficulties and expense of teaching through direct experience, desirable as it might be, schools have substituted more expedient modes: reading, mathematics, science, history, and the arts—the great repositories of human wisdom and achievement.

If, for example, students were studying the Grand Canyon, and we wanted to give them a general idea of it without actually going there, we could resort to a verbal description: "The Grand Canyon, the world's largest gorge, is a spectacle of multicolored layers of rock carved out over the millennia by the Colorado River." If we wanted to convey its vastness, we might use measurements: "The Grand Canyon is more than 1 mile deep, 4 to 18 miles wide, and more than 200 miles long." Each of these symbolic systems—words and numbers—permits us to reveal important aspects, though a picture or painting might prove to be equally telling (Figure 5.1).

The arts—creative writing, dance, music, theater/film, and the visual arts—serve as ways that we react to, record, and share our impressions of the world. Students can be asked to express their own reaction to and interpretation of the Grand Canyon, using, say, poetry as the communicative vehicle. Whereas mathematics gives us precise quantitative measures of magnitude, poetry explores our various personal reactions. Both views are valid. Both contribute to understanding. Together, they prescribe a larger overall conception of, in this case, one of nature's masterpieces.

We need every possible way to represent, interpret, and convey our world because of a very simple but powerful reason: No one of these ways can provide a complete picture. Individually, mathematics, science, and history convey only part of the reality of the world. Nor do the arts alone suffice. Rather, a multiplicity of symbol systems are required to provide a more complete picture and a more comprehensive education.

A MORE ENGAGING WAY TO LEARN

The arts complement the sciences because they nurture different modes of reasoning. The arts teach divergent rather than convergent thinking. They ask students to come up with different, rather than similar, solutions. Unlike many other subjects that students study, the arts usually do not demand one

FIGURE 5.1. It's been said that "one picture is worth a thousand words." American artist Thomas Moran painted the glory of *The Grand Canyon of the Yellowstone* in 1872. (Used by permission of the National Museum of American Art, Smithsonian Institution. Lent by U.S. Department of the Interior, Office of the Secretary)

correct response (Figure 5.2). In this way, the arts are able to break through the true–false, name-this, memorize-that confines of public education because for every problem, there may be many correct answers. This kind of reasoning is far more common in the real world, in which there often are many ways to do any one thing well. American business needs both kinds of reasoning, not just the standard answer.

When we involve students in creative problem solving, we invite their participation as partners in the learning process. Instead of being told what to think, the arts require students to sort out their own reactions and articulate them through the medium at hand. Their beings become absorbed into the task so that they learn from the inside out rather than from the outside in. They discover the answers for themselves through their own inventions. Such figuring out requires critical thinking, analysis, and judgment, and students tend to stay on task because they are creating their own world, not

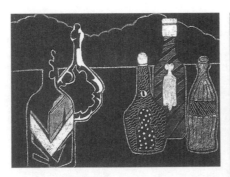

FIGURE 5.2. Under the excellent teaching of Nelle Elam, students at Starkville (Mississippi) High School invent their own ways of solving the same problem—producing a visually pleasing and creative statement using five personally selected, symmetrically drawn bottles and the technique of crayon etching. In learning to solve such problems, students must exercise judgment, explore options, and arrive at appropriate solutions. (Used by permission)

replicating someone else's. Being able to think independently is the basis of creativity. It is also an engaging way to learn.

The arts invite students to be active participants in their world rather than mere observers of it. But it's not busyness alone that matters: In the process of creating their own visions, the arts teach students craftsmanship. Arts curricula teach students how all the expressive details work together, and how important those details are. For example, fine workmanship is really the centerpiece of Japan's economic triumph. "Made in Japan" evokes a vastly different, and far more positive, image today than it did in the 1930s. Why? Because the Japanese applied craftsmanship to industry. The arts require students to apply standards to their own work, to be self-critical, and to be able to self-correct. Through the arts, students learn self-discipline and how to handle frustration and failure in pursuit of their goals. These attributes are essential to a competent workforce and well-made products.

Workmanship requires a personal commitment to excellence. The arts call for students to stretch their inner resources and put them to work to attain their own image of perfection. Through the arts students learn that they can make their own unexceptional beings extraordinary and uncommon. They can invent a broader universe in which they can see new dimensions and create their own visions of the world as it was, is, and might be. By using their imagination, students begin to realize that they can make themselves and their world what they envision. Because the arts cultivate the imaginative thought processes—the source of creativity—they energize the motivation to learn. These mental capacities are basic to America's success in the competitive global economy.

A MORE COHESIVE CURRICULUM

The subject matter of the arts is as broad as life itself, and therefore the arts easily relate to aspects of almost everything else that is taught. But the arts are generally not conveyors of information. Dance and music do not add to our information overload. Their purpose is not to convey data but to supply insight and wisdom, in a word, *meaning*. Their power is that they can *move* us. They serve as connectors that give understanding a human dimension. They tell us about people: how they thought and felt and what they valued. They help us define ourselves and our times, as well as other people and other times.

The arts are powerful tools of communication. Each of the arts functions as a communications system that has allowed people through the ages to articulate observations, interpretations, and possibilities. Furthermore, the arts of the past will continue to communicate to us if we learn how to "read" their symbolic codes. For example, to understand the difference between the way people thought and lived during the Renaissance and Baroque periods, we can use the arts to enrich historical descriptions and accounts. For instance, comparing styles of architecture and design during these periods can be instructive, providing more insight and clarity.

Through the arts, we can see that the systematic, ordered thinking that prevailed in the Renaissance was replaced by the dynamic and elaborate drama of the Baroque, the latter exemplified by the music of J. S. Bach. The move was from light and small to heavy and massive, from simple to complex (Figure 5.3). Students can make these comparisons and discoveries themselves, and they can experiment with their own designs, contrasting the more controlled Classical view with the freer Romantic vision. In this way, the arts overlap and reinforce learning in other areas.

The arts also convey a sense of time and place that transport students, helping them travel beyond mere facts to experience the past in a more personal way. Music, for example, evokes how people of other times and places felt and thought. Through their music, the people of past ages come alive

FIGURE 5.3.   Architecture and design reveal differences in the way humans lived and thought at other times. Whereas the fifteenth-century Renaissance Pazzi Chapel in Florence, designed by Filippo Brunelleschi (left), is symmetrical, square, clean lined, and functional, the seventeenth-century Baroque church of Santa Maria della Salute in Venice, designed by Baldassare Longhena, is multifronted, octagonal, heavily ornamented, and theatrical—a new spirit evoking a new age. (Used by permission of Alinari/Art Resource, New York)

FIGURE 5.4.   Dawn of a new day symbolizes the hope of western migration in this nineteenth-century painting, *Emigrants Crossing the Plains* by Albert Bierstadt. (Used by permission of the National Cowboy Hall of Fame and Western Heritage Center, Oklahoma City, Oklahoma)

again, projecting their spirit across the centuries. In this way, the arts can enliven history, giving it a human dimension that draws students in.

The arts can also extend an understanding of science. If students are studying the nature of our solar system and how the earth turning on its axis every twenty-four hours causes the sun to appear to rise and set, science can provide part of the truth about sunrises and sunsets, but the exhilaration we feel at the birth of a new day is another part of the meaning or truth of a sunrise (Figure 5.4). The British aesthetician and critic Herbert Read once commented, "Art is the representation, science the explanation—of the same reality." That is, the arts and the sciences relate different aspects of that reality.

When used well, the arts are the cement that joins all the disparate curricular areas together. In the best schools this is often the case. The arts are valued for their interdisciplinary potential, and the result is a more cohesive curriculum in which students explore relationships among disciplines. Truth and understanding are recognized as a composite of perspectives, not just one partial and tentative view. Science, after all, is in a constant state of flux. In this sense, the arts, in conjunction with other aspects of the curriculum, afford students more complete and compelling conceptions. They provide another panorama of meaning and knowing.

BRIDGES TO THE BROADER CULTURE

Because the arts often express a sense of community and ethnicity, they are one of the main ways in which humans define who they are. Because the arts convey the spirit of the people who created them, they can help young people acquire inter- and intracultural understanding. The arts are not just multicultural, they are transcultural, inviting cross-cultural communication and understanding and teaching openness toward those who are different from us (Figure 5.5).

By putting us in touch with our own and other people's feelings, the arts teach one of the great civilizing capacities—how to be empathetic. To the extent that the arts teach empathy, they develop our capacity for compassion and humaneness. Whereas intelligence can be used as a tool of greed and deception, empathy intercedes, reining in such uses of intelligence. Empathy permits us to assume another person's point of view. When we listen to the lyrical loneliness of an ancient melody played on an American Indian

FIGURE 5.5.   African-American artist Beauford Delaney captures the plight of the homeless in his painting, *Can Fire in the Park* (1946), creating empathy and understanding in the viewer of a lifestyle different from our own. (Used by permission of the National Museum of American Art, Smithsonian Institution)

flute, the sounds evoke the spirit of the tribe. Native American dances have the same effect. Experiencing this part of their civilization makes it easier for us to understand that Native Americans have often been wrongfully stereotyped.

There is a near miracle here, because as soon as we have a glimpse of another people's humanity, we have crossed the cultural chasm that separates us. It isn't intellect that connects us to other people; it is feeling. Because people define themselves through their artistic expressions, these expressions communicate their human essence. This explains why the arts serve as ways that we connect ourselves to those who came before us and those who live beside us. The arts teach respect.

A MORE HUMANISTIC CURRICULUM

One of the arts' most important contributions to the development of young people is the cultivation of their emotional and spiritual well-being. The human spirit in all its manifestations is central to the arts. Think of the great cathedrals, mosques, and temples, the paintings, sculpture, and music that have been created around the world to put us in touch, and to sustain our contact, with the spiritual world. Students can be inspired by the arts to reach deeper within themselves to stand in awe of dimensions of life we cannot fully understand or grasp, of our own fragile and temporal being, and of life itself in the vastness of the cosmos.

The arts introduce us to human perceptions and understanding we could not acquire any other way. At their best, they always enlighten. Theater, for example, explores the foibles and triumphs of humanity past and present. What is behind the velvet curtain? A slice of life that we can view from a distance and, we hope, with greater objectivity. We see ourselves reenacted. By experiencing human situations and their consequences, we can better understand ourselves and others.

Through the arts, students can relate directly to the essence of people who lived before them. Auguste Rodin's sculpture *The Burghers of Calais*, for example, re-creates a tragic episode in the Hundred Years' War between England and France. Five male figures, each a study of despair, are shown as they prepare for an audience with the English king, Edward III, who was laying siege to Calais in 1347. These citizens sacrificed their lives to save the city. In their slow and agonizing dance, we confront the human suffering wrought by war and the nobility of these citizens, evoking the nature of that distant conflict so that we all can relate to it (Figure 5.6).

But such artworks accomplish something even more important. By example, they show us extraordinary human possibilities. The burghers demonstrate the human capacity to withstand adversity and to triumph over it. Like many other artworks, Rodin's sculpture shows students that they can

FIGURE 5.6.   We are there. Auguste Rodin's sculpture *The Burghers of Calais* (1886)
takes us back to 1347 to show the suffering caused by the Hundred Years' War and
the nobility of those who sacrificed their lives to save others. (Used by permission of
the Hirshhorn Museum and Sculpture Garden, Smithsonian Institution, Gift of
Joseph H. Hirshorn, 1966. Photograph by Lee Stalsworth)

reach beyond the ordinary and the mundane to discover their own magna-
nimity and capacity for humaneness.

We are creatures of feeling as well as thought, and schools that recognize this fact, and address it, are better schools. Science and technology do
not tend to our spirit, but the arts do. That is their role, and it is why and
how they complement and counterbalance the rest of the curriculum. Our

spirit needs as much nurturing as does any other part of our mind, and schools that ignore it are cold and desolate places. Remember that if we fail to touch the humanity of students, we have not really touched them at all. And schools that do not teach the arts are, quite literally, creating a generation that is less civilized than it could be, more barbaric than it should be.

SUMMARY

The arts provide a more comprehensive and insightful education because they invite students to explore the emotional, intuitive, and irrational aspects of life that science is hard pressed to explain. Humans invented each of the arts as a way of representing particular aspects of reality in order to understand and make sense of the world, manage life better, and be able to share these perceptions with others. The arts therefore enrich the curriculum by adding important extensions of awareness and comprehension at the same time that they affirm the interconnectedness of all forms of knowing. This is why an education without the arts is incomplete.

The Necessity for the Arts

The arts are necessary in our lives and in our schools because they

:: *Teach us divergent, rather than convergent, thinking*
:: *Develop craftsmanship, the ability to apply aesthetics*
:: *Introduce us to perceptions and understandings we could not acquire in any other way*
:: *Enlighten our understanding, making it deeper and more comprehensive*
:: *Facilitate human communication within and across cultures*
:: *Help us define who we are and articulate our own very special sense of being*
:: *Characterize their age, distinguishing our relationship to time by showing us as we were yesterday and as we are today*
:: *Replenish our spirit and, by nurturing it, consoling it, and inspiring it, affirm our humanity*

As processes for distilling certain kinds of personal meaning, the arts can function as vehicles for imaginative learning, captivating students by activating their creative mental resources. The arts are self-enablers that involve students in exploring the life around them, past and present, and in constructing and inventing the future. Through the arts, students learn to see themselves as functioning members of the human race, persons who share a bond across different cultures with people who also express themselves and communicate through their indigenous artistic expressions. In these ways, the arts enhance the students' capacities to participate significantly in their world. No wonder, then, that schools that give comparable attention to the arts are better schools.

Strong arts, strong schools. Where this relationship is understood, the arts are not the first to go when budgets are tightened. Rather, the arts are viewed as essential components of a general education. They are not just for the gifted and talented. Like math and science, they can benefit everyone. When cuts have to be made, they are not made unilaterally but across the board. Enlightened school boards know that without a sufficient arts education, students are deprived of a whole fundamental world of understanding.

The arts are not pretty bulletin boards. They are not turkeys and bunny rabbits. They are not frivolous entertainment. Rather, the arts represent humanity. They are the languages of civilization through which we express our fears, our anxieties, our hungers, our struggles, our hopes. They are systems of meaning that have real and important utility, which is why schools that give students the means and encouragement to explore these realms provide a better education. This explains, too, why the arts are a mark of excellence in American schooling.

_ chapter six _

CHEATING OUR CHILDREN:
WHY EVERY CHILD NEEDS THE ARTS

Like other subjects in the curriculum of American schools, the arts provide an opportunity for children to realize certain talents and potentials. Particularly in their creative modes, the arts ask students to reach inside themselves to explore their own fascinations and perceptions and to give them suitable and precise representation. In the process of translating their inner discernments and revelations into a symbolic form, children discover and develop their capabilities and uncover some of their human possibilities. Because they are so personal in what they require of each would-be artist, the arts can disclose important insights and impart crucial—and practical— habits of thought that are generally not taught as well through other subjects.

It is precisely because the creative act flows from the inside out rather than the outside in that it helps youngsters discover their own resources, develop their own attributes, and realize their own personal potential. Education generally does not do this. That is, usually students are told, "Here is the way the world is," rather than asked, "What do you think the world is or might be?" Through the process of refining their own personal visions, students discover and develop their own intellectual resources. Because the arts ask students to determine their own abilities, they are self-motivating. They propel and stimulate, fascinate and captivate because they engage students personally with their true inner selves, not some concept of self imposed from outside. All human beings want to know what they can do. By having to draw on their own ideas, students discover and explore their own cognitive capacities.

I believe that engagements with the arts can contribute significantly and uniquely to personal development in several essential ways, changing people's inlook and outlook, thought processes and abilities, and generally making them more capable of coping with the world around them. Therefore, every child needs the arts, for some or all of the following reasons.

TO HELP THEM DEFINE WHO THEY ARE

As individuals, we all are originals, but how and when do we realize this? Much of education teaches us to mold our lives to the demands of external conformity. Our individual uniqueness emerges gradually as we probe our personal resources. We have to find it internally by listening to our own inner voice. We have to discover and learn to savor our original way of being human. Charles Taylor, a professor of philosophy and political science at McGill University, notes:

> There is a certain way of being human that is *my* way. I am called upon to live my life in this way, and not in imitation of anyone else's life. But this notion gives a new importance to being true to myself. If I am not, I miss the point of my life; I miss what being human is for *me*.[1]

Taylor believes that we define ourselves "through our acquisition of rich human languages of expression," including the "languages" of the arts. These modes of expression must be acquired, largely through exchanges with others:

> We define our identity always in dialogue with, sometimes in struggle against, the things our significant others want to see in us. Even after we outgrow some of these others—our parents, for instance— and they disappear from our lives, the conversation with them continues within us as long as we live.[2]

This interchange between people, facilitated by our ability to express and communicate, lies at the center of making and sustaining our identity, of recognizing our authenticity. Each person is unique and deserving of respect because of this shared universal human potential.

The arts invite us to express our own visions and values and to explore the world from our own viewpoint and perception. They help us cultivate particularity and individuality. Through creative involvements in the arts, we make choices, and in the process we determine our own self. We come to respect diversity because we learn to respect our own differences and singularity.

Self-esteem is established by just such inner searches. By recognizing who we are and by giving voice to our personal inner life, arts education induces self-respect. It legitimizes self-identity. Doubts about ourselves operate conversely, causing degrees of self-denigration, whereas self-respect grows through positive reinforcement. We tap our inner resources and, because of them, are able to command affirmation and recognition. Our dignity and self-respect as individuals reside in achievement, and the arts provide legitimate ways to achieve and to win recognition.

TO SEE THEMSELVES AS PART OF A LARGER CULTURE

Our culture—defined as the way in which we choose to live and what we choose to value—is a human creation. At the same time that we learn our idiosyncratic nature, experiences with the arts teach us to appreciate the commonalities that undergird our collective life: our right to express and communicate, our belief in our individuality and our freedom to assert it, our respect for our differences, and our right to dissent. The arts establish our relationship with what is universal in human existence—love, human dignity, and caring and also hate, greed, suffering, and so on.

Artistic expressions introduce students to a wider world. They help students comprehend the human condition, by showing perspectives that can stretch and challenge their viewpoint. They help students learn to exist in a broadened horizon, recognizing and respecting an expanded universe consisting of options outside their own traditions and their individual points of view.

A culture's artifacts necessarily reveal the nature of that culture, how and what it expresses and its general characteristics. Through artistic representations, we share our humanity. What would life be without such shared expressions? How would such understanding be conveyed? If we are to survive, we will need all the symbolic forms at our command because they permit us not only to preserve and pass along our accumulated wisdom but also to give voice to the invention of new visions.

The arts help students see beyond the limits of their own cultural story. By introducing them to the multiple facets of their own and other civilizations, past and present, their horizons are extended. They learn to respect values other than their own. By learning to respect the distinctive arts of others, students learn to respect the people who created them as equals.

TO CULTIVATE AND BROADEN THEIR PERCEPTION

One of the reasons we read novels is that the characters in them are drawn sharply, clearly, and vividly. We can understand them in a way that is less possible in real life, and these revelations help us see all people and ourselves better. We can experience pain and suffering at arm's length. The arts awaken us to our feelings and to nuances of sensation. They make us more alert to the world around us.

Increasingly, the arts are being viewed as *systems of meaning*, as living histories of eras and peoples and as records and revelations of the human spirit. They are being viewed as symbol systems as important as mathematics and science. Harvard professor emeritus Nelson Goodman points out that science doesn't have the edge on truth, only one perspective out of an infinite number of possibilities.[3] Science is always self-correcting. Its truths evolve and change. But that doesn't negate its importance. In this sense, science is like art, always presenting new views and new responses to the world.

The arts are *acts of intelligence* no less than other subjects are. They are forms of thought as potent in what they convey as mathematical and scientific symbols are. The Egyptian pyramids can be "described" in mathematical measurements, and history can hypothesize about how, why, and when they were built, but a photograph or painting of them can show us other equally important aspects of their reality. The arts are symbol systems that enable us to represent our ideas, concepts, and feelings in a variety of forms that can be "read" by other people. The arts were invented to enable us to react to the world, to analyze it, and to record our impressions so that they can be shared.

Is there a better way to gain an understanding of ancient Greek civilization than through its magnificent temples, statues, pottery, and poetry? The Gothic cathedrals tell us about the Middle Ages just as clearly as the skyscraper reveals the modern age. The arts may well be the most telling imprints of any civilization. In this sense, they are living histories of eras and peoples and records and revelations of the human spirit. One might well ask how history could possibly be taught without including them.

Today's schools are concerned, as they rightly should be, with teaching literacy. But literacy should not—must not—be limited to the written word. It should also encompass the symbol systems of the arts. If our concept of literacy is defined too narrowly as referring to just the symbol systems of language, mathematics, and science, children will not be equipped with the breadth of symbolic tools they need to represent, express, and communicate the full spectrum of human life.

What constitutes a good and adequate education? Today, the goal has become very practical: employability. But is that enough? Few would take issue with the notion that children should know how to read, write, and compute. But what about developing human values, such as the ability to get along with other people, to respect human life, to maintain integrity, to be fair and just? The arts affect the mind and spirit. They bring enlightenment to the area of human values and the meaning and possibilities of our existence.

The arts can expand consciousness. They can open eyes, ears, feelings, minds. Encounters with the arts invite students to explore new meanings of themselves and the human condition. They awaken curiosity, present new perspectives, stimulate personal involvement, and convey different ways of looking at themselves and the world. Through their encounters with a work of art, students learn that the more of themselves they put into it, the more they will derive from it. The more they probe and explore, the more they will discover and understand. The payoff is built right in. Students feel the excitement in bringing a work alive, of learning to use their energies for the reward of revelation, and this is an attribute that has important applications in any work situation.

It is one of the important provinces of the arts that they challenge the status quo. The continuing political turmoil over the National Endowment for the Arts and the controversy surrounding grants to photographer Andres Serrano and other artists because of works that some critics have labeled blasphemous and indecent reside in this miscalculation (misconception) of what the arts are and whether public funds should be used to support them. By their nature, the arts seek to show us new dimensions. They critique life. They make judgments of the world, some of which we may not find compatible with our own views.

Irwin Edman tells us that through art, we learn to see the world in new and hitherto undreamed-of patterns: "A picture by Cézanne of a snow-laden tree among fallen snows may give us for the first time an inexpungeable sense of the reality of a tree."[4] The arts continually attempt to rescue us from our delusions, counter our smug complacency, challenge the commonplace, and give us a new and sometimes contentious account of life. Do people benefit from being confronted by such options? These new ways to view the world stretch and sometimes squash our accustomed way of seeing and believing. They challenge us to see and to think differently. We can either accommodate these new views or reject them. In a democracy, alternatives are an essential part of our freedom to express and even our right to offend.

TO EXPAND THEIR ABILITY
TO EXPRESS AND COMMUNICATE

Every symbol system functions as both a system of meaning and a means of understanding. The arts are areas of inquiry, ways of knowing that all humans need. As human beings, we are unique among all forms of life because we capture our experience through symbol systems. We cannot adequately convey the range of human experience through written and spoken words alone. How could we express our religious beliefs and our deepest human joys and sorrows if it were not for the arts?

All art forms function as tools of expression and communication, the ways in which we humans seek to know. They permit us to cast our own perceptions and to capture the perceptions of others. To become an expressive, communicative being is the essence of our personal human spirit. When that possibility is denied to young people, they acquire little pride and less enthusiasm. Perhaps that is why drugs, crime, hostility, indifference, and insensitivity tend to run rampant in schools that deprive students of instruction in the arts.

One of the major requirements of education is to give children the breadth of symbolic tools they need to represent, express, and communicate every aspect of human life. If our concept of literacy is defined too narrowly as referring to just the symbol systems of language, mathematics, and science, children will be shortchanged. Howard Gardner pointed out that schools restrict the development of the human intellect by concentrating on nurturing only the linguistic and mathematical/logical parts of the brain. Children must have access to these forms because, as Elliot Eisner observed, "The apotheoses of human achievement have been couched in such forms."

The arts, like the sciences, are windows on the world. Creative writing, music, theater, visual arts, media (film, photography, and television), architecture, and dance reveal aspects about ourselves, the world around us, and the relationship between the two. The arts constitute "an ensemble of stories we tell ourselves about ourselves."[5] In 1937, German planes flying for Franco in the Spanish Civil War bombed a defenseless village as a laboratory experiment, killing many of the inhabitants. In *Guérnica*, Pablo Picasso painted his outrage in the form of a vicious bull surveying a scene of human beings screaming, suffering, and dying. These powerful images etch in our minds the horror of a senseless act of war.

Similar themes have been represented in other art forms. Benjamin Britten's *War Requiem* gives poignant musical and poetic expression to the unpredictable misfortunes of war's carnage. Britten juxtaposes the verses of Wilfred Owens, a poet killed during World War I, with the ancient scriptures of the Mass for the Dead. In Euripides' play *The Trojan Women*, the ancient art of theater expresses the grievous sacrifices that war forces humans to endure. The film *Platoon*, written and directed by Oliver Stone, is a more recent exposition of the "meaning" of war, a theme that has been treated again and again with telling effect in literature throughout the ages. The theme of humans inflicting suffering on humans has also been expressed through dance. One example is *Dreams*, a modern dance choreographed by Anna Sokolow, in which the dreams become nightmares of Nazi concentration camps.

This theme and many others are investigated, expressed, and communicated through the arts. The arts erase nothingness. Even if they deal with the subject of nothingness, they evoke somethingness. They provide expanded awareness. They intensify and extend consciousness. They bring us face to face with our lives, what we have avoided, and what we may not have personally experienced or felt—not always comfortable revelations, but certainly instructive. They help us transcend our blandness. In this way, the arts can function as an antidote for wasted, meaningless lives. It is always amazes me how little many people ask of life. They seem content with everyday routine and a lack of self-exploration and fulfillment. The arts break through such dullness.

TO ESCAPE THE MUNDANE

Paradoxically, at the same time that the arts can clarify reality, drawing our attention to what we might have overlooked or simply missed—say, the horrors and hurts of war—they can also take us into new and unexpected worlds, like the joy of Mr. Bojangles dancing. The music that young people choose to listen to helps them transcend the sometimes harsh and unaccommodating world they may live in. Through the arts, they enter another state, one that is distracting and nonthreatening and one that they can control.

The arts sharpen reality; they can also provide a temporary mental release from actuality. Movies and novels, in particular, enable us to lose ourselves in another environment and time, inhabited by characters who are fascinatingly different from the people we know. All of us benefit from having a respite from the trials and tribulations of our everyday lives. The experience of entering a different universe gives us perspective on our own existence. It helps us break loose from our own limited sphere to enter into and realize the potentials and predicaments of the unknown and unfamiliar.

Such respites are an important way that we renew and refresh ourselves, a necessary function of personal rejuvenation. The arts stretch us beyond the mundane and commonplace by activating our imaginations to create a wholly different existence. A love song, for example, can tell us that the joyous state of love is larger than life, certainly bigger than life without it. These imaginative states are compelling because they show the possibilities of life in positive ways, a psychologically necessary and reassuring process. The paradox is that in losing ourselves, we regain self, a being refreshed and renewed by the simple act of diversion.

TO DEVELOP THEIR IMAGINATION

Of all the capacities of the human mind, imagination may be the most unusual and momentous. By exercising imagination, humans have been able to transform and reinvent the world in infinite arrangements. Our evolving adaptations, adjustments, recyclings, and inventions enable us to cope and to survive. By using our capacity to imagine, we reinvent our lives every day, and we invent our future as well. Imagination enables us to burst the confines of the ordinary. It allows us to rise up to meet new challenges and to improve the human condition. One of the valuable outcomes of education, then, is an expansion of imagination.[6]

It is the capacity for invention that carries a civilization to new plateaus. Our searches for new solutions depend on our ability to look at our situation anew, to fabricate alternatives, and to reconceive our lives. We literally formulate our possibilities. In the play of children, invention is abundant, but it is a quality seldom cultivated in schooling. By the fourth grade, students generally have lost much of their will to invent, as though it is a childish propensity best to be relinquished. Schools and teachers generally discourage the inclination to think out and see beyond. We tend to teach unquestioning acceptance and shut out critical and creative reevaluation, rethinking, and reformulation, and in the process, modern civilization loses some of its options and flexibility.

Every human being should not only be aware of, but also learn to apply and to venerate, his or her inventive possibilities. The quality of imagination is a treasure that each of us should savor and respect. Young people are, by nature, explorers, eager to encounter the untried and investigate their quiescent (latent) possibilities. It is the human mind operating at its best. When it is respected and explored, the originality of each human being becomes a way to save the schools from the irrelevance and boredom that prevail in so many classrooms. Personal invention is self-absorptive and wholly involving, human engagement in a necessarily meaningful context.

The arts and human imagination are irrevocably interlocked. Artists are always trying to create something new. As a painter, "you're always trying to make something that has never been seen," declares Brice Marden. "You're trying to make something you'd like to see. You do not see it anywhere else, so you make it. When it's not a surprise for you to see, you do not make it."[7] Only the capacity to wonder and to daydream—not usually qualities that are respected in schooling—permits us to create such surprises.

The problems posed by artistic creation do not have easy answers, and in this regard they are analogous to life. Indeed, they may have more than one correct answer and certainly many ineffectual ones. Understanding such ambiguities can have many applications at home and at work. Two plus two equals four is not relevant to the kinds of difficult thinking and decision making we are required to make so often in the adult world. Through encounters with the arts, students experience the exhilaration of traveling beyond the simplistic true–false and right–wrong litanies that prevail in most American classrooms.

Joyous as it may be, the act of creation demands enormous self-discipline and teaches students to learn how to handle frustration and failure in pursuit of their idea. It requires setting goals, determining a technique, figuring out how to apply it, and continually making evaluations and revisions, in other words, thinking and solving problems.

TO LEARN TO EVALUATE AND MAKE JUDGMENTS

A student who is attempting to translate, say, the battle of Gettysburg into a pictorial representation faces an infinite number of options—and decisions.

What is the message? What moment of the battle should be depicted in order to convey that message? What technique, size, scale, color, and form are appropriate? The student makes these decisions because there is no way to proceed without doing so. Early on, these judgments may be made by intuition, by guesswork, or by personal preference rather than by application of an established set of criteria. But some kind of criteria must be used to make such decisions and to justify them, even if it is limited to "I like it" or "I don't like it." The justification for our preferences and tastes has to be educated.

Some of these judgments or preferences will prove easier to make than others. The students may not have a choice of different sizes of paper and so must accept what is available and make the best of it. On the matter of what to depict, however, there may be difficult choices and decisions. The students must imagine various possibilities and make a choice based on what will work best to accomplish their goals and what they can do given their personal limitations and competencies and their consequences. In later stages of development, the students will have acquired a more explicit set of criteria by which to make such determinations. Some decisions may become more automatic while others continue to be anguished. Through the creative process, students are forced to make judgments, and they necessarily develop a set of criteria by which to make them. They learn how to exercise judgment and how to justify their decisions.

In the process of making such judgments, a person's value system is developed. A constant critiquing of results (consequences) may suggest and necessitate adjustments and midcourse corrections, changes of purpose or message, or possibly even abandonment. Students learn to appraise, that is, to judge the worth of operating one way or another. Leaning on the thoughts of John Dewey, Mary J. Reichling, a professor at the University of Southwestern Louisiana, ties such judgments directly to imagination:

> How one selects among various means and consequences is by using imagination. Perhaps this defines one aspect of the teacher's role: that is, to assist students in imagining all eventualities possible to insure that the desired consequences will actually result and be prized when they do occur. . . . While teachers cannot impose values, they can help students to see the results of their actions or dispositions if they are able to envisage the consequences.[8]

In making aesthetic judgments, students learn that their creative attempts have to be exercised within boundaries that they establish. In the process of creation, being too open ended can be debilitating. Most creation is accomplished within limitations and for good reason. Eliminating some of the options simplifies the complex decision-making process. Painters start with a certain-size canvas and palette of colors. Composers start with an established form and have in mind a particular performance medium. Writers start with a poem, a short story, or a novel in mind. These decisions still leave many judgments to be made, but they don't leave the artist floating in total uncertainty. Learning to make these judgments is a capability that all humans require, because life forces us to make difficult decisions in every realm of our lives every day.

Because they are inherently personal, the arts provide a strong means for schools to activate and inspire students, to encourage self-motivation and discipline, and to help them discover the originality of their beings, the wonders and possibilities of life, the joys of learning, the satisfaction of achievement, and the revelations that literacy, broadly defined, provides. The arts are a central and fundamental means of attaining these objectives. The challenge is to carry a message to every superintendent, principal, school-board member, and parent to the effect that the arts should be an essential educational resource for every child in every school system. The educational potential of the arts is too great not to be fully exploited.

chapter seven

IMPROVING GENERAL EDUCATION THROUGH THE ARTS

Discrete study of the various individual arts, as we saw in Chapters 5 and 6, can enhance human perception and understanding uniquely and significantly. These dimensions qualify the arts to be an important part of general education for all students, but they are not the whole story. There is another application that can provide impressive educational dividends: the arts used as vehicles to enhance learning in other subjects. In addition to being treated as subjects worthy of study in their own right, the arts can function in tandem with the entire curriculum, enlivening it and ensuring the student's engagement in the learning process.

Imagine the scene: The auditorium is bristling with anticipation. The "press" has assembled for a momentous occasion—President "Teddy" Roosevelt's final press conference before leaving office. The Secret Service agents glare at the reporters. Suddenly the band strikes up "Hail to the Chief." Applause greets the president as he walks through the crowd toward the podium, shaking the hands of reporters along the way. Placards urge "TR" to "Finish the Canal" and "Hang Loose for Bull Moose." The president is surrounded by grim-looking agents. His press secretary introduces him.

Reporter Tom Cisewski of the *Providence Journal Bulletin* asks, "What do you think of giving up control over the Panama Canal?" Pounding on the podium, the president shouts that American "control of the canal is essential, and I would fight to maintain it."

The questions probe every facet of the times, and the answers reveal the history of the period: the assassination of President William McKinley, conservation, the "Big Stick" policy, and how two bicycle makers made a "machine that flies."

A chorus sings the 1904 campaign song "We Want Teddy for Four Years More." The band plays patriotic songs of the period. Television crews record the whole event.

This scene takes place in the cafeteria at the Washington Irving Intermediate School in Springfield, Virginia. Roosevelt is played by Bob Boyd, a professional actor; the agents, press secretary, TV crews, members of the band and chorus, and the hundreds of reporters are seventh, eighth, and ninth graders. Some 100 posters depicting events during the Roosevelt years, researched in the library and drawn in the art classes, decorate the school halls.

The event was coordinated by the social studies department. Student reporters studied the period for two weeks, and each prepared three questions to stump the president. The teachers and cafeteria staff wore costumes of the period to lend an air of authenticity.

What was the result? William Costolo, principal of the school, summed it up:

> The students were deeply involved. They were active participants in the events of history. This was an exciting and emotional learning experience. The arts brought a sense of feeling to the period that is missing in the traditional history lesson. These students will remember facts about TR for a long time to come.

Music, the visual arts, the media, and theater were used as the means of learning history. They were fused with the subject matter, relating them to the subject being studied and, in the process, enlarging and invigorating learning. This "integration" of the arts can be taken to a more profound dimension in which the classroom creates an environment in which the arts are treated as a primary context for learning to take place. The approach draws connections between the arts and the subject being learned, what Ron Berger, a sixth-grade teacher in western Massachusetts refers to as "knitting it all together."[1] Such a holistic view is in keeping with real life, in which events seldom unfold in isolation. Wedding the arts to learning makes sense because the arts can fuel academic interest. But more important, Berger maintains, "they can be at the core of a [school] culture of high standards." In this framework, the arts function as "an entire structure of creating, critiquing, and sharing all academic work within an aesthetic model":

> I've argued that arts can form the basis of school norms and standards for work in a manner which is incredibly powerful. Student work is strong not just because they have more energy for it, and not because there is a clear transfer of intelligences, but rather because academic work is embodied in projects which are viewed artistically at all points in their creation.

This approach immediately liberates the arts from their usual restrictive and independent existence, although students still have to master technique in order to use the arts effectively. Students learn how to communicate through an art form in order to explore a subject area. They learn the subject, and they learn the art. But the arts are not separated from life; they are made a part of it. Berger explains:

> To understand this entails a shift in a conception of art from something which dwells in museums or concert halls, which is how most adults in this society view it, or something which lasts from 1:45 to 2:30 on Thursday afternoon (barring budget cuts), which is how most students in this society view it. It means seeing art as inextricably a part of all that we produce and share, which is how many kindergartners view it. Kindergartners may not articulate this in the abstract, but they may be happy to paint a picture, sing a song, and create a fantasy play to share with you their ideas and feelings.

Such a concept takes the arts out of the elitist world that seems to say that art is just for the gifted few and makes it a democratic expressive tool that all people can create, use to communicate, and share their own and others' perceptions. This concept, variously referred to as *arts in general education (AGE)* or *integrated arts*, dates back to the late 1960s and the experiments of the now-defunct Arts in Education Program of the John D. Rockefeller (JDR) III Fund. It is based on the theory that an arts program, viewed comprehensively, fulfills four functions:

1. It provides specialized education. (The arts are taught as separate disciplines worthy of study in their own right.)
2. It serves the needs of exceptional students. (The arts offer a variety of means to meet the special needs of the handicapped, the culturally deprived, and the talented.)
3. It establishes educational linkages with the community. (The arts provide a means to open and maintain productive lines of communication between the school and the community.)
4. It enhances general education. (The arts become enmeshed with all the other subject matters in the curriculum in such a way that they enliven the whole educational enterprise.)

AN INTERDISCIPLINARY APPROACH

When the arts are viewed as interdisciplinary studies and used as helpful tools in all learning, they assume an additional function that can reinforce learning in general. This "interdisciplinary" approach—the designation I prefer—is this aspect of the program that often is neglected or wholly ignored. An arts program that concentrates on only the first three functions tends to remain isolated, even though it may appear to be educationally sound strictly as education in the art. Integrating the arts with the school's fundamental goals and priorities has the potential to demonstrate their value to members of the school board, administrators, classroom teachers, parents, and students.

The theory that music and the other arts enhance general learning can be a powerful way to establish their educational usefulness. For this reason, the concept can improve the role and status of the arts in education in those schools that adopt this approach. Before that can happen, however, arts educators themselves must be persuaded.

An interdisciplinary arts program is not a substitute for the discrete learning of the various arts, although it may be incorporated as a part of it. Instead, an interdisciplinary approach uses the arts in tandem with other subjects to enhance learning in those areas. Here the arts refer not only to music and the visual arts but also to dance (movement), theater, creative writing, media, and environmental arts. Filtering the arts throughout the entire curriculum has an obvious educational use, as it integrates them with the school's goals and priorities and, in the process, demonstrates their educational value. This interdisciplinary approach combines learning in the arts with learning in other fields.

Some people regard the interdisciplinary technique as a means of enhancing basic education, by subordinating the arts to serve learning in the traditional subjects. In fact, in an effective interdisciplinary program, students learn as much about the arts as they do the subject that is their focus. In this respect, they may serve as a methodology, but not one that has no substance in its own right.

Interdisciplinary arts is an infusion of the arts with other subject matter in the general curriculum. By enlisting all the senses in the learning process, the arts provide a self-generated and self-propelled approach to learning. Infusing the arts into other subjects is mutually beneficial: The arts enhance learning in other subjects, and at the same time their infiltration into other subjects improves learning in the arts. The arts process should not, however, be distorted for the sake of learning something other than the arts. Fortunately, the subject matter of the arts explores multiple facets of the world and human life and can quite naturally relate to learning in general and add dimensions that are compelling and insightful.

ENCODING AND DECODING

The arts process encompasses the actions of encoding (perceiving, reacting, and creating) and decoding (re-creating, interpreting, and evaluating.) To encode is to transmit. Each art form represents a different symbolic system that students learn to use expressively. In dance, for example, the elements that make up the code are sound, movement, line, pattern, form, space, shape, rhythm, time, and energy. Just as meaning in prose language requires building forms from letters, words, sentences, and paragraphs, meaning in dance or any other art depends on combining the elements of its code to fashion forms that express and communicate.

Coding in the arts is analogous to coding in mathematics and science, in which students learn to use numbers and formulas to represent observations about the real world. Encoding is the process of translating thoughts, feelings, and observations into symbolic form. After children draw a picture of a house, they learn that there is another way, a verbal way, to indicate "house." The personal symbol (the picture) becomes a clue to learning the impersonal one (the word). Both the picture and the word are abstract; that is, they are not the reality but a convenient stand-in that conveys meaning in clear and convenient forms. The advantage of working through the arts is that they offer a variety of captivating ways to draw the students into the world of symbolization. Used in this way, the arts reinforce the development of the ability to manipulate symbols.

The process of coding in the arts can be applied to almost any subject. Suppose, for example, a classroom teacher is trying to get her second-grade class to understand the geometric concept of symmetry. Children may find this a difficult concept to grasp. Artistic codes can help. Through the visual arts, the children can arrange squares of different sizes and shapes on paper so that they make a symmetrical design. Through movement, each child can create a symmetrical shape with his or her body and then change the shape so that it is asymmetrical. Students can make symmetrical and asymmetrical shapes with a partner and then create group designs. In this case, movement (dance) can be used to introduce a mathematical concept in a personal and self-involving way.

Structure or form is a basic element of storytelling. A first-grade teacher might ask children to reorder a shuffled group of pictures so that they tell a (coherent) story. In the process, the children discover that stories have a beginning, a middle, and an end. The goal here is to build a logical sequence of parts in a linear time frame. Theater and music can reinforce this understanding. Stories can be acted out so that children feel the logic of the events and their culmination. Using music, students can create their own rhythmic (and, later, melodic) canons, inventing sequential order through the discovery of repetition and alternation.

Decoding is the means of receiving or "reading" what others "say" through the pictures they draw or the music they create. The receiver translates the code, thereby interpreting the meaning of the symbols. The decoding of the various artistic systems is a process of communication. Again, the process of decoding in the arts is analogous to learning to decode in science, mathematics, and the written word. But whereas coding is a creative act, decoding is generally re-creative and interpretive.

Deriving meaning from artistic symbols in the decoding process signifies that the viewer understands the content. The subject matter of the arts—their content—is life in all its manifestations. The arts are the means that humans have invented to convey their world as they experience it. Since the arts are the ways that people represent their perceptions of the world, they also are ways of knowing that world. In this sense they qualify as basic education.

Because the arts are usually not about art but about many other subjects, the argument that it is a bastardization to use them to teach those other subjects just doesn't hold water. The subject matter of the arts, revealed through the decoding process, can easily and naturally relate to most, if not all, the subjects in the curriculum.

The process of decoding in the arts can be applied to almost any subject. In reading, comprehension often depends on students' sensing the emotional content of the story. In music, identifying the changing moods can help children understand the changing moods in the poems and stories they are learning to read. Selecting appropriate music to accompany their stories or dramatizations helps students understand the meaning to be communicated.

In science, a study of textures on a nature walk helps reinforce the words that describe them—rough, smooth, fuzzy, spiny, and so on. The aesthetic dimensions are explored for their educational potential. Later, when children verbally describe the different textures that they see in one another's graphite rubbings of textures, they are decoding the arts and learning vocabulary at the same time.

These techniques work at every level. In high school, students can use the arts to study each period of American history in much the same way as the students at Washington Irving did. By singing and dancing to the music of a particular period, interpreting events through the visual arts, studying films about the period, and dramatizing literature, debates, and documents, students sense the spirit of the times and enter into it in a personal and emotional way. This direct contact is far more compelling than historical accounts alone.

Applying the study of the arts as a process for investigating and sharing their worlds of learning draws students into the subject matter and gives them ownership of it. Instead of being outwardly directed by the teacher, they become inwardly directed by themselves. They are not just regurgitating information handed to them but are also constructing their own meaning for themselves.

The arts engage students and summon their personal involvement. Used in this interdisciplinary way, they motivate students to want to learn and to be excited by it. Such engagement can reduce truancy and vandalism and even violence, because students like going to school better when they are using their own personal development and creative thought processes. They are making learning their own rather than having it foist on them.

_ chapter eight _

DEVELOPING NEW AUDIENCES

It is time that our symphony orchestras, opera companies, and other arts presentation enterprises realize that they cannot thrive, perhaps not even survive, by continuing to operate in the same old ways. The world, our values, our educational priorities, and our culture have been changing, but they, by and large, have not. Based on the number of performances, opera audiences declined by almost 6 percent during 1992 and 1993, compared with 1991 and 1992.[1] But there are hopeful signs: Ticket sales increased by 11 percent, even though main-stage and festival attendance decreased by 4 percent. Audiences for ballet and modern dance and symphony orchestras have tapered off and appear to be shrinking.

THE PROBLEMS

But the problem is bigger than the performing arts and therefore more insidious. The proportion of Americans who read serious contemporary literature is dwindling, and museum attendance is down. It is as though thousands of Americans are deliberately turning their backs on the arts, certainly in their classical forms. A 1989 *Washington Post*–ABC poll revealed that federal aid to public television and radio and assistance to the arts and music are at the bottom of America's shopping list, with fewer than one in five respondents favoring higher spending for these areas. Apparently, there is no longer enough public interest or support to sustain all these cultural institutions. Consequently, many of them are threatened with financial strangulation.

Some people would have us believe that our dwindling audiences for the arts are due to the anarchy of today's art, detached as much of it is from public purpose, meaning, and understanding. Certainly the fact that art has gone its private way has not helped it in the marketplace. Nor does it serve the interest of the marketer, in this case the opera companies and symphony orchestras that try to relate to the twentieth century and look like they belong to it by occasionally performing works so socially defiant that they offend their conservative patrons.

But the artist's anarchy, as damaging as it is to the vibrancy of these institutions, is not the crux of the problem. What we must remember is that even when subscription seasons sold out, the new art still was no more or less appealing to the public. What we are facing is a cultural upheaval.[2] Our values are in flux. As public taste embraces the sensational, the commercial, and the gross, aesthetic quality is being trashed in favor of the expedient— fast food, the quick fix, and easy entertainment. There is an ongoing, pervasive struggle—a cultural divide—between the values of those who support the arts and those who denounce them.

Today's audiences become bored more quickly. It seems to take more to attract their interest, captivate them, and sustain their attention. They tend to be restless and less easily satisfied for very long, maybe because the world is moving at dizzying speed, and they are innundated by images. Shouldn't the arts and entertainment keep pace?

Today we demand constant action, diversity, fascination, stimulation, and revelation, all in less time. The ideal of delayed gratification has been telescoped to embrace immediacy. The balance between unity and variety has tipped in favor of variety. Beauty as an ideal has been replaced by adventure. Perhaps something about communicative technique can be learned from films, television, and popular music that play to contemporary audiences in the tens of millions. These mass entertainments leave nothing to chance in trying to reach potential clients. If nothing more, they have an attitude and a determination that might be applied beneficially.

The world of America looking toward the new millennium is an increasingly barbaric place, with slaughter on the streets, drugs perverting lives in almost every family, and constant revelations of deceit and crime in high places. It seems to be growing cruder and more insensitive. The honesty and integrity of arts are fundamentally at odds with these conditions. They reside in a society that seems increasingly hostile to their presence. In light of these devastating circumstances, what are our arts institutions doing to save themselves? Museums do their blockbuster retrospective on Van Gogh or Tutankhamen but contemplate adopting theme-park approaches in order to attract more regular attendance. Ballet companies, intent on keeping themselves financially solvent, stage lengthy runs of *The Nutcracker* every Christmas season. Similarly, the National Symphony gives not one but two performances of Tchaikovsky's *1812 Overture*, with cannons, at Wolf Trap every July to accommodate all the fans. In 1992, the orchestra performed

Prokofiev's *Alexander Nevsky* along with a reprint of the classic Russian film to an overflow audience, a standing ovation, and rave reviews. These tactics show that there is still an audience out there whose interest can be tapped by certain kinds of events. But is it enough? Do we pander when we give the audience what it will support? Or asked in another way, is quality compromised more by serving a broader audience or an ever-diminishing one? Just what must we do to secure audiences in the future?

CLASSICAL MUSIC: SINGING THE BLUES

The traditional institutions of what used to be called "high culture" are in serious trouble. The Buffalo Philharmonic and the Rochester Philharmonic, among other small city orchestras, have serious financial problems. Indeed, in the last six years the country's orchestras as a whole have run deficits totaling $100 million. From 1989 to 1993, the money given to dance by New York State dropped 59 percent and by California 29 percent. High culture today survives chiefly because of the support of wealthy corporate patrons. In Buffalo, which lacks wealthy donors, high culture is dying, and culture is becoming less and less accessible. The symphony is one of the few attractions the city can use to lure new businesses to what is otherwise an aging, rust-belt town.[3]

Marcia Friedmutter, director of the cultural arts unit of the New York City School System's Division of Curriculum and Instruction, lays the blame on "budgetary constraints." Although there are funds to support other subjects, music education is simply not sufficiently valued. In the 1984/1985 school year New York City cut the number of its music teachers from 2,200 to 793. And in regard to budgets, curricular considerations, staffing, and scheduling, music doesn't command much priority. But the adult population of the United States doesn't think very highly of classical music, either.

The survey of public participation in the arts conducted by the National Endowment for the Arts in 1985 showed that of the 54 million Americans who did go to museums or live performances, 13 percent went to live performances of classical music, 18.6 percent to musicals, 9.6 percent to jazz, and 3 percent to opera. Many more people, however, are participating in the arts via television, radio, and recordings. The survey revealed that "the mass media reach a wider arts audience—typically twice as large—than do live performances." It noted the large number of commercial radio stations devoted to classical music and jazz and the great dependence of opera on television and radio to expand its audience. The higher the level of education and income, the greater the interest and participation. Nevertheless, audiences for opera and symphonic music in live performances and on the media generally consist of the affluent and better educated.[4]

The reason is that music education programs are reaching the brighter, more affluent students, who become the audiences for classical music in the future. But music, particularly at the high school level, typically reaches only a small percentage of the students. Music teachers should ask themselves why they insist on being so selective. It might well be that the parents of these brighter, better-off students convey their tastes to their offspring and also support music programs in the schools. And their children tend to follow their example. But music teachers may prefer working with the brighter students and deliberately seek them out. That kind of exclusivity creates a major problem for developing audiences for opera, symphonies, and other forms of classical music.

NEW APPROACHES

What seems to be needed is a whole set of new approaches that can attack this complex problem simultaneously on several fronts. If opera has benefited from titling (projecting a translation simultaneously with the foreign language being sung), what more might be done? Perhaps the arts would be wise to commence a massive redevelopment effort designed to look freshly and thoroughly at our own ingrained habits and practices to see where they may be hindering us. For example, one reviewer of *Alexander Nevsky* suggested that it "could easily become [Tchaikovsky's] counterpart each August." This may be precisely what is wrong with the whole mentality of the classical arts. They are continually in pursuit of tradition. When we find something that works, we repeat it until it wears out its welcome. We tend to inundate people with sameness. The symphony orchestra suffers from bankruptcy of the imagination. What it needs in order to attract audiences is not two unusual ideas that excite public interest but dozens of them. It needs change.

The symphony orchestra can no longer afford to have a bad performance—not that it ever could. One bad performance can kill all interest in live music for all newcomers for all time. Rather, the symphony orchestra must seize every opportunity to recapture music's vibrancy, to return the art to a form of communication, not just personal expression. Effective communication today commands and sustains interest, excites the emotions, awakens the spirit, and engages the mind, all at the same time. The challenge is to succeed with people who are deluged with communications of all kinds.

In music, to be willing and eager to experiment may not be as easy as it sounds. Collectively, musicians are among the most obstinately habitual of all professionals. Suggest such simple devices as relighting or reseating the orchestra, warming up offstage, or moving the orchestra to another venue, and you will hear grownups whimper like infants. But the threat of going out of business can make even musicians more receptive. The penchant of musicians and opera singers to feed their own egos by presenting themselves as the only ones "in the know"—the musical literati—has alienated them from the people they should befriend. "Cinderella," said her two ugly stepsisters in a television production of the classic, "We is going to the ball, and you is not!" The difference today is that Cinderella does not want to go to the concert hall or opera house, because they no longer have a special status. To turn around this public indifference and disregard, the real communicative importance of music must be reasserted, and to do this, the audience must be moved. They must come first.

The National Endowment for the Arts (NEA) can help lead this redevelopment effort by requiring grants in music, opera, musical theater, and the other arts to support new ways of operating, programming, and presenting. In music, grants should give some priority to innovation in such areas as repertoire (including new music and the ignored repertoire of well-established composers), presentation format, new venues, educational initiatives, and outreach. The NEA has not done the field of music any favors by shoring it up, *as is*, for the past two decades. If anything, it has made musical enterprises less aware of the need to adapt and alter their practice to fit our changing times. The handouts have insulated the field from the vicissitudes that would have necessitated adjustments and corrections along the way. Now, with falling attendance and higher costs, this shoring up is not sufficient to overcome two decades of denial. Lack of responsiveness to the public has fed the music world's disdain. But these problems are not new. The NEA would have been of far greater service to orchestras and opera companies if it had made them face the music all along. Perhaps the arts must reclaim their own leadership.

Redevelopment efforts, new leadership, and changes born of experimentation and innovation, important as they are, are short-term adjustments and gains, Band-Aids in the face of an epidemic. To deal realistically with cultural upheaval, we need to apply long-term solutions as well.

EDUCATION

A survey of the attitudes of sixth- and tenth-grade students toward classical music reveals that many young people don't like it, don't understand it, and don't even know what it is. Their opinions range from an all-too-rare "wondrous sound" to "it stinks" and is "boring" and "dull." A significant 35.6 percent of the responses described classical music as soft and/or slow, and their misdefinitions ranged from big band, ballroom, and rock and roll, to music heard in hospitals, dentists' offices, elevators, and supermarkets.[5] To many of these young people, classical music is a dead language, a subject akin to Latin.

Such negative attitudes toward classical music are a result of ignorance, proving that an understanding of classical music requires study. Unlike rock music or rap—which so many of these students find immediately accessible and understandable, classical music poses challenges comparable to learning a foreign language. After all, the musical language of popular music is deliberately in the public vernacular, whereas classical music is more complex, more structured and developed, and sometimes more subtle, profound, or sublime in content. Accordingly, a person must know more to get the message, like the extra effort it takes to understand Shakespeare or Spenser or Milton.

Let us give education another chance. Those of us who regard the arts as important believe that they improve human perception and understanding, creativity and communication, and thought and feeling, which are essential to the conduct of life and society. How did we arrive at such a notion? We *learned* it.

According to the "Survey of Public Participation in the Arts," conducted by the National Endowment for the Arts in 1985, 53 percent of those polled had never had lessons or classes in music, and 80 percent had never studied music appreciation. Music appreciation courses were likely to have been taken only in college.[6]

Our public schools no longer have enough interest in, respect for, or understanding of music to provide the quality or quantity of public support that is necessary for the arts to be sustained as an essential ingredient of our culture. In many public schools, vast numbers of children are being denied access to their musical heritage. In some of our largest cities, the number of music specialists at the elementary level has been dropping for nearly two decades. String programs and orchestras are becoming extinct. In secondary schools, music programs usually do not reach all students. As a result, a downtrodden army of cultureless children is marching toward a barren and depleted adulthood and taking the future of our civilization with them.

As increasing numbers of children grow up with little or no experience, knowledge, and understanding of music, our public performing arts are becoming an ever more exclusive reclusion for a dwindling educated elite.

Why study classical music? Because the apotheoses of human achievement in musical art are found in works such as Bach's B minor Mass, Beethoven's Ninth Symphony, and Britten's *War Requiem*. We should offer every person the right to climb those mountains. Where are the new audiences going to come from if not from our schools? Until provisions are made in America's public schools for all students to understand classical music, it will continue to be an art of a small, and perhaps dwindling, adult elite, with growing numbers of young detractors.

With the demise of music programs, we are losing a major civilizing force. Even though the study of the arts may not make people more moral, it does put them in touch with some of the highest achievements of humankind. It shows what can be done. It teaches students to reach, to live up to something, to embrace a wider universe. Encounters with music and the other arts permit students to unlock some of the great stored wisdom of the ages.

The arts are part of what make people well educated. Take the arts away, and they will inevitably become less well educated. There is no replacement. They either acquire the capacity to unlock these insights and meanings, or they are deprived of them. Children made to do without them are the lesser for it. That is why every young person, without exception, should be given access to the study of the arts: not so they will become artists but so they will become better educated. In visual arts and music, teachers have made this serious error for many years: They concentrate their efforts on the talented, on those who already have been won over. In the arts and certainly in music, we cannot afford to have any enemies. We must reach the people who are the future cab drivers, salespersons, plumbers, politicians, school administrators, and lawyers. This means that symphony orchestras, opera companies, ballet and theater companies, and all the other public arts enterprises have to take greater responsibility. Who is going to persuade schools if not those most affected? Who is going to take the leadership if not those who have an understanding of the arts and a commitment to them?

How can arts education be revitalized? Certainly not through the token efforts of the past: one-shot student matinees, school-assembly presentations, artists visiting schools, and special events for very talented young performers. Although these approaches may be useful, they do not begin to do the job. Building a real understanding of the classical arts among young people requires a wholly different and far more comprehensive commitment. OPERA America, a professional organization representing more than 100 opera companies in North America, is attempting to do this, by developing a series of materials to teach opera at every grade level. With these materials in hand, opera companies can become a resource for ongoing, in-school arts education programs. Faced with annihilation, opera companies and orchestras must assume far more responsibility for education. They must be accountable. It is their world. In contrast, science does not sit by the wayside when it comes to taking educational responsibility and action. The National Science Foundation is deeply involved in education and thoroughly committed. It assembles the troops and assumes leadership.

Unless we can persuade the schools to assume the responsibility of passing on the culture to the younger generation, to think beyond just employability as the goal of education, we will be forced to depend totally on private-sector alternatives. And that prospect poses far more difficulties than do new coalitions with exiting state and local educational agencies. Again, we must turn to the NEA for leadership. This, too, will call for some major adjustments.

The reason that the NEA in the past focused its support on artists and arts institutions and not on education is that artists and arts institutions did not, until recently, connect with education the well-being of their own enterprises. This neglect of music in American schools is already having serious effects on our performing arts institutions and our culture as a whole. In truth, there can be no art or artists without some form of education, nor would there be any arts institutions in American society without the infrastructure of education to sustain them. The well-being of our cultural enterprises depends directly on the effectiveness of education in the arts. The reverse is equally true: The place and pertinence of the arts in education depends directly on the well-being of the arts in society. If there were no arts in society, there would be no need for any in education. The two are therefore interlocking and interdependent components of the same universe. The arts and education are allies, two sides of the same coin.

What is at stake is nothing less than a whole way of life. The classical arts represent a value system that should be prized but increasingly is not. One hope is to gather all the forces, scant as they are, and join together in a massive effort to reverse the current trends. If we don't, we stand to lose a precious part of our cultivated human existence. The world could get coarser, crueler, and more uncouth. We could lose altogether our mechanisms for communicating both the ennobling and the starkly revealing purviews of human life. We could cease to value the "languages" of civilization through which we express our feelings, dreams, outrages, and intuitive understandings. Science does not and cannot provide us with this insight.

In this technological age, music and the other arts are needed more than ever to reaffirm our humanity. With satellite TV transmission and the Internet, cellular phones and modems, faxes and e-mail, and other electronic advances, communication among people worldwide is easier than ever before.

This pluralistic, multiethnic culture requires more, not less, cultural understanding. The arts can bridge ethnic differences and open the avenues of human understanding. They can give American youth and society, now charged with a dehumanizing and primitive machismo, a balancing dimension of humaneness. These are powerful reasons to fight for the arts' survival. The future of our civilization and the quality of our culture depend on the health and vibrancy of our performing arts and their counterpart in our schools. In this regard, concerted efforts on both the artistic and educational fronts by everyone involved in the arts, including the NEA, are imperative. They alone will determine whether these forms of communication count for much just around the corner in the twenty-first century.

part three

CURRICULUM

Encounters with the arts can take many forms, some stressing one set of aspects, some another. A school curriculum consists of all the courses and content offered in a particular subject. It defines the centers of concentration that are taught and learned. The choices that face arts teachers as they invent a curriculum must take into account such practical conditions as the circumstances in the school, the background of the students, the number of arts teachers, the extent of teacher/student contact, and the availability and type of equipment, instructional materials, and community resources. Many different influences impinge on the arts curriculum, dictating what can be expected and accomplished. The curriculum is determined (and sometimes compromised) by the quality and the quantity of instruction, the resources consigned to the arts, and the status with which the arts are held in a school.

Practical matters aside, the curriculum itself is usually grounded in a set of beliefs about what education in each art form should be. Teachers must know what they want to accomplish through arts education, and the best way to achieve maximum educational impact given the limitations of their circumstances, their own abilities and interests, and their beliefs regarding the focus and purpose of arts study.

What constitutes excellence in creative writing, dance, music, theater, and visual arts education? One answer is provided by the national standards for the arts (minus creative writing, which will be included with the standards for English) developed by a consortium of arts education organizations in 1994. The standards concentrate on the processes of achieving specific arts skills and knowledge and determine what every young American should know and be able to do in each of the arts. These are suggested guideposts that leave it up to individual schools and teachers to decide on the specific curricula to produce these results. How much emphasis should be put on developing technique (production); understanding the historical, cultural, and aesthetic aspects of each art; refining critical abilities; and establishing the value of the arts?

The curriculum is what teachers teach after their classroom door is closed, rather than a list of standards or a printed syllabus. It is what is covered in class and what students actually learn. The curriculum must take into account how much emphasis should be given to intracultural understanding, the amount of attention that will be paid to one area or another, how community resources should be incorporated, how the art will be used to assist students in general learning, and many other issues. Is there agreement and continuity throughout the arts program? Figuring all this out requires considerable thought and planning, which is no simple task.

Part III explores some of the issues that must be decided when creating an arts curriculum. What are the intrinsic and distinctive characteristics of each art form, and how can these be translated into what and how students learn? The dilemma posed by the many options of the diverse cultures in our country requires teachers to select what should be stressed. Because arts educators usually claim to develop students' creativity, the lack of emphasis on doing so in the curriculum poses a serious problem of credibility. There must be continuity between theory and practice. How do the arts relate to academic achievement in general? All these issues and more determine what an arts curriculum should be. Such curricular decisions are sometimes difficult because the choices are extensive and the ramifications so momentous.

_ chapter nine _

ALL ARTS, ALL STUDENTS

The erosion of the arts in American elementary schools is pervasive.
Although music and visual arts programs in grades 1 through 6 exist
in most schools, the time allotted to them has dropped alarmingly during the past three decades.[1] Opportunities to study the other arts are
meager. Dance is rarely taught. Almost 93 percent of elementary schools
do not offer it, and when it is offered it is generally taught by a physical
education teacher rather than a certified dance specialist. The situation is
similar in drama/theater. Almost 84 percent of elementary schools do not
have a drama/theater program as such, although classroom teachers frequently dramatize stories or use dramatic activities in teaching subjects
other than drama/theater.[2]

EQUALITY OF ACCESS AND OPPORTUNITY

Across the country, access to study of the arts is blatantly uneven. According
to Judith M. Burton, professor and coordinator of the program in art and
art education at Teachers College, Columbia University,

> At the elementary level art is mandated by most states, but provision
> is inequitable; in fact, many children across the land have no access to
> formal art instruction, and many teachers at this level have little or
> no formal training in the arts or arts education. Few good instruc-
> tional resources are available to help teachers, apart from commercial
> productions whose artistic authenticity and educational substance is
> often minimal, biased, and, not infrequently, erroneous.[3]

A study conducted by the National Center for Education Statistics that analyzed all high school graduates in the class of 1982 shows that there is a marked inequality of opportunity in the availability of arts instruction in American schools.[4] Nearly one-third of these seniors—more than 1 million—received no instruction whatsoever in any of the arts during their four years of high school. Almost 10 percent of our high schools do not offer a single course in music; 15 percent offer no instruction in the visual arts; more than one-half provide no instruction in crafts or dramatic arts; and more than two-thirds offer no creative writing, graphic and commercial arts, dance, or design courses.[5]

Then, too, arts offerings differ according to where a student happens to live. In general, schools in the South offer far fewer courses in the arts than do schools elsewhere. High schools there are less likely to offer instruction in dramatic arts, design, crafts, and creative writing. Courses in music and art appreciation are found more often in northern schools, and western schools are more likely to give instruction in dance. About one-half the secondary schools in the United States offer basic courses such as music and art appreciation, with schools in the suburbs providing far more opportunities to be educated in the arts. Whereas virtually all larger schools—those with 1,500 or more students—offer dramatic arts and design, only 31 percent of smaller schools offer instruction in these areas. Schools with 10 percent or higher concentrations of black or Latino students offer fewer arts and humanities courses. Schools with high numbers of college-bound students offer more courses in the arts. But even in exceptional high schools that might be considered to have ample courses in the arts, relatively few students enroll in them. They are often advised to concentrate on academics and to elect additional courses in science and math rather than the arts.

Nonetheless, many of our outstanding programs of arts instruction are world-class models of their type. Few school systems in other countries, for example, produce the level of musical performance achieved by some of our school bands, choruses, and orchestras. Some school systems can also boast about their work in the visual arts, dance, theater, and creative writing. Nor are all urban programs deficient. Pittsburgh and Dallas, among other cities, have excellent arts programs. But these tend to be the exceptions rather than the rule.

Equality of opportunity remains one of the fundamental principles of American education. Yet individually, the arts are seldom accorded equal treatment in school curricula, with music and visual arts being far more prevalent than dance, media arts, theater, or creative writing.

THE INDIVIDUALITY OF ART FORMS

Collectively, the arts represent a variety of ways to conceptualize meaning. Individually, however, they "speak" in their own languages, with the messages and meanings tailored to their medium. They help us see, hear, move, and use these capacities to signify meaning. Even when they deal with the same subject, each art form provides its own aesthetic perspective.

Creative Writing

When literature sets us to thinking about the human condition, social change may well be the result. John Steinbeck's novel *The Grapes of Wrath* (1939) uses the plight of Dust Bowl farmers turned migrant laborers in the 1930s to represent all victims of disaster. By putting ourselves in these circumstances, we may form new understanding that alters our attitudes and leads to social change. Although this is not always the case, it is so frequently enough to characterize the art. Jane Alexander, chairman of the National Endowment for the Arts, observed: "Because they often tap into the very issues that society is grappling with, the arts can cause outrage, fear and anger. They're only doing their job."[6]

Poetry is another story. Through juxtapositions of images, analogies, and imaginative visions, poetry creates its own reality. Words become their own excuse for being. The needs of creative writing are unique. Of all the arts it is the easiest to teach in school, since it readily relates to the most sanctified of the basics, the language arts. Yet it is surprising how few schools offer creative writing. The support of poets and writers in residence by the National Endowment for the Arts education program and state arts agencies has been a main force in delivering this art to students.

Why teach poetry? Through it, students express through language their visions of the world. Flora Arnstein, a poet and teacher, noted that "poetry is recorded experience—or imagined experience." She believes that the only way to get kids to write is to have them write about their own experiences and what they've felt.[7] Oddly enough, even though poetry, essays, and short stories relate directly to the language arts, creative writing is rarely emphasized in the public schools, perhaps because it takes up a lot of time, particularly on the teacher's part.

Dance

Dance is a good way for students to develop a sense of themselves and a perspective on life. Movement is the essence of dance, and perhaps the essence of life itself. Maybe that is why dance has been a part of human cultures as far back as records exist. It is one of the rituals that celebrate significant life passages, and it is a way we release our aesthetic expressivity through our physical being, an exuberant and compelling form of communication.

Like the other arts, dance demands discipline and control. The dancer has to learn how the body moves, how to call up that movement, repeat it, and understand its expressive use. Dance expression is a repertoire of movements in frameworks of time, energy, and form. It requires students to exercise their creative imaginations, their ability to think and to figure out, to develop a sense of form, and to seek meaning through their own life force. Students learn dance by actually dancing and also by being an observer of or audience for dance performances.

Dance is an enigmatic, often misperceived, art. For one thing, most people have never studied it, and so all they know about it is their experience with social dancing, certainly not a representative or complete example of the art. As a result, the public tends to be ambivalent, and sometimes hostile, about including dance in the public school curriculum.

A school doesn't always need to hire a dance specialist in order to offer dance instruction. For example, if a town has a fine school of dance that caters to young people, the public school might well use those expert teachers and facilities to set up a cooperative program that enables every student in the school system to have some instruction in dance. This outside program would supplement, not supplant, the dance component that is often a regular part of the school's physical education program. Community dancers and dance groups can be brought into the schools on a temporary basis to work with students and to demonstrate the art. The school acts as the coordinating agency, making certain that all students are scheduled for this particular learning experience. The aim here is to expose students to this art by letting them experience it firsthand.

Music

Whether music is explored by singing, playing an instrument, composing on synthesizer and computer, or listening, students learn the art of expression and communication through sound. They learn to create, perform, listen perceptively, and analyze. Where technology is used, it individualizes and expands instruction. A comprehensive program of music instruction encompasses instrumental and vocal music as well as general music. The latter is a survey intended to convey to students the varied subject matter of music, its technical requirements, and its emotional message. They learn that if music isn't expressive, it is worthless.[8] In the best music programs, students learn the art of improvisation, interpretation, and creation, but such programs are rare.

For more than a century, classical music has prided itself on what the composer/commentator Lawrence Kramer calls its "transcendental apartness" and its disdain for nonmusical meaning. But classical music is no longer the dominant cultural high art that it once was. The attempt to retain its esoteric stature by "denying music discursive meaning mystifies rather than enhances it, and this prevalent attitude has increasingly encouraged people to believe that classical music has nothing to say to them." Kramer argues that music "is radically enveloped and interwoven with meanings," and he is intent on retrieving music from its traditional self-containment and uncovering those meanings.[9] What is important is that this symbol system we call music speaks to us and that it conveys meaning in a compelling way.

Today, music education explores a multitude of musical styles, including not just classical music but also folk and ethnic music, religious music, jazz, blues, gospel, rock, and other popular forms. Students learn to identify the source of the sound, whether solo or ensemble, the different instruments and voices, and their combinations into bands, choruses, and orchestras, and a variety of small ensembles. They explore the historical periods and their distinctive styles, as well as the music of other cultures. They also learn the art of musical expression—how sound can be used to communicate feelings.

Theater

The prominence of television drama in children's lives encourages their natural desire to act. Theater, the art of people, conveys the meaning of its words made vibrant with the colors and sounds of the human voice and the coordinated rhythm of the moving body. Drama invites children to imitate the actions and character traits of people around them, observations that propel the child from a purely egocentric being to a more worldly understanding. Acting ties students to their inner and outer worlds, and the play is used as an instrument of growth.

Creative drama or play making refers to improvised drama. It may be used by a group of any age and is not exhibitional; that is, it is not intended as a formal presentation for an audience. According to educational theater expert Nellie McCaslin, for junior and senior high school students, however, a play is often the desired culmination of a semester's work. To deprive students of the experience would be to withhold the ultimate satisfaction."[10]

Creating a character calls for keen observation, imagination, insight, and often remarkable understanding. In addition to heightening social awareness, creating a character enhances cooperation, communicative movements, and better habits of speech. In addition to developing acting skills and inventing situations and their resolution, theater students learn the supportive arts of scenery, costume, and lighting design.

Barbara Salisbury Wills, executive director of the American Alliance for Theater and Education, observes that few classroom teachers have had any background in drama; rather "they often equate drama with putting on a play for the PTA." Administrators often have the same limited view. Wills believes that teachers think they are addressing drama when their students put on "skits" based on social studies events. Teachers use drama only as a tool to teach other subjects; they do not view it as a discipline in its own right, nor do they know how to assess it.[11]

Theater, like dance, needs support for curricular development. Universities or state theater associations that might initiate these efforts generally lack the necessary funds to bring the relevant people together. Curricular development is a long-term undertaking requiring the coordinated efforts of imaginative and seasoned teachers.

Understanding oneself and others is at the apex of the theater experience. By seeing a representation of life reenacted, we explore another perspective on other humans and their reactions, foibles, and solutions, satisfactory and not. This slice of life forms a world that draws us inward and outward at the same time.

Visual and Media Arts

Today, especially, the most affecting art is visual—photographs, advertising, computer graphics, design, drawing, painting, pottery, and sculpture. Media arts, such as television and film, are multiart forms with a strong, often dominant, visual component. Design is an essential and powerful element of the world of commerce, to which people readily respond. Drawing and painting develop basic perceptions of the world. Indeed, the visual arts may be the most dominant art mode of our culture at this time, certainly among youth, although the allure of music (sound) also cannot be underestimated.

Education in visual and media arts can take many forms and and have several aims. Students are usually taught a specific technique in some visual medium—pencil or paint or video imaging or collage (a combination of bits of objects pasted together on a surface to create an effect). But learning skills is just part of an education in visual arts, not the whole story. The better programs are more comprehensive.

In its preliminary review of art programs, the Getty Center identified those features that characterize the customary content and practice of art education:

> Chief among these is the traditional emphasis in visual arts education on fostering creative expression and developing artistic skills, such as drawing, painting and sculpting. This approach is evidenced in programs that stress hands-on production activities to the virtual exclusion of teaching children about the cultural and historical contributions of art or how to value, analyze, and interpret works of art.[12]

The Getty Center criticizes these programs: "While recent reports on the quality of education cry out for courses with greater substance and rigor, and while traditional 'academic' courses stress thought, reason, and ideas, art courses have sought traditionally to engage children's imaginations, feelings, and emotions."[13] The center's solution is to devise visual art programs that encompass art history, art criticism, aesthetics, and art production. The center is trying to make art programs more academic, to design art courses that "stress thought, reason, and ideas," in other words, to counter the public notion that the arts are mindless play and pleasure.

The emphasis of these efforts is currently on teacher in-service education, with much of the focus on elementary classroom teachers. Already the general philosophy of broadening the curriculum and making it "discipline based"[14] is affecting curricular development in all the arts in many state departments of education and local school districts. Although it is still too early to tell, the Getty Center's effort appears now to be an excellent model of how to effect change in the arts, because it has made art educators throughout the country aware of the need to enlarge their conceptual base, and it has used the mechanism of teacher in-service education to instill a discipline-based approach.

Photography, video, computer programs, and multimedia often are expressive tools that excite student's interest. Some students suddenly come alive when the emphasis is not on book learning but on creating visual images. At the O'Loughlin Elementary School in Hays, Kansas, for example, students begin developing multimedia presentations in kindergarten. By the third grade, they're operating an in-school TV station that produces a morning newscast.

SERVING ALL THE STUDENTS

The population of American schools is heterogenous. Students differ in their background, nurturing at home, family stability, parental support, interest in learning, motivation, race, self-respect, respect for parents' and teachers' authority, amount of time they spend passively watching television, and other factors. The schools must fulfill the special needs of all kinds of students whether the subject is mathematics or the arts.

Although most students are lumped into the category of "average," each possesses unique qualities of intellectual capacity, personality, and deportment, and there is no better vehicle for accommodating individuality than the arts. The old idea of a uniform education for everybody seems to be fading. It has not worked. One out of every three students in America leaves high school without a diploma; in some metropolitan areas the drop-out rate is more than 50 percent. This is educational failure of extraordinary magnitude.

"Special Needs" Students

"Special needs" students who are physically and/or mentally disabled can benefit from the arts. Their impairments cover a wide range of problems, from a disability such as autism that causes students to disrupt classrooms, to students who are emotionally disturbed and those who exhibit very mild retardation. Some public schools try to accommodate these children by creating special programs and special classrooms and hiring teacher aides and specialists. Schools place these students in separate classrooms so that they can be taught individually by experts.

Financial considerations have forced some schools to abandon these costly special programs and "mainstream" disabled students in regular classrooms, a harsher and probably less productive solution. Has the generation-old, congressionally mandated effort to educate physically and mentally disabled children in ordinary classrooms worked? A federal five-year study of high school students found that disabled students who spend all their time in regular classrooms fail 10 percent more frequently than do those who spend only half their time there. The question that must be addressed is to what extent the needs of handicapped students should be permitted to impinge on the majority of children and vice versa. According to a recent survey, the public is concerned that "average students don't get the attention they need because the teacher is distracted trying to deal with the youngsters at the extremes."[15]

How do the arts serve this population? The need to express and communicate transcends most disabilities. Autism, for example, may be an obstacle, but it does not destroy talent. Children with handicaps can find the arts stimulating, as they distract them from their physical and mental condition and involve them in activities that awaken their latent abilities. This may account for the observable relationship between disability and heightened creativity. The arts can also play a restorative role, assisting physical healing and giving students greater self-confidence. In an interview, a student who had suffered head injuries and other disabilities, observed, "When they see my art, they don't see my disability. They see who I am."[16] For people with disabilities who are viewed (and may view themselves) as helpless, dependent, and worthless, the arts are often empowering. Few, if any, physical or mental challenges can limit the human potential to create and to feel better because of it.[17] Given that the arts can counter pain and misfortune, schools should offer these students opportunities to give their lives joy and meaning.

Juvenile Delinquents

American youth constitute the fastest-growing segment of our criminal population. According to the Federal Bureau of Investigation, juvenile arrests have nearly quadrupled in the twenty-five years from 1965 to 1990, and these young offenders not only are the "disadvantaged minority youth in urban areas" but also include "all races, all social classes and life styles."[18]

Almost three-quarters of Americans (72 percent) say that drugs and violence are serious problems in their schools. Their principal requirements for improved education are for a safe, orderly environment and effective teaching of the basics (defined as reading, writing, and arithmetic). They cite the lack of discipline and violence as the biggest problems facing the public schools.[19] Only a disciplined environment free of drugs, violence, and firearms can be conducive to learning.

Again, the arts can provide a way, not a panacea, but certainly a positive influence and remedy for many lost and foundering students. Unfortunately, the dearth of city public school arts programs has left many young blacks, Latinos, Asians, and whites with few or no opportunities to become involved in the arts. More than 90 percent of the nation's school districts receive funds under Chapter 1, a compensatory program that provides extra instruction for educationally disadvantaged students, but rarely does this mean instruction in the arts. Impoverished students benefit from compensatory assistance. Social, economic, educational, environmental, and cultural differences all are part of the influences that cause violence among today's youth. We need sweeping changes to save these youths. American society neglects racial minorities and the poor, heaping undeserved misery on them. Journalist Steve L. Dash, who has spent years studying the urban crisis, wrote:

> The adolescent drug sellers and their destitute adult clients are just the observable symptoms of continuing inner-city decay. This decay is intricately interwoven with other dead-end ingredients of life within America's bottom tier of poverty: adolescent childbearing, child abuse and neglect, foster care, dropping out of school, welfare dependence, single parenthood, chronic unemployment and neighborhood crime and violence.[20]

According to studies by the Urban Institute, during the last generation, America's urban underclass population tripled in size, to an estimated 2.7 million persons, and it is growing at the rate of 8 percent a decade. Black Americans make up 57 percent of this underclass, whites and Latinos 20 percent each. The remaining 3 percent is made up of Asians and Native Americans.

Many of these students are "at risk"; that is, they are resisting the system and are likely to drop out of school. Because of their limited proficiency in English, poverty, single-parent families, geographic location, or economic disadvantage, more than 5 million U.S. students face a greater risk of lower educational achievement than do more fortunate students. According to a report by the U.S. Department of Education in 1994, 27.5 percent of Latinos aged sixteen to twenty-four dropped out of school, compared with 16 percent of blacks and 10 percent of whites. If we are going to help such students achieve their full educational potential, they must be identified early and given special attention and special programs. Crime and violence are products of these failures. Bringing these students into the system and helping them achieve success is a sure way to intercede before they become adult offenders.

Substance abuse among inmates in Washington, D.C., amounts to 15 to 20 percent of the prison population, who are responsible for 60 to 75 percent of the country's criminal activity. Jasper Ormond, a clinical psychologist, maintains that this population views crime as a way out of poverty. The average age of these inmates, who grew up in the city's poorest neighborhoods and read just above the third-grade level, is between eighteen and twenty-four.[21] Prison is not a deterrent for teenaged criminals, who go right back to committing more crimes when they return to the street.

What is the solution? According to Dash,

> Intensive work with children in the first six years of elementary school can begin to make a difference. Many of these prisoners went on to junior high school without the academic foundation to do junior high-level work much less be able to function academically at the high school level. . . .
>
> Of course, providing a basic education won't save all of them. But it will give many more of them an avenue into stable employment and conventional American life. After that, you can see the connections just as you can see the connections to a life of crime— and society should see why it needs to make sure they acquire that basic ability. There are, after all, very few high school graduates in prison.[22]

Survival itself for many of these students depends on the kind of education they receive and whether they can connect personally and substantially with it. When schools care about these youth, they can counter the cycle of despair by showing that there are alternatives to a life of poverty, drug abuse, illiteracy, and crime. We must produce healthy people if we want to reduce the alienation and disenfranchisement that pervade the youthful poor. One of the inescapable facts is that it costs far more to process and incarcerate these young criminals than it does to educate them so that they do not enter the public judicial system in the first place. Prevention rather than punishment is the cost-effective way to go.

What does this have to do with the arts? Judge Isabel Gomey of the Hennepin County (Minnesota) Judicial System believes that education in the arts can have a direct and important bearing. She regularly presides over juvenile cases and has made a point of talking with these young murderers, rapists, drug dealers, robbers, burglars, car thieves—people prone to violence. Among these young offenders, she finds a common thread: "They are dead inside," Judge Gomey says. "They have no spark. There is no light." She thinks that the arts can break through this void in a way that mathematics, science, geography, and other subjects cannot. The arts can ignite the spark by directly engaging the internal self, urging their beings to life. They can help develop these young people's imagination and talent and give them a personal and meaningful focus.

Educators have perpetuated the myth that kids do not achieve because of low self-esteem and that the way to get them to do better in school and in society is to first make them feel better about themselves. But self-confidence must be based on real accomplishments, not phony praise or inflated grades. Respecting oneself can block destructive behavior by diffusing anger and demonstrating self-worth. But self-esteem cannot just be handed to students; it must be earned.

The arts can function as a positive intervention in the lives of poor minority children who live in crime- and drug-infested environments and in one-parent homes in which there is little caring and no encouragement to learn. When they turn to criminal activity, the system punishes them but rarely attempts to show them that they can achieve and even excel.

THE POTENTIAL OF TECHNOLOGY

During the decade from 1984 to 1994, an estimated $2 billion was spent on more than 2 million computers for America's classrooms. With the right software, the new computer technologies can make learning more engaging and thorough, more tailored to the individual's needs and interests, and more substantive. The technology-rich curriculum at the G. W. Childs Elementary School in Philadelphia has virtually eradicated absenteeism. By the third grade, these computer-literate kids are printing their own prose in classroom collections.

Through computers, the information superhighway enters the schools, dispensing digitized bits and bytes that are electronically transportable. Among these technologies are the CD-ROM *interactive multimedia* (*interactive* means that students can choose among a variety of options, including still and moving images; *multimedia* refers to a combination of text, graphics, sound, and video), *hypermedia* (displaying documents on screen without imposing a linear start-to-finish order), *virtual space* (a "you are there" visual semblance of reality), and *high-definition television* (a far clearer and more detailed reproduction). These technologies, and others under development, have the potential of extending the curriculum to neglected areas like the arts. Students read about American composer Aaron Copland's use of American subject matter, and then they can immediately hear examples such as *Billy the Kid* and *Rodeo*. The printed word is thereby enhanced and reinforced by audio and visual extensions that are readily at hand.

Computers can also facilitate creativity. In music, for example, students can compose while the computer, synthesizer (a sound-producing keyboard), and sequencer (a tape deck that stores data regarding the music) records the sounds and prints out a score. Students who might normally shun the study of music enthusiastically embrace the use of the computer in composition.

But there are limitations. Just as computer software does mathematical calculations and corrects spelling and grammar—thereby eliminating the need for students to learn these skills—the computer and digital sound processor do all the work so that students no longer have to learn how to notate their musical creations. In art, design and animation are facilitated by the software without the students having to learn to draft or draw. Students, bound by the software, create in that framework, letting the computer do the real work.

Even though we may fret about students learning basic skills, calculators and computers do reduce the need to learn how to read, by substituting pictures for words. Then, too, software has a tendency to complicate and corrupt its possibilities by being too comprehensive. An interactive multimedia compact disk for Igor Stravinsky's *Rite of Spring*[23] permits the student to follow the score and illustrates the complex changing rhythmic accents, at the same time offering the student options to access the work on several levels, including information about the musical, historical, cultural, and political contexts. There is more information than anybody probably needs, as if students could learn all there is to know about music through one work. The hundreds of options for exploring details raises the question of how students decide what they want to pursue without getting lost, distracted, or overwhelmed. The single musical work becomes a smorgasbord for a musical cuisine, with the choices sending students in multiple directions to pursue details that can disembody rather than clarify the subject. The boundary between education and entertainment is crossed at the expense of learning how to work. No doubt these problems will be corrected in time so that the educational potential of technology is more effective. Meanwhile, the use of technology in schools continues to grow: In 1993, more than 5,000 schools had satellite dishes.

It may be too early in the electronic revolution to assess its educational potential, but computers are redefining the arts, and the combination of words and images facilitated by video is creating a new literacy. These new possibilities enable the arts to explore new dimensions of meaning. Technology facilitates personal expression. It helps us comprehend and relate the story of our lives. Young people are fascinated by technology, and it can engage them in ways that traditional approaches cannot. Integrated with the arts, it can be a powerful tool.[24] It can propel students to make compelling connections with the arts and to become involved in learning.

MAGNET SCHOOLS OF THE ARTS

The concept of the magnet school is well established and growing across the country. There are now between 300 and 400 arts magnet schools in the United States. But even though most arts educators agree that these programs are worthwhile and should be encouraged, some have criticized them for draining the talent from all other schools and for concentrating arts resources on relatively few students. If a magnet school forces a compromise in the arts programs of other high schools or monopolizes the arts resources, its fairness can be questioned. Magnet schools should not be an excuse for a depleted arts program in other schools, just as a science magnet should not take away the science curriculum from all other students.

Some children have special talents in the arts, and for them, studying the arts is a priority. One way to provide this instruction is through special electives in the arts at the secondary level; another is through private-sector alternatives; still another is by organizing a magnet school in the arts that caters to these students. From all accounts, the effect of Proposition 13 in California, which reduced arts instruction in many schools, is waiting lists for private music instruction. There just is not enough arts instruction in schools or enough magnet schools for the arts to satisfy the demand. School systems have not reduced the arts in the schools because they have a magnet school of the arts; rather, it is more likely the other way around. Systems have set up the magnet school because of the depletion of arts programs and the demands of parents to provide opportunities for the talented.

The magnet school forces are too often content to stay in their oasis, forgetting that the desert around them threatens to encroach and eradicate. The magnet schools must therefore find ways to bring the enriching, life-enhancing waters of the arts out into the desert and also invite the desert dwellers in to feast. Rather than seal itself off as a special enclave, the magnet school has an obligation to the larger school system beyond, to all the students, and to the community.

The arts complement the academic program, and the reverse is equally true. In some magnet schools, the academics are treated with the same disdain that the arts are accorded in schools where academics reign supreme. The Davidson Arts Magnet School in Augusta, Georgia, for example, a school composed of 500 students in grades 5 to 12, half African American and half white, has received the highest test scores in the county, including those of the private schools, for the past eight years. Even with more than 60 percent of its students classified as at risk, daily instruction in the arts has created a productive classroom learning environment with significant improvements in academic performance. In the better arts magnet schools, the arts are not viewed as an "easy" A.

— chapter ten —

THE ARTS AS ACADEMIC, BASIC, AND COMPREHENSIVE

You can't examine education today without realizing that we are in the midst of an intense battle for the minds of American youth. American industry is asserting that many of its difficulties—such as its struggle to compete in world markets and its challenge to leadership in the electronics, steel, automotive, and computer industries—are due to failures in American education. Corporate leaders lay the blame for America's loss of its competitive edge on the unemployability of American youth, their illiteracy, and their inability to be innovative.

Despite the narrowness of corporate claims on education and their call for more emphasis on the basics (devoid of the arts), education is a broad cerebral universe. As John Goodlad pointed out, American parents don't want a bare-bones curriculum. Rather, they want it all: a solid academic program plus physical education for the body and the arts for creativity.[1] They want every possible opportunity for their children, including the arts. But more than this, three major trends in the United States hold enormous promise to establish the arts as substantive and mindful.

THE ARTS AS ACADEMIC

The first trend is toward making the arts more academic, which originated in large measure in *A Nation at Risk* and other reports on education. It is now the call also of the J. Paul Getty Center for Education in the Arts, the National Endowment for the Arts, and a number of state legislatures.

There are some good reasons for this. Often the arts have not been viewed as intellectual endeavors but largely as hands-on activities. Indeed, parents and some educators see them as being more akin to elation than edification. The Getty Center decided to make arts programs more academic, to develop courses in art that "stress thought, reason, and ideas." We know that in the arts, technique can become an end in itself. Students learn to dance the steps, to play the tune. That's it. In schools devoted to the development of mentation, such activities are viewed as having only marginal importance.

Thomas Ewens, professor of philosophy at the Rhode Island School of Design, described what he calls the "philosophic bias" that underlies the Getty Center's reasoning: "Understanding, substance, rigor, thought, reason, ideas, and intellectual capacities are good, [whereas] engaging children's imagination, feelings, and emotions, if not bad, is at least woefully inadequate." This rhetoric about rigor reveals the "old split between the intellect and emotions" that underlies the Getty philosophy,

> a bias in favor of intellect which undergirds the principal reasons given in favor of discipline-based art education. . . . The attempt to lay the blame for the low priority accorded art education in our schools on the fact that it is oriented to art production is misguided. There may be a lot of things wrong with contemporary art education but the fact that it is primarily concerned with making art is not one of them.[2]

A correction is now under way in all the arts and in education itself. But such adjustments should be a matter of degree. The fact that Ewens has raised the issue may prevent the Getty Center from going too far in the opposite direction. Ideally, students should be able to make art and appreciate it, perform music and acquire knowledge of it, at the same time. What we really seek is balance.

In the hands of better teachers, the arts can have academic aspects, such as considerations of style, history, culture, theory, and criticism that reveal the intent and the message of the work. And I would guess that if taken to the ultimate and rightly directed, these considerations would culminate in the engagement of children's imaginations, feelings, and emotion, those elements that traditionally have been sought. And that is as it should be. Let's not take the heart out of the arts, but let's not be satisfied with just goose bumps, either.

At the same time, I think we must recognize that the arts have their own academic aspects, that they can be academic and experiential at the same time, and that by no means need one be given up for the other. Educational expectations for children are simply not substantial enough when all the band does is play marches and fanfares at the football game's half-time show. If it is treated primarily as a vehicle for entertainment, band *is* extracurricular. Depending on how it is approached, band doesn't have to be superficial, and in many schools it is not. The study of instrumental music can give students one of the best means for exploring music to its greatest depths: learning about musical form, style, and expression, as well as developing skill. Although students may use their reading, writing, and other academic competencies in the process, they are subordinate to the central, artistic goals at hand.

The play element, so often a natural, innate part of arts expression, can and should captivate and delight children. At the same time, it should provide the impetus and motivation to delve beneath the surface to explore the artistic craft, the ingeniousness of the expression. As in any subject, achievement in the arts can fascinate and reward; it can also demand discipline and hard work. The latter should not be lost on children.

In response, educators are now attempting to counteract these views by making arts education more academic. The Getty Center wants to expand art programs "to include art history, art criticism, and aesthetics, along with art production," because it no longer is enough "to engage children's imaginations, feelings, and emotions."[3] I am concerned, and rightly so, that arts courses have been considered "frills." But I believe that by giving arts courses greater substance, they will acquire more educational credibility. However, I think we need to decide very carefully what that substance, that academic dimension, should be.

What is arts education for? Maxine Greene, a professor at Teachers College, Columbia University, observed that if young people are to renew their worlds, they must live fully and be interested in the possibilities of life.

> For this to happen, they have to be enabled to break with confinement in the domains of popular culture, mass entertainment, televised realities, and private cynicism or hopelessness. Offered concrete and significant alternatives, windows through which to see beyond the actual, they may refuse their own submergence in the typical and the everyday.... It is not only the thought of *having* more that moves the young to reach beyond themselves; it is the idea of *being* more, becoming different, experiencing more deeply, overcoming the humdrum, the plain ordinariness and repetitions of everyday life.[4]

It is here that we begin to get a hint of what the arts, at their best, are all about. They are the application of human imagination, thought, and feeling, through a range of languages, for the purpose of illuminating life in all its mystery, misery, delight, pity, and wonder.

There is a great danger, it seems to me, that the term *academic* will be misappropriated and misapplied. It is certainly a possibility at the high school level if arts teachers take the advice of the College Board's booklet, "Academic Preparation in the Arts," the so-called Red Book. This booklet pictures kids in band and orchestra classes keeping project books that are "filled with reports, critiques, and musical analyses." The booklet goes on to promote the

> relationship between a mastery of the arts and the development of the broad academic competencies that students will need in all college subjects—reading, writing, speaking and listening, mathematics, reasoning, studying, using computers, and observing. . . . It is important to study the arts for their own sake; it is also important to recognize that they provide additional opportunities to enhance these basic skills.[5]

I agree that all students should recognize that the arts demand serious study, but not the same kind of serious study required in their other subjects. We are in danger of overcorrecting. My concern is that we will misinterpret "academic" to mean all those insufferable things we had to endure in school and that the arts will lose its one advantage over academics—that they are refreshingly different in the way they are taught and learned.

The arts have their own academic aspects, but they can be academic and experiential at the same time. They can be vehicles for teaching certain other subjects. The arts convey meaning about the world and provide a means to engage with that world, just as science helps us understand ourselves, the world, and their interrelationship.

Are the arts just about arts? Well, sometimes they are. The musical *A Chorus Line* is about musical theater, but it is also about people. Is music only about music? We have been led by some historians and theorists to believe that music is pure abstraction. It's not so. Is dance about dance, theater about theater, visual arts about visual art, writing about writing?

All the arts are conveyances of insight beyond themselves. Even emotion can be viewed as a form of knowing and understanding. In this sense, all music is programmatic. It tells us something about ourselves, something about life, something about the people who created it, something about the culture from which it sprang. The arts are a natural adjunct to the study of history and civilization. Rather than corrupting their integrity, such a use of the arts realizes their intrinsic qualities.

To view the arts as vehicles for understanding the world, to recognize that the arts provide some of the best ways to enliven learning and make students respond, is to realize their true educational potential and importance. Viewing the arts more academically is an acknowledgment that they are more than mere enrichment. They are important studies in their own right.

THE ARTS AS BASIC

If approaching the arts more academically is a first trend, considering them basic is a second. Viewing the arts as forms of human intelligence and as systems of meaning has already begun to have an effect on school curriculum, on what and how the arts are taught. If the arts are basic, the corollary is that they must be for everyone. Currently, about twenty-eight states require some arts for high school graduation, although in some cases, students can choose courses other than the arts, such as vocational education, foreign language, and humanities. The trend in these states represents a fundamental change in philosophy: a move from a highly specialized, performance- or product-oriented arts program focused on the few toward a broadened, more academic program serving the many. This outlook balances the emphasis on skill development coupled with the acquisition of knowledge.

If the arts are to achieve anything more than marginal status, the conflict between entertainment and substantive education must be resolved in favor of substance. Arts educators must make sure that concentrating solely on performance and production does not result in the public's equating the arts with the frivolous world of TV and entertainment and not with the technological future that has become the serious business of education. Ways must be found to make clear connections between the arts and national educational priorities.

In 1988 at the behest of Congress, the NEA issued a report on arts education stating flatly that "basic arts education does not exist in the United States today."[6] This report defines a basic arts education as a curriculum that provides all students, not only the gifted and talented, with knowledge of, and skills in, the arts. In light of their penchant to emphasize performance programs for the talented, arts educators would find it difficult to take issue with this assessment. This bias toward performance probably contributes to the perception that the performing arts are more akin to entertainment than to serious learning. When the development of skill and technique becomes an end in itself, knowledge of the art is given little attention.

Defining What Is Basic

The curriculum of American schools stresses a core of common knowledge and understanding important to every citizen. What is this basic curriculum? Ernest L. Boyer gives one answer: "Broadly defined, it is a study of those consequential ideas, experiences, and traditions common to all of us by virtue of our membership in the human family at a particular moment in history."[7] These common learnings teach the next generation about their human heritage. If the arts are part of this heritage—and who could argue sensibly that they are not?—then they should be included in the basic curriculum and should be required of all students.

If our current situation were as simple as this logic suggests, the arts would now have the status of science and mathematics in American schools. In truth, it should be that simple, but reality and practice intercede. In the performing arts, the goal has not been education through performance so much as performance as an end in itself. The goal has not been to teach all students their artistic heritage but, rather, to teach production to the talented. Arts education has been remarkably effective at achieving the latter and outrageously negligent at providing the former.

Some critics would have us believe that performance and appreciation are at odds, that we must choose one or the other, and that those who speak for one are necessarily the enemy of the other. In recent years, a conflict between making art and appreciating it has arisen and intensified. The traditional emphasis on skill development is being challenged. This conflict, which elevates performance for the talented and minimizes appreciation for the many, still prevails. But there is evidence that this ingrained national educational penchant for developing artistic skills ("doing" art) at the expense of understanding it ("learning about" art) is being overturned. Harry S. Broudy, professor emeritus of philosophy of education at the University of Illinois, explained: The issue today is "whether performance is an end in itself or whether it is ancillary to something else."[8]

Performance remains an essential means of learning about music, dance, and theater, just as production in visual arts and the creation of poetry and stories in creative writing—"doing" art—is central to learning in these areas. With the artist as model—in this case performers and creators—learning by doing has been a central strength of all the arts.

Today, the attempt to make the arts basic is the galvanizing goal of arts education. To achieve this status, arts curricula cannot be limited to just skill development. As soon as arts teachers are persuaded that the arts are part of general education, that arts education is basic education, they must accept the idea that the arts are worthy study for every student. What is basic, by definition, must be for all. Visual art, then, is no different from math or science. No person can be truly educated without some understanding of the arts.

But there is another compelling reason for arts teachers to be part of general education: Arts education cannot afford to have any enemies. It is almost always the people who have not been reached in the arts who end up being state legislators, mayors, school-board members, school administrators, and nonsupportive members of Congress. Paradoxically, these are the people who often make the rules and set the policies regarding the arts in spite of, and even because of, their scant knowledge of them. Their ignorance comes back to haunt arts teachers, who only victimize themselves when they deny students an adequate education. The indifference returns in the form of curtailments, slashed budgets, and lack of general support for arts education programs; insufficient audiences for live music performance; indifference to the visual arts; lack of interest in theater and dance; lack of desire to read;

attacks on the National Endowment for the Arts; and financial problems for the arts all around.

If the arts are basic, they must be taught as basics. They must strike a better balance between the development of skills and the acquisition of knowledge. We must recognize creativity as an essential tool for developing musical thought and understanding, and we must offer courses to all students, not just the talented.

What Makes the Arts Basic?

Because the public, school administrators, and board members decide what the school curriculum will include, arts teachers must show them precisely why the arts are basic. From a practical perspective, arts education provides the human family with at least three fundamental pillars in the foundation for a humane education:

Studying the arts encourages all students to cultivate and refine their sensibilities. We have many indications that the schools' failure to cultivate and refine the sensibilities has had adverse affects on the younger generation. Drugs, crime, hostility, indifference, and insensitivity run rampant in schools that do not provide sufficient instruction in the arts.[9] In the process of over-selling science, mathematics, and technology as the salvation of commerce, schools have denied students something more precious—access to their inner beings and their personal spirit. As Elliot Eisner claimed, when we deny children access to a major expressive mode such as music, we deprive them of "the meanings that the making of music makes possible."[10] The result is a form of human deprivation. Without attending to the human spirit, schools tend to turn out insensitive citizens who lack compassion, people whose aggressiveness is not tempered by the controlling forces of sensitivity and caring about others. Many of today's schools, devoid of the arts, are cultivating a generation of modern-day barbarians. American society is the casualty.

Studying the arts establishes a basic relationship between the individual and the cultural heritage of the human family. American society today is a microcosm of the entire world. Our multiculturalism is an American fact of life, and the arts are pervasive and persuasive ways we express it. The arts provide fundamental ways to understand our own and other people's humanness. We neglect such enlightenment at our own peril. Schools that do not provide sufficient education in the arts are not teaching youths the tradition of community values that unite the society. Nor are they providing a basis to study and appreciate or, at the very least, to understand the values of other societies.

Because the arts are an expression of the beings that create them, they reflect their thinking and values as well as the social milieu in which they originate. Even if it is not the overt intent of the composer who created it, the music we listen to defines who we are and gives us identity as a social group. Because it reflects identity, music also provides the basis for understanding identity. All the arts are ways that humans express the individuality of their social character.

Our youth are the targets of a multimillion-dollar industry. Television and radio broadcasting, pop concerts and recordings have made music ubiquitous and diverse for youth, without help from the schools. In music, "pop" lyrics are written in the vernacular, everyday "language" tailored to appeal and to communicate easily.

Like any of the many genres of music, some of this commercial music is fine by any standard; some is merely good; and much of it is vacuous and ephemeral. Harry Broudy asked: "Do public school pupils in a democratic society need 'fine' art or will the popular brands do just as well?"[11] It is the pervasiveness and command of this music—its capacity to saturate and satiate—that poses the challenge for music education. Our youth must be given opportunities to sample the full range of music that is their rich heritage, not just one form or style, however varied by new releases.

The arts are nothing if not responsive to people. To think of the various art forms as systems of communication is vastly different from thinking of them as self-expression, a kind of self-indulgence that can be socially irresponsible and, therefore, little regarded. Arts that communicate put us in touch with others; they reach out to embrace people. They are of the people, by the people, and for the people. Communication shuts down the ivory towers. It makes our symphony orchestras and other presentation arts enterprises responsive to the public, something they sometimes forget. And it makes our arts programs in schools touch everyone, ensuring connections between people, all kinds of people. These connections are part of basic education.

Studing the arts furnishes students with a crucial aesthetic metaphor of what life at its best might be. Each art form gives students an aesthetic frame of reference that has broad applicability; those persons who have been educated artistically think differently because of it. The arts can provide an aesthetic value orientation. Ideally, the aesthetics of creative writing, dance, music, theater, and visual arts become ingrained habits of thought. Through the study of an art, students learn to strive for perfection, to self-correct, and to create a satisfactory solution to the challenges at hand.

The act of perception we learn by studying an art becomes part of our lifestyle. It is a mode of thinking, observing, and reacting. Personal taste and our expression of it are basic elements of the human condition; the applications are daily and infinite. Aesthetic considerations are essential to the satis-factory conduct of society. The aesthetic viewpoint empowers us to create our own best state of existence, to realize our finest human possibilities. When the aesthetic component is ignored, we denigrate life. We dehuman-ize our environments, bombard people with ugliness, and deprive them of the comforts and satisfactions they need for their psychological well-being. Aesthetics is a natural and important part of our encounter with life. It is the way we bring our sensual and rational beings to come to terms with the world around us.

The important point here is the significant transfer of aesthetic under-standing from the arts to other realms of life. The quality of aesthetic thought, expectations, and satisfactions learned from studying the arts can make a substantial difference in the quality of life. This is why the arts are not the domain of the privileged, the rich, or the talented but belong to us all.

VIEWING THE ARTS COMPREHENSIVELY

So far, we've looked at two trends: the arts as both academic and basic. They also are being viewed more comprehensively. I call these trends the ABCs of the arts: viewing the arts as academic, basic, and comprehensive.

Comprehensive arts education refers to a curriculum of all the arts for all the children, and much more. Comprehensive means that our programs study all aspects of an art form—creativity, skill, theory, history, appreciation, aesthetics, and criticism. It means a program that incorporates community arts resources. And it refers to a curriculum that ranges from discrete arts to an infusion of the arts into the other courses in the humanities curriculum and to arts programs for special populations—the very young, seniors, the disabled, and the talented. That is a tall order.

As a curriculum, the arts have rarely been considered comparable to or the equivalent of other major areas, such as the language arts, social studies, or sciences. One of the reasons, I suspect, is that most arts people have not advanced the arts as such. Arts teachers generally have been quite content in their specialism, in the pleasures and problems of visual arts, or media, or music, or dance, or theater, or creative writing. By and large, they don't think holistically to the degree that biologists, chemists, and physicists accept the generic banner of "science."

Still, the concept of comprehensive arts has been bantered about for many years. Oddly enough, many arts educators have not yet accepted the idea. Some dance and theater educators, for example, do not think of dance or theater education in the larger context of the arts. Viewing the arts comprehensively permits us to view them as an important area of human knowledge and insight. By thinking of the arts in this way instead of as isolated individual subjects such as the visual arts or dance, they immediately assume the status of a curricular area comparable to the sciences, social studies, even the language arts. That is as it should be.

To be truly comprehensive, the arts curriculum in the schools must form new alliances and alignments and join in new kinds of transactions that will make this larger curriculum a reality. The arts do not have to sacrifice their individuality to work together or to be organized as a fine arts department, but they do have to work together to design a curriculum that is equivalent in importance to the sciences.

Can school systems aspire to having a comprehensive arts education program? Many school districts in the United States offer some visual art and music instruction on all grade levels. The concept of comprehensive arts suggests that schools should extend this arts instruction to include dance, media, theater, and creative writing. At a minimum, quality learning experiences in all the arts should be made available through visiting artists and by attachments to programs outside the schools. Given the proliferation of other requirements and the financial constraints, it is probably unrealistic to expect schools to hire dance, theater, media, and creative-writing specialists in addition to specialists in music and visual arts.

Comprehensive programs are also reaching beyond the age boundaries of kindergarten to grade 12. With the enormous increase of single parents and working parents, day-care centers, nursery schools, and preprimary schools have sprung up in every community. The arts should be a strong part of these programs if for no other reason than they teach basic perception, social cooperation, and the delights and rewards of learning.

Equally important is the development of arts education programs for the growing population of older Americans. Arts education can be a desirable and valued entity in adult communities. Retired persons with knowledge of and ability in the arts can be invited to work with their peers and with younger students. Long-term goals and objectives that encompass whole communities should be developed, and arts and education agencies and personnel should reevaluate their areas of responsibility.

Arts programs for the talented and the disabled have special merit. The disabled are often stereotyped as devoid of any talent or ability. But given the opportunity, many blind children show a special sensitivity to music. Similarly, if given the opportunity, deaf children often develop special abilities in visual arts. The especially talented also deserve special programs; otherwise, much extraordinary talent is stymied and lost, to the detriment of society.

Community-Based Resources

In some school districts in which arts programs were seriously curtailed in recent years and arts specialists were removed from the staff, a hodge podge of activities largely organized from arts agencies outside the schools have arisen in their place. In their desperation to give their students some kind of art experience, these schools grab at any straw—a visiting artist who works with a class or two for a brief period, an ensemble of performers who put on an educational program for the students, or a field trip to a local museum or an event at a performing arts center. Such experiences can expose students to the arts and artists, but they are no substitute for an ongoing, sequential program of arts instruction.

Ideally, a sequential arts program is primarily school based but also incorporates community arts resources. Many communities offer ample opportunities for learning in depth about the arts—through community schools of the arts, private teachers of voice and instruments, dance and theater schools for children and youth, church youth choirs, community bands and orchestras, or drum and bugle corps, or through children's arts education programs sponsored by museums, symphony orchestras, opera, dance, and theater companies, as well as city and county recreation departments.

To be sure, the extent of these out-of-school educational opportunities differs from community to community according to the particular arts resources available. But most communities have some. The question of whether the emphasis should be placed on the in- or out-of-school program depends on the effectiveness of these efforts.

Goodlad and other educators view education as a collaboration between the schools and other agencies, and he believes such collaboration should be promoted. "There is not one agency," Goodlad states, "but an ecology of institutions educating—school, home, places of worship, television, press, museums, libraries, businesses, factories, and more."[12] Boyer, too, recommends that high schools "establish connections with learning places beyond the schools—such as libraries, museums, art galleries, colleges and industrial laboratories," because the realities of the community can teach what the isolated school cannot.[13]

Goodlad acknowledges that "cooperative functioning of agencies and institutions so far has proved to be difficult, in part because we have not recognized the urgency of the need and in part because as yet we have only a glimmer of the potential." And where have schools seen that glimmer? "Networks in the arts all across this country," Goodlad observes, "educate in their own right as well as help the schools to educate in and through the arts."[14]

The idea of schools and community agencies working together, of schools using community arts resources, not only works, it makes good sense. But such partnerships between the schools and community arts enterprises must be based on thoughtfully coordinated efforts between the in-school program and the resources outside.

The lack of adequate resources inside schools may have caused arts teachers to look outside in the first place. For example, field trips have always been more important to the arts than to other courses because they have taken the place, in many schools, of aspects of learning that were hardly in the curriculum at all. According to Junius Eddy,

> Occasional visits to art or historical museums, to libraries and cultural centers, and to children's concerts and other performing arts events were, until recently, the major instrumentalities through which many schools provided youngsters with any kind of learning experiences at all in the arts—passive though such experiences often were.[15]

The real experience of a symphony orchestra, a ballet, and an art gallery and the exhilaration of working with a real poet, dancer, or sculptor enlarge and enrich the program well beyond what the schools alone can provide.

On the one hand, artists and community arts organizations can give students opportunities to experience and understand directly works of art and various types of performances, to discover how artists create, and to examine the technical caliber of their work. Or schools can give students opportunities to investigate various art forms, develop their own talents and appreciation, and experience their own creativity and performance. Together, schools and community arts organizations can more adequately and effectively cover the history, theory, criticism, and performance of the several arts.

Community arts resources should not be used merely as adjunct enrichment activities bearing little or no relation to the in-school educational program. Rather, such activities should be incorporated into the sequential arts curriculum so that they are contiguous with program goals and relate to the planned scope of work. Few such community-based programs offer complete and structured curricula in a particular art for students of all ages. But even those that do, rarely, if ever, reach every student. Curriculum-based instruction serves as the central coordinating program. Only the schools can ensure that all children have the kinds of arts experiences that constitute an adequate program of instruction, whether that instruction is school or community based.

Rather than being a mere supplement to the in-school program, community arts resources can be integrated into the in-school curriculum to extend, enliven, broaden, and deepen it and give it a sense of reality and presence that only come from experiencing the arts as they exist and function in society. The schools do not own arts education. It would be sheer recklessness for in-school arts programs to ignore the assistance that artists and community arts organizations and institutions can provide. But each community must assess its own advantages and set up its own agreements regarding program provisions and shared responsibilities.

The fragmentation of knowledge is a flaw of American schools. The arts have been part of that fragmentation. Each of the arts wants its own little corner of the world. Insulation and isolation may be comforting, but they are unrealistic. There must be a time for specialization in any field, but it is usually later in the course of study. By enlarging our vision of the arts as academic, basic, and comprehensive, the arts immediately gather greater educational substance and significance, and they demonstrate to young people that there is an aesthetic dimension to everything in life. That is a lesson too few people seem to have learned.

_ chapter eleven _

WHOSE CULTURE SHOULD BE TAUGHT?

Intolerance in American society is brazen and growing more so. Fractious factions, ethnic tensions, religious bigotry, and conflicts between people of different genders and lifestyles seem everywhere to be "in your face." Americans seem to need someone or something to hate in order to rise to a higher status. Insistent vocal forces of pro and con meet head on, people and organizations fighting for their own self-interest and empowerment. This is a dynamic process, the results of which determine our culture, particularly its future. The stakes are high, and media expert Fred Inglis tells us how high: "Arguments over culture are inherent to its nature, and are then compounded by the conflicts of class, generation, gender, race, and so forth. Making a culture produces the great human benefits of identity, membership, mutuality, patriotism, loyalty. These values entail by definition exclusion, enemies, rejection, quarrels, betrayal, warfare."[1] Inglis explains that culture is competitive: "We tell ourselves our stories, some true, some false, some ennobling, some degrading, in order to win the moment of illumination, the freedom and empowerment that go with it." Each generation imagines, invents, and fights for its vision of its future. All of us are participants in this process of creating culture according to our personal vision of the good society. The arts are part of this process, and so squabbles about their role and importance, their nature and prominence, are one of the continuing modern-day struggles.

WHOSE CULTURE?

Americans bicker about "the degree of fairness with which their ethnic or affective group is depicted in school curricula."[2] David Rieff, senior fellow at the World Policy Institute, observes that "only people who live in a closeted enclave quite divorced from what is happening in the rest of the world could treat these questions with such anguished seriousness." The paradox is "this quintessentially American ability to ignore reality, or give it the spin of one's individual choosing, that has provided American culture with its unique global reach and seductiveness."[3]

America's culture is a vast and complex mosaic of arts with multiethnic and multinational origins, and the tension among them presents the public schools with difficult choices. Which arts—whose culture—should be taught?

In 1977 the Rockefeller panel report *Coming to Our Senses: The Significance of the Arts for American Education* defined American culture as "a quilted fabric with numerous national minorities interspersed." The panel viewed the artistic creations of our ethnic peoples as "the most visible expressions of this variegated culture," and they saw these creations as "an invaluable resource for arts education."[4] The ethnic arts movement, they stated, is "a central force in American culture," and they urged the schools to "take advantage of such programs to improve their own arts education efforts." The panel expressed reservations, however, about the possible limitations of arts programs designed for those with the same social or economic conditions. The danger, they said, is that "such programs can become isolated and segregated from the rest of the society, thus running the risk of stagnating without the interchange of ideas." They also felt that "programs directed at particular ethnic or racial groups may only temporarily satisfy the need to strengthen a sense of self or to articulate fully the messages and forms which derive from social and historical heritage."[5]

What was not said here, but needs to be said, is that arts programs that isolate people from the totality of American culture not only repudiate that culture but also, by the sin of omission, perpetrate cultural deprivation. This is true whether the narrow vision of the world is that of the minority sectors of society or the white Anglo-Saxon majority. Such programs put blinders on children and teach them to look at only their own footsteps.

We must be careful not to move toward cultural separatism, particularly in our cities. Here, where many children attend schools that do not provide adequate arts instruction and where they are not introduced to prevailing traditions and practices of artistic culture, they are apt instead to be engulfed in the particular culture of their community. For many children, this is the culture of the ghetto, often rich in itself, but certainly not representative of the larger society outside. Those who teach the arts must make sure that the many ethnic elements of our culture do not separate us but that all students have access to the universal elements of culture that bind us as a civilization.

What we do not want in the United States is a dissolution of our many ethnic cultures or a fusion of them into one indistinguishable mass. The diverse riches of mind, spirit, and imagination make a dynamic whole only if there is a shared culture at the base. If we are not to be a country of many separate peoples, we must establish commonalities of culture as well as some understanding across our many artistic legacies.

Shall we uphold a school district's right to teach mainly black arts, Latino arts, Asian arts, European arts because of the particular ethnic demographics of the local population? E. D. Hirsch Jr., a professor of English Literature at the University of Virigina and the author of *Cultural Literacy: What Every American Needs to Know*, asserts, "Our diversity has been represented by the motto on all our coins—E Pluribus Unum, 'out of many one.' Our debate has been over whether to stress the *many* or the *one*." He further amplifies the argument for a balanced view of American culture:

> If we *had* to make a choice between the *one* and the *many*, most Americans would choose the principle of unity, since we cannot function as a nation without it. Indeed, we have already fought a civil war over that question. Few of us accept the extreme and impractical idea that our unity can be a purely legal umbrella, which formally contains but does not integrate our diversity. On the other side, the specific content of our larger national culture is not and must not be detailed, unchanging, or coercive, because that would impinge on our equally fundamental principles of diversity, localism, and toleration. A balanced, moderate position is the only workable American position, and it is bound to be the one that will prevail.[6]

We must know ourselves as both the many and the one. (Sometimes we have to be reminded that we are far more alike than we are different, and it is the similar qualities that we so often overlook.)

Hirsch goes on to say that above all, schools should teach the commonalities of mainstream culture, but

> to acknowledge the importance of minority and local cultures of all sorts, to insist on their protection and nurture, to give them demonstrations of respect in the public sphere are traditional aims that should be stressed even when one is concerned, as I am, with national culture and literacy.... It is for the Amish to decide what Amish traditions are, but it is for all of us to decide collectively what our American traditions are, to decide what "American" means on the other side of the hyphen in Italo-American or Asian-American. What national values and traditions really belong to national cultural literacy?[7]

No doubt Hirsch would agree that the inculcation of national cultural literacy should take precedence over any ethnic considerations but not that these
subcultures should be homogenized or obliterated. On the contrary, people
need to wed their personal cultural identity to a strong sense of national cultural identity. They must see their own uniqueness as an important slice of
the whole and see themselves in the context of the larger world.

Defining that larger world poses difficulties. What exactly constitutes
mainstream American culture? Hirsch offers a fifty-four-page list, "What
Literate Americans Know," which contains 154 words related to music, 53
to art, 37 to theater, 10 to dance, and more than 300 from literature or areas
related to the arts. That is a total of about 555 terms representing the arts
out of some 4,650 entries, or about 12 percent. But why Brahms and not
Bernstein and Copland? Why Caruso and not *Carmen*? Why Gilbert and
Sullivan and not Rogers and Hammerstein? Why Prokofiev and not
Rachmaninoff, Verdi and not Wagner? Such questions could be asked end-
lessly, with little agreement. Literacy would be better defined in terms of
the broad traditions of culture: the musical works, say, of many periods and
styles, the principal composers through the ages, and familiarity with the
traditions of music making.

What Hirsch does not acknowledge is that children should be introduced to the *un*commonalities of artistic culture—humankind's extraordinary achievements in architecture, ballet, chamber music, drama, jazz,
modern dance, opera, painting, poetry, prose, sculpture, symphonic literature, and so forth. But we must not make the mistake of believing, as does
Allan Bloom, author of *The Closing of the American Mind*, that American culture is derived entirely from the traditions of Greece and Western Europe.
Eurocentrism is as unsuitable a view of American culture as the relativistic
pandering to everything and anything. Nor is our culture tied primarily to
literature and philosophy, as both Hirsch and Bloom would have us believe.
All the arts, including literature, are at the core.

By their nature, all the arts represent a culture, and therefore it may be
more important for a largely Latino community to stress other aesthetic
manifestations of cultural diversity than just the Latino element. The black
person who knows only African-American music and the white person who
knows only European painting and architecture are equally deprived. Yet we
must recognize that this country has its roots deep in the traditions of
Greece, Rome, and the rest of Europe. Every citizen of this nation has a right
and an obligation to that heritage, just as we all have a right and an obligation
to jazz, ragtime, and gospel. In this regard, our artistic eclecticism is a fact of
American life, and the cross-fertilization between types and styles of art is the
basis of much of our creative vitality. What helps bind us as a nation and a
people are the universal elements of our pluralistic artistic heritage.

What, then, should the schools do? Should they pass on all the existing manifestations of art as though all are of equal value? To the extent that all these artistic expressions are part of our heritage, yes, they have a viable claim to a share of arts education. Indeed, the main function of arts education is to transmit to new generations the breadth and richness of American culture. But constraints of time and resources force arts educators to make certain choices. What, then, should we pass on, and what should we pass over?

TRANSCULTURAL UNDERSTANDING

The arts can have an important role in today's multicultural schools if they capitalize on their capacity for teaching transcultural understanding. The global economy and the changing ethnicity of American society make such education imperative. Because the arts are one of the main ways that people define their sense of themselves, they are tailor made for teaching ethnic empathy.

Music, like every art, can be a force for defining and emphasizing our differences and divisions or a force for seeing and expressing our cultural cohesiveness. Barbara Jordon noted that "the arts can help us painlessly to articulate and showcase our oneness."[8] How can this happen? Flutist John Rainer, Jr., a member of the Taos tribe in New Mexico, performs traditional Native American music, communicating the essence of his people. The soothing, lyrical quality of these old melodies contradicts the stereotypes that have depicted Native Americans as primitive and savage. Through their music, we experience their sensitivity and humanity. One of the qualities of music is its capacity to connect us with people who are different from us. This is true of the other arts as well.

Multiculturalism should be a mechanism to break down the walls of ethnic separatism and to transform diversity into unity, a mechanism that is rejected by those whom Arthur Schlesinger, Jr., calls "the ideologues of ethnicity."

> The ethnic revolt against the melting pot has reached the point, in rhetoric at least, though not I think in reality, of a denial of the idea of a common culture and a single society. If large numbers of people really accept this, the republic would be in serious trouble. The question poses itself: how to restore the balance between *unum* and *pluribus*?[9]

We are in a position in arts education to choose between promoting wholeness or fragmentation. I'm on the side of wholeness, of illuminating a common culture that happens to be multicultural.

Like it or not, rap music is often a raw expression of anger and disenfranchisement. Music conveys a sense of hope and hostility, of moral courage and rebuke.[10] Because rap musicians reveal how they think and feel, their music defines who they are. Liking or not liking this music does not negate its function. As an expression of the outlook and beliefs and soul of black youths, it is a revelation of their ethnicity. Although rap music sometimes expresses racial divisiveness, it usually does so in the context of the commonly held American belief in the movement from exclusion to inclusion.

How far can we go in teaching a multiplicity of musical cultures, in teaching an in-depth understanding of such music?[11] There are limitations. In spite of these limitations, we can help our young people emerge from their musical cocoons to experience a wider world of cultural expression. At the least, we can acquaint youth with the distinctive inheritances that enrich our culture as Americans, inheritances that are the contributions of all our ethnic groups. As Schlesinger reminds us, "Belief in one's own culture does not require disdain for other cultures."[12] And he advises us to master our own culture before we explore the world. Music can help students to define their collective sense of themselves. That is one of its most valuable capacities.

There are great differences among children in what arts they have been exposed to and what they know about them. Accordingly, communities and schools will differ in what they need to stress. People should understand their own ethnic culture as well as the cultural traditions of the nation, but arts curricula do not have to stress what students already know and like. Young people will benefit from studying popular culture if they gain new perceptions and insights. More important, young people quite often do need the schools to help them understand their own ethnic artistic heritage and to introduce them to the artistic heritage of other cultures, including the European traditions that are the basis for so much of our artistic expression. To these ends, arts education is the irreplaceable conduit for conveying the artistic heritage of African-, Asian-, European-, Hispanic-, and Native Americans to citizens of the next generation.

A second criterion of limitation and choice is the degree of abstractness or difficulty of the artistic "language." If a particular example of an art form is simple to perform (or readily understood), students may not benefit from studying it. Some popular and folk art is immediately decipherable, as these artistic codes are deliberately in the public vernacular. In comparison, understanding African sculpture, Asian dance, Greek theater, Hispanic literature, or European artistic traditions poses challenges comparable to learning a foreign language. These codes tend to be more complex, more highly structured and developed, or sometimes more subtle or profound in content. Accordingly, they demand more attention in education.

THE VALUE OF THINGS

All the claims for more emphasis on a particular culture rather than another should be weighed and evaluated. Everything is not of equal value. Rembrandt's portraits are far better than anything I could do, and better than many other artists. Lynne V. Cheney, former chairwoman of the National Endowment for the Humanities, states the case:

> The world is not a relativistic stew where everything is of equal importance. Learning to sort out the more valuable from the less, the significant from the trivial, the enduring from the ephemeral is difficult—but it is also one of the highest purposes of education. When such choices are not made, colleges and universities—and the schools that look to them for leadership—fall all too easily into the notion that their purpose is simply to teach students *how* to think, a crucial skill, but one unlikely to be developed when there is no decision as to what students should think about.

The fact of our pluralistic artistic culture, then, does not translate into equal claims on the educational curriculum. Every citizen should have the means to understand the greatest artistic traditions of America, those that represent the ultimate human achievements. Accordingly, the time has come for Americans to acknowledge the tremendous contributions of African Americans to our culture. What people around the world characterize as American in music is inevitably the influences of jazz, gospel, soul, blues, rap, and ragtime. The contributions of blacks to our artistic culture have been pervasive and impressive, and we all are richer for them. At the same time, we must acknowledge the central importance of the Western tradition that forms our heritage. According to Cheney,

> It is sometimes argued that the story of our nation's past and the Western tradition that forms our heritage is irrelevant to a population that increasingly comes from other traditions, but I would argue that the opposite is true. While we need to know as much as we can about all people everywhere, our first goal has to be to comprehend this nation, all its virtues and faults, all its glories and failures. We can only build from where we are, and to do so intelligently requires that we—that all of us—know where we are.[13]

Students should be given all the pieces of the cultural puzzle, not just those they can easily relate to, are already familiar with, or can readily become interested in. Some of those pieces are especially representative of the range, character, and concentration of American arts; others are difficult to understand. The curriculum must be adjusted accordingly. Arts education is a celebration of diversity, and it is the exploration of that diversity that rewards learning in the arts.

_ chapter twelve _

THE SHAMEFUL
NEGLECT OF CREATIVITY

When teaching students to be creative thinkers, most American schools are derelict. All too rarely are young people asked to solve problems, be innovative, and figure out new solutions. The arts are one of the best means for teaching these skills. But in this regard, most schools have not lived up to their responsibility, and many arts programs have not fulfilled their potential.

CREATIVITY AND THE ARTS

American schools as a whole do not ask students to be creative. Of course, in certain subjects—spelling and history come to mind—too much creativity would be inappropriate. But in mathematics and science it should be an integral part of the challenge. Discussions of problems, conflicts, and issues in social studies require reasoning and call for students to come up with and justify their own viewpoint. But too often, students are simply told what to think.

In the arts, we expect creativity to be an integral part of the curriculum, and sometimes it is. Dance is generally taught as creative movement, although it may be far more imitative than creative. The art of theater is developed through improvisational techniques. Creative writing is learned by writing original essays, poems, and stories. The visual arts are taught largely through the process of inventing images. In music, students may be asked to compose their own compositions, but, for the most part, music is presented to youth as a given. According to Judith M. Burton, professor and coordinator of the program in arts and art education at Teachers College, Columbia University,

Of all the concepts that we lean on in our discipline, "creativity" is, perhaps, the most overused and least understood; it is a concept about which there is more disagreement than almost any other.... Our judgments about what is and what is not creative are often colored by unusual, strange, haphazard, or unexpected outcomes, or by products made by children which mirror those works of mature artists that we happen to admire. Either way, it seems that creativity in the art studio is often promoted by a teacher's vision of particular kinds of products and learning is simply directed toward their accomplishment. In short, we are driven by our appreciation of outcomes and end products, rather than by a concern to promote inner habits of mind.[1]

In observing arts classes in his study of American schools, John I. Goodlad found that the arts "did not convey the picture of individual expression and artistic creativity toward which one is led by the rhetoric of forward-looking practice in the field."[2] Like much of what goes on in American classrooms, students in the arts are handed the answers. They are given preprinted turkey outlines to color in. Too seldom are students in performing groups in dance, music, and theater asked to find ways to be more effective in their interpretation and communication, more dynamic and appropriate in their expression. Yet arts teachers believe that interpretation is a creative act, and perhaps it is for them, but certainly not for their students. Rather, the arts teacher—the "director"—tells the students exactly what to do, and they do it. Students are not asked to use their minds. They are not involved in experimentation, evaluation, trial-and-error corrections, or their own inventions.

The role of the imagination is seldom acknowledged. As Burton noted,

It is the imagination that allows us to take journeys in thought, to probe the hidden and undiscovered dimension of things, to enlarge our horizons and transcend limits. It is the imagination, moreover, that allows us to play with ideas, draw new conclusions, test them in thought and action, and transform what is empirically given to us in our world into our own personal symbolic realities. The imagination is one of humankind's most precious capacities, one to which we need to give a privileged place in our schools.[3]

It is precisely in the act of being creative with an art form that we come to exercise our real intelligence, to translate our observations symbolically in the process of formulating and conveying our understandings. This process of translating our intuitions, feelings, and spirit into musical constructs— that is, encoding them with sound, words, visual images, movements—

requires exercising judgment, estimating possible outcomes, weighing the result of various choices, deciding among unlimited options, making modifications, and taking action based on such estimates. This is problem solving of the most difficult kind, which gives rigor and substance to the study of any art.

WHAT CREATIVITY CAN DO

A classroom teacher tells this story: For two and one-half hours a week for approximately eight weeks, my classroom was transformed into an art studio. I watched as my thirty-seven "artisans" worked diligently to create family "Memory Trees." These are individual, five-foot-tall totems constructed from hollow cardboard tubes that are brightly painted and decorated with ancestral masks and several symbols, including an expressive hand gesture. Each is designed to "tell" the life of a relative. As their classroom teacher, I looked on quite proudly as my children worked enthusiastically and cooperatively. I enjoyed observing both their amazement and pleasure as each child discovered his or her own creativity.

The artists involved—Shari Davis and Ben Ferdman of the Children's Museum of Manhattan—were immediately accepted and welcomed by the children. Davis and Ferdman began the project with a discussion of the meanings of terms such as *cultures, traditions,* and *symbols.* The children were expected to interview family members or friends about a relative, living or dead. I willingly permitted the children to interview me about my Italian grandmother. It soon became obvious that the children thoroughly enjoyed learning about my grandma, and I loved sharing her with them.

During our next session, the children drew preliminary drawings of their relatives, using their notes and interviews as a guide. It was interesting to see how the children depicted their relatives from their written descriptions. They then sculpted clay masks. I knew that this session would require serious concentration and care. I hadn't anticipated that my room would be as quiet as it was. I could see the determination in each child as he or she worked to create a lifelike face. They were determined that no detail would be omitted!

Writing skills were reinforced when the children were asked to write essays about their relative, some of which they read aloud. By sharing these essays and discussing them, the children developed a greater awareness that we all come from various cultures with different traditions and values. Even I was amazed at the number of different cultures sitting before me every day.

We reviewed the concept of the symbol. Since we had recently finished a lesson on map symbols, the children were familiar with this concept. Ferdman and Davis asked the children to choose the two animals whose character would best symbolize that of their relative. I followed through by listing, with the children's help, the names of approximately thirty animals. Together, we decided on the character of each animal. One boy chose a bird to represent his grandmother because she "is never home and she likes to be free." He also chose a fish because "she loves to be clean." He called his animal a *fird*. Another student created a *snouse*, a combination of a snake and a mouse, because his grandmother "was quiet" and because "she was small and moved fast." We all enjoyed a good laugh during this session.

Next, the children were asked to think about gestures that might "say" something about their relatives. Their next addition to the Memory Tree was hands. Some constructed clenched fists, symbolizing power. One Haitian boy explained that his clenched fist depicted his grandfather, who "had to learn how to fight in the streets of Haiti." Others constructed open hands, reaching out because, as one girl explained, "my grandmother was always giving. She shared her stuff."

"Symbol leaves" were attached to the "trees" to explain the life of the children's relatives. Some Latino children constructed palm trees and chickens. An Arab boy created a model of his grandfather's house in Syria. A student from Ghana proudly displayed his country's flag, and another student taped on a book because his grandmother used "to sing and tell me stories."

This program was a huge success. When the trees were completed, the children's self-esteem soared. They had created a significant work of art. As Shari Davis remarked, "To have a personal, unique, and monumental final project impressed the children." They had worked cooperatively, shared with one another, criticized, and made suggestions. We learned more about one another and gained a greater respect and understanding of our cultures.

The children began receiving praise and attention that was well deserved. One of my girls commented that she liked doing this because "it made me feel good about myself." Another explained, "It gave me a chance to know my ancestor better." Tyrese liked the project because "we shared paint and didn't fight." Larry enjoyed the classes because "it was the greatest experience in my life. It was like going to my ancestor's house."

Few things are more important to me than seeing my children feel great about themselves. The arts provided a vehicle for me to get to know these children better by learning more about their backgrounds. I feel a great sense of happiness for them and, needless to say, a tremendous amount of pride in their achievement![4]

HOW CREATIVE ARE YOU?

The creative person is a natural problem solver, but also one who comes up with new solutions. The answers tend to be unconventional. Instead of thinking convergently, that is, in the customary and expected way, the creative person thinks divergently, finding different or unusual ways to think and operate. Creative people tend to deviate from the normal or typical in their thinking. They look for new connections, new orders, and new possibilities. They do not copy; they invent.

> The already minimal funds withdrawn from curriculum based instruction in many states and districts have often been directed towards other solutions, largely towards the infusion into the school of visiting artists: performer programs which, under the umbrella of audience development or enrichment opportunities, offer short term exposure to artistry and performance often supported by corporate funding. Such flying visits, while exposing children to the arts, once unglued from full and continuous curriculum provision, do little to reinforced serious learning, even worse, these cursory "tastes" often succeed in breeding contempt for the arts as "entertainment" or as "elitist" enterprises unrelated to the ebb and flow of the everyday challenges of living in the world.[5]

Artists vary in the degree of their originality. Some prefer to work in the prevailing styles and modes of their day. Others, like Arnold Schoenberg, formulated wholly new ways to use sound expressively. When Paul Cézanne chose to paint a fallen, snow-covered tree he saw what others had failed to see. By finding beauty where no one had done so before, he reclaimed that moment of nature for us all. This kind of unconventional thinking has permitted humans to achieve new marvels. Creative people—both artists and scientists—have a high tolerance for ambiguity, irregularity, disorganization, and asymmetry, which seem to challenge and inspire them to seek new orders and meanings.

Every human being has some sense of creativity. We all have enjoyed doodling or building forms out of Lego blocks. Again, it is a matter of degree. If our creativity is not encouraged—and it often is not—we can turn it off. A true creative genius, however, like Mozart, is not only extremely rare but probably unstoppable.

To see how creative you might be, think of the kind of explanation or description you might attach to a photograph of a man sitting in a reclining seat on an airplane, returning from a business trip or professional conference. Here is the way a very bright high school student described the picture:

> Mr. Smith is on his way home from a successful business trip. He is very happy and he is thinking about his wonderful family and how glad he will be to see them again. He can picture it, about an hour from now, his plane landing at the airport and Mrs. Smith and their three children all there welcoming him home again.

In contrast, here is the way a highly creative high school student described the picture:

> This man is flying back from Reno where he has just won a divorce from his wife. He couldn't stand to live with her anymore, he told the judge, because she wore so much cold cream on her face at night that her head would skid across the pillow and hit him in the head. He is now contemplating a new skid-proof face cream.[6]

The creative student is unconventional, revealing an ability to go off in new directions, to "diverge" from the customary and the known.

THE SPECIAL PROBLEMS OF MUSIC

Of all the arts, music is often taught in the least creative way. At every level, kindergarten through graduate school, music is presented to students as a preexisting body of literature with which the student must become familiar. An acquaintance with and an understanding of that repertoire of musical "standards" are acquired slowly over many years, primarily by learning to sing, play an instrument, and read musical symbols. Seldom, if ever, are students invited to use the medium of sound to fashion their own totally original musical expressions. Incredibly, most doctoral programs in music do not require any courses in musical composition.

Certainly, music education programs that are content with simply passing on the classical and ethnic musical culture as is are prosaic and staid. Maintaining the status quo isn't a particularly stimulating business. Without investing in its creative aspects, we consign music to history. By preoccupying our young talent and our audiences with the standard repertoire, we sap the vitality of the art. In contrast, theater does not restrict itself to Molière and Shakespeare, or the visual arts to Leonardo da Vinci and Rembrandt.

The study of music, we often hear, develops creative self-expression. This is a goal that most parents, school administrators, and board members find highly desirable. Unfortunately, the rhetoric is seldom matched in practice. By and large, music teachers, many of whom had little creative music making in their own education, think of their subject primarily as an art of re-creation. As far as students are concerned, composers are dead people, and music is a fairly finished art.

Many music teachers delude themselves into thinking that interpretation is the equivalent of creativity. Music teachers tend to regard performance as a creative act. It may be so for the teacher, but is it for the students? True, some decisions in the process of interpreting a piece of music do invite some creative choice. But for the most part, these decisions are made by the conductor and presented to students as a *fait accompli*.

In performance groups, students learn to communicate the composer's meaning. Although they may identify with the thought and emotion expressed, such performance does not teach students that they can use sound as a medium for conveying their own impressions. Teachers rarely invite students to try performing a piece in a number of different ways, evaluate the various effects, and decide which approach is the most affecting. Instead, the "director" dictates how the music should be played and interpreted, and the students follow orders. They are not involved in interpretive decision making.

In most music study, improvisation—the spontaneous creation of a melodic composition or variations on a theme—is not an integral part of the curriculum. Almost invariably, students are taught to read the printed notes. Even in high school and college jazz bands, where one might expect that improvisation would be the rule, students are taught to adhere to the charts.

Music textbooks for elementary and junior high schools do make a modest nod to creativity. Book 6 of the *Share the Music* series, for example, asks students to create an original accompaniment, to create appropriate background music for a scene, create a melody in 3/4 time, write a patriotic text, and create a performance using the appropriate tone color, articulation, dynamics, and tempo.[7] This is typical of today's texts, so the situation in regard to musical creativity is improving. But some music teachers insist that the rules of musical notation be mastered before any attempts are made at personal musical expression. Such teachers emphasize music as primarily an art of performance, a way of decoding what others have expressed. In a sense, they reduce music to a secondhand art, forgetting that first the music was created, and then the notational systems for it were devised. We seem to have forgotten that music is an aural art and that only for purposes of easy and accurate recall were musical symbols invented. Following this sequence, students should learn to use sound to express their own original musical "thoughts" and then create their own encoding of them. In this way they will come to see the need for musical notation. In this way, too, the act of musical creation can serve as the impetus for learning the means to record music in symbols, just as we learn to speak before we write. In any case, the act of creating music need not be constrained by the students' knowledge of notation, or their lack of it. Creation can be a totally aural process.

In opera education, students are sometimes asked to create their own opera—to write the story, the libretto, and the melodies and then to create a production, including the costumes, scenery, lighting, and music. The Metropolitan Opera's Education Program sends opera education experts into the schools to work with students and teachers and show how this can be done. Similarly, OPERA America, the umbrella organization for more than 100 opera companies in North America, has produced educational materials with a component called "Create and Produce" that introduces students to storytelling by having them write and perform their own opera based on a story and music of their own creation.[8]

In music the model has been the artist as a performer. If music teachers have been negligent, it is in ignoring the model of the artist as composer. Students respond excitedly to the challenge of creating their own musical compositions, sometimes with the help of technology (synthesizers and computers), and they learn the substance of musical expression and communication in the process. Being creative is another good way for students to learn to understand music.

If music is to be a living art that communicates in our own time, students of the art must become involved in its creative aspects. They must learn to use sound as a medium for their own communication. Whether by exploiting the technique of improvisation, experimenting with the organization of sound with the help of computers and synthesizers, or simply inventing their own musical expressions, students can experience music as an art of *self*-creation rather an art of *re*-creation.

The ability to develop one's own musical constructs lies at the heart of musical literacy and musical intelligence. It is basic to the understanding of music as an art, just as learning to draw and paint and sculpt are basic to an understanding of the visual arts. Musical literacy is not just the capacity to interpret or to master the technique of playing and singing what others have created. It is also the ability to create and to use sound as a means of self-expression and communication. Learning to use sound to represent their own meaning allows students to exercise and develop their musical intelligence, a way for them to react to their own lives and times. More important, in coming to terms with how and what one can "say" with music, students naturally come to value and to better understand the musical creations of others.

POTENTIAL

Learning the value of all our various symbolic systems is one of the functions of education. But to acquire real understanding, students must be able to use the systems to express their own meaning. It is not enough merely to learn to admire the way others have used images, sound, movement, and words to express and convey their own meaning, however universal. The real challenge in mastering an art is in employing its technique to one's own ends, to be able to use these techniques of representation to convey one's own personal feelings about, observations of, reactions to, and understandings about the world.

What goes on in classrooms in the arts determines the worth of an arts program. What teachers teach and students learn, in, through, and about the arts, is the measure of a program's quality and the justification for its existence. An effective arts program introduces students to the broad arts culture and gives them the tools and the necessary knowledge to understand it. Learning to use the arts as tools of expression is an essential part of arts education. Indeed, the arts are an invaluable resource for teaching students to use their own minds and imaginations to fashion new and better worlds.

_ chapter thirteen _

CULTIVATING THE ARTS
IN HIGH SCHOOL

The failure of arts delivery systems is having a deleterious effect on the arts, particularly on the high school level. The lack of certification in dance and theater and the closer alignment of these areas to the world of professional performance than to education are damaging these arts, because they lack adequate representation in the curriculum.

In the visual arts, teachers perpetuate the practice of teaching to their strengths and interests rather than offering a comprehensive program of instruction. They may concentrate on ceramics, drawing, or jewelry making and little else. Teachers teach what pleases them and often what is easiest. The result is that the students are shortchanged. This abuse is widespread.

Music education in American high schools is so entrenched that all programs are similar. As do art teachers, music teachers concentrate on what they like to teach, in this case, performance. Even so, many students are left out. More than 30 percent of small secondary schools do not even offer marching band and mixed chorus, and fewer than 10 percent offer orchestra, related arts, music history, class piano, class voice, or other courses. Students who do not qualify for band, chorus, or orchestra are therefore systematically excluded from the study of music. As might be expected, unattractive elective courses are shunned by students and soon eliminated. There are exceptions: Band programs are growing at the rate of 7 to 10 percent a year, and enrollment in music theory courses has had an enormous increase in recent years.

THE STATE OF THE ARTS

Large secondary schools usually have several performing groups, but not much else. Although enrollment in choral groups has increased in 42 percent

128

of the schools, concert band in 33 percent, marching band in 32 percent, and orchestra in 41 percent, fewer schools are offering general music, music appreciation, music history, and other academic courses. Since 1962, the percentage of high schools offering music appreciation has dropped from 47 to 22 percent, and that of high schools offering general music has declined from 44 to 22 percent. This may account for the alarming 25 percent decrease in enrollments in music in both small and large high schools. Perhaps music teachers don't offer courses that excite students, or they focus the music curriculum on performance, with the result that opportunities for other kinds of music study have been reduced or eliminated. One of the glaring inadequacies of high school music is the neglect of students who do not participate in performance ensembles. Today, high school music reaches, on average, about 7 to 10 percent of the students.

A survey of schools reveals that "increases in academic requirements or other factors appear to be having a negative effect on enrollment in arts classes and activities."[1] Indeed, the increasingly tangential position of the arts in the curricula of American schools is cause for concern. There is little dance and theater, and opportunities to study creative writing (essays, poems, short stories, and novels) are generally scarce and inconsistent. Meaning in the arts tends to come from performance and production—informed engagement. Even though the best way to understand the arts is having the experience of doing them, students will be shortchanged if the emphasis is strictly on production. An approach that gives a broader perspective does not need to ignore creation and production (performance).

The first of the different levels of experiencing the arts is a kind of oblivious, vague, and inattentive haze. Then comes the emotional or sensuous level, a conscious awareness. The third level is analytical and perceptive, revealing the work's expressive power. Finally, the better the work is understood, the more likely the result will be a heightened response, a peak experience. Informed engagement with varied works of arts is central to understanding.

What are the benefits of work in the arts? There is a great, diverse range of expressive results, many of them shocking, grotesque, violent, paradoxical, contradictory, even absurd. Strong arts imply a comprehensive program of art instruction, including access to dance and theater at some point during the high school years. What can be done to reestablish the education credibility of the arts? If change is called for, how can we persuade arts teachers to alter their ways?

One thing is certain: The education world of which the arts are a tenuous part does not put any priority on reforming the arts, even though it might agree that they need it. There are more urgent priorities. If we are going to create a better tomorrow for the arts, the impetus will instead have to come from artists working closely with the public and school administrators. Will including the arts in the new federal education reform bill, establishing national standards, and having the support of the current secretary of education solve the problems? They will help, but I am convinced that the education community itself will have to take the initiative if the current trends are to be reversed.

EXCLUSIVITY

The fact that most high school students do not have an opportunity to study music is one of the clearest and most devastating indictments of music education. Later, as adults, those students who are left out come to believe that music study is unnecessary and irrelevant. The result is a public inadequately educated in the subject and offer only lukewarm or no support. Schools that offer only performance programs consign the majority of students to discover their musical heritage in the commercial culture that surrounds them. When music study is not provided, students are denied access to a major form of human insight and understanding.

WHAT NEEDS FIXING

Performance is where American music education shines. But in many high schools, music is suffering from what might be called *paradigm blindness*, a regimen of ensembles with few if any options for students who do not qualify. When music education concentrates solely on performance, its educational potential is compromised and its impact is diluted. As effective as performing can be in teaching students about music, this single-focused persistence impoverishes music education if only because it excludes so many students.

The problem is not new. Almost twenty years ago Jack E. Schaeffer, former director of music education for the Seattle public schools, laid the blame on music educators: "Frequently they see their mission purely as the development of perfection in performing groups. They give low priority to developing a quality program in general music for students who cannot qualify for performing groups. They are failing to broaden the base of music education." And he chastised college and universities for giving "higher status to studies for the development of band, choir, and orchestra directors than to those that prepare the general music teacher."[2]

Music educators who are wedded to performance and only performance, seem oblivious to other ways to illuminate musical understanding or serve the student population. Performance may be the best way to learn music, but it is certainly not the only way. As important as the performing experiences can be for the students involved in them, these ensembles constitute an inhospitable landscape for those who are not involved.

Why do we need anything more than performing ensembles at the high school level? There are three main reasons:

1. They explore music from perspectives that provide musical insight not generally conveyed through performance.
2. They permit students who are not adept at performing either vocally or instrumentally to acquire musical understanding through other means, such as learning to listen perceptively, analyzing what they hear, creating and communicating with sound, and developing criteria that enable them to substantiate their musical opinions and judgments.
3. They give all students the option of studying music.

A broader array of electives immediately establishes music as a serious curricular study, a subject of real learning, not entertainment. Thus the concept of "general" music has to change. Rather than loading the curriculum with broad surveys that lack substantive content, the course should be exploratory and introductory but also challenging, explicit, highly focused, and concrete in insight.

Performing groups convey the idea that learning about music depends directly on singing or playing, and there is no doubt that the only way to learn to play a trumpet is to do it. But many students do not aspire to learn to sing or to master an instrument. It makes sense, therefore, that if music is to be established as an indispensable part of general education for all students, it must go beyond a performance-dominated curriculum.

Music educators fought for the establishment of high school graduation requirements in fine arts and, then failed to provide alternative ways to fulfill them. These requirements vary from state to state and can usually be met by a wide variety of courses, music being just one possibility. Students can earn credits from performance ensembles or other music courses. But the curriculums' emphasis on performance and the lack of other options sends students the message that they cannot fulfill the requirement through music if they do not sing or play an instrument. Instead, they must do this through some other course of study, say, in art, theater, or dance. Instead of opening the door to music study, the result of these new requirements is often to send students elsewhere.

Many high school administrators, board members, and parents are reticent to fund a curriculum that reaches so few students. They fail to see its universal value. By involving more students, the music education program increases its status and, at the same time, the likelihood of developing a supportive public. The most effective advocacy is one's own acquired understanding. Ensuring the future of music education, like the future of science and mathematics, depends on the value the public assigns it.

NATIONAL STANDARDS IN THE ARTS

After more than two years of hearings and deliberations, national standards for arts education were agreed on and published in 1994. The national movement to develop standards in every subject is sponsored by the U.S. Department of Education as part of the Goals 2000: Educate America Act, designed to set national achievement standards and encourage innovation. This legislation includes the arts as one of the nine core subjects, officially making the arts a component of a complete education for all children. Each of the nine subjects—English, mathematics, science, foreign languages, civics and government, economics, arts, history, and geography—will have voluntary national academic and performance standards.

Developed by a consortium of national arts education associations, the standards in the arts outline what every young American should know and be able to do in dance, music, theater, and the visual arts.[3] (The standards for creative writing will be included in the standards for English.) The standards, which specify an array of skills, knowledge, and techniques in each art, are organized on three levels: grades K through 4, grades 5 through 8, and grades 9 through 12, progressing to ever more sophisticated learnings. Determining the curriculum and the specific instructional activities necessary to achieve the standards is the responsibility of the states, local school districts, and individual teachers. These voluntary standards are a step toward helping the states and local school districts create their own Goals 2000 plan, tailored to their own curricular program, student needs, and available resources. These standards are based on the belief that higher expectations produce better performance.

In theater, for example, the intent is to develop theater literacy, or learning to see the created world of theater through the eyes of the playwright, actor, designer, and director. Students become active participants in the processes of performing and creating theater. Likewise, dance has seven content standards:

1. Identifying and demonstrating movement elements and skills in performing dance.
2. Understanding choreographic principles, processes, and structures.
3. Understanding dance as a way to create and communicate meaning.
4. Applying and demonstrating critical and creative thinking skills in dance.

5. Demonstrating and understanding dance in various cultures and historical periods.
6. Making connections between dance and healthful living.
7. Making connections between dance and other disciplines.

The new national standards for music make clear that programs for just the talented are insufficient.

> Arts courses for the specially motivated do not quality as basic or adequate arts instruction. They certainly cannot prepare all students to meet the standards [suggested]. These standards assume that students in all grades will be actively involved in comprehensive, sequential programs that include creating, performing, and producing on the one hand, and study, analysis, and reflection on the other. Both kinds of activities are indispensable elements of a well-rounded education in the arts.[4]

What is clear from the standards in music for grades 9 to 12 is that they cannot be achieved solely through the usual performing groups. "Every course in music, including performance courses, should provide instruction in creating, performing, listening to, and analyzing music, in addition to focusing on its specific subject matter."[5] But performing groups are probably not the best vehicles for students to learn to analyze and describe "a varied repertoire of music, representing diverse genres and cultures"; to demonstrate "extensive knowledge of the technical vocabulary of music"; or to "identify and explain compositional devices and techniques used to provide unity and variety and tension and release in a musical work."[6] Performing ensembles may not provide the most effective forum for understanding the relationship between music and the other arts or between music and history and culture. In essence, these standards support broadening the base of high school music to encompass more than just performance.

The standards stress skill development, which is where the emphasis has been during the past two or three decades in all the arts. But technical development reinforces the status quo and does not articulate the relationship of the art to general education. What has been slighted is any emphasis on value. The thought was to subsume value under the other categories, but instead, it was promptly forgotten. Eventually, the U.S. Department of Education will draw up school-to-work standards and opportunity-to-learn standards, with the former demonstrating how the arts and others subjects contribute to educating an effective workforce and the latter articulating the conditions for quality teaching, such as safe schools, sufficient time on task, and adequate materials and facilities.

But some refreshingly new and different areas of emphasis extend the music curriculum and make it more comprehensive. Among them is the suggestion that students learn to improvise melodies, variations, and accompaniment; compose and arrange music; read and notate music; listen to, analyze, and describe music; evaluate music and music performances; understand the relationships among music, the other arts, and disciplines outside the arts; and understand music in relation to history and culture.

Establishing national standards may turn out to be a curse as well as a cure. Elliot Eisner asked: "Is it reasonable to expect that there is a single version of art, music, drama, dance, mathematics, science, physics, chemistry, biology, social studies, and geography? A one-version program that's good for 47 million youngsters working in 110 thousand schools?"[7] Eisner reasons that youngsters in different locales and situations and with different backgrounds may require different educational programs, and he questions the idea that there is "one kind of program that is good for everybody in schools everywhere for all time." He eschews uniformity as a strategic educational aim, particularly in the arts, which should stress innovation, surprise, and creative thinking skills "that do not fit prespecified norms. . . . A cookie cutter model of educational outcomes does not fit a culturally pluralistic culture."[8] He believes that what we desperately need is better teaching, but better teaching cannot be mandated.

Eisner makes a case for relevance. "I'd say things would be better in education, if what [students] learned in school related to the problems they have to deal with in life."[9] The arts tend to overlook their own significance. Teaching students to value the arts is not something arts teachers have stressed, nor do the standards. The idea is that as students develop skill, they will automatically acquire a sense of value. But value does not automatically follow as an outcome of technical competency. Creating a mural, learning a dance, and playing a clarinet does not guarantee that students will value these arts. Evidently, the thought of many, if not most music teachers, is that playing a clarinet automatically conveys its importance and that students who sing in the choir will automatically learn to value music. If this is the thinking, it is fallacious. I know too many adults who spend years in the band and choir and, years later, do not give the arts their due. This is particularly disturbing when they sit on school boards. They, too, see music as fun, as extracurricular, and not as a subject with real substance. Students may simply enjoy themselves and never connect their experience to the value of these particular arts. This is decidedly not the case with math and science, whose value is not taken for granted. The first standard in mathematics, for example, states that "students should learn to value mathematics."[10]

Clearly, Eisner sees the standards as missing the mark educationally. Education, he writes, is about learning to deal with uncertainty and ambiguity. It is about learning how to savor the quality of the journey. It is about becoming critically minded, intellectually curious and learning how to frame and pursue your own educational aims. It is not about regaining our competitive edge.[11]

The national standards are voluntary, and they invite states and local school systems to adapt them to the students in the community, their needs, the aims of education, and the resources that can be assembled. The standards provide a means of determining the competency of students in the arts and other subjects, how students measure up to these standards that define what students should know and be able to do. Students will be assessed at ages nine, thirteen, and seventeen (grades 4, 8, and 12) by the National Assessment of Educational Progress (NAEP), providing the public with data about the condition and progress of student achievement.[12] The first national assessment of the competencies that students are expected to achieve through these standards is planned for 1997.

Teachers must make clear why an education in music is significant. Why should I study music? What will it do for me? Joy E. Lawrence, professor of music education at Kent State University, advises, "We need to change our thinking, change our focus, and change our approaches to make music exciting, relevant, and rewarding—an art form to be experienced and enjoyed by teenagers."[13] The rewards of music study emerge from understanding music as a form of human communication, a link with past civilizations and other cultures. Students learn to see music in the larger context of human culture, not as mere entertainment.

Music must be conceived and perceived as part of general education. Music teachers must treat it as a basic. This is the only justification for including music study in public schooling. The fact that all students do not take chemistry and physics does not eliminate them as basics in general education. Moreover, science does not concentrate on training scientists or mathematics on creating mathematicians but, rather, a public that understands the relevance of science and mathematics and how they are used to enhance our lives. The arts should be no different. The aim of music studies is to produce better educated human beings, not more and better artists.

We must cultivate a richer landscape for the arts in high school. Electives, designed for the entire student body, have to enrich and broaden the curriculum to encompass opportunities for all students to study pivotal aspect of the arts. Ultimately, we want students to value the arts—to gain an understanding of, and respect for, the role and importance of the arts in their lives and in the lives of all humans. Whatever the particular focus of study, the connection of the arts to the world of today should be central. Achieving relevance means that students relate in-school arts with out-of-school arts and that they interrelate the arts on a highly personal level. By learning to be perceptive about the music they hear, for example, they will recognize sound as a powerful form of communication that traverses all human cultures, what musicologist Edith Borroff calls a "luminous window."[14] An intracultural or a transcultural approach demonstrates the diversity of American culture and the startling confluence of music in human life.

Schools with Comprehensive Programs

Fortunately, several public high schools around the country deliberately reach beyond the talented, offering all students a variety of ways to study music. These schools actively counter the claim that music education is elitist. Here are some examples:

:: In addition to performing ensembles, the Area High School in Altoona, Pennsylvania, a moderate-size railroad town, offers "Electronic Music," "Theory and Harmony," "Survey of Music," and "Electronic Studio Arts," the last an interdisciplinary course encompassing music, art, and technology.

:: The California High School in San Ramon, California, offers its students a number of courses that meet University of California and California State University admission requirements in the arts. A general music course is designed to open up a world of music for every student who enrolls. According to music teacher James M. Cauter, when students hear music played on an outstanding stereo system, "They experience a marked increase in their desire to listen to music of all styles! They begin to develop and expand their own personal collection of recordings, and they leave your room every day with a positive feeling." Cauter also offers a course called "Music Today" that surveys a variety of historical musical examples. This school also has a fine arts course called "Interrelating the Arts," generally team taught, which explores the basic concepts and uniqueness of dance, drama, music, and the visual arts.

:: The LaCrosse, Wisconsin, High School offers a popular course, "Soundscapes," that replaces "Music Survey," a course that failed to attract sufficient student enrollment. In "Soundscapes," students cover the same curriculum, but they use contemporary technology to compose their own musical works. Some 170 students signed up for the course for the 1993/1994 school year. Bix Swerman, who taught band in LaCrosse for ten years, teaches this class exclusively. He now has five sections of "Soundscapes" and enough interested students for two more. "Instead of lecturing to inattentive students, I have students asking specific questions about components of music in the works they are creating."*

:: In addition to a wide array of small and large ensembles, Miami's Palmetto Senior High School, which has an enrollment of about 1,900 students in grades 10 through 12, offers courses for nonperformers, including "Introduction to Music," a one-semester course that meets for one hour each day. In some years, four sections are needed with about thirty students in each. This class fulfills the state's one-half credit graduation requirement in the fine arts. There are also classes in theory, guitar, and, occasionally, electronic music.

:: The course "Austin Live Music Scene" is one of several in music at the Anderson High School in Austin, Texas. This general music or appreciation course (note the deliberate avoidance of those terms) includes five evening field trips to live performances. A year's course in theory, taught on electronic keyboards, also is offered.

:: At the Moravia, New York, Central High School, a rural school with 1,400 students in grades K through 12 (and 650 students in the high school), "Music in Our Lives," a general course mandated by the state, meets for one hour every day all year long. According to music teacher Denise Abbattista, the course has been so successful that it has led to the development of other courses, including a guitar and synthesizer ensemble. There also are courses in music theory and appreciation, the latter using a traditional historical approach. These courses have attracted an amazing 67 percent of the high school students.

* Bix Swerman, "With Soundscapes, Imagination is the Only Limit," *Wisconsin School Musician*, September 1993, p. 69.

_ chapter fourteen _

THE CORRELATION
WITH ACADEMIC ACHIEVEMENT

The effect of arts study on learning in general, though not yet substantiated sufficiently, can be surprisingly positive. Students that study the arts seem to do better overall. Apparently there is a critical, though as yet not adequately explained or documented, link between the extent of arts engagement and the quality of academic performance. In a variety of programs across the country, the arts have been credited with helping young minds perform well and encouraging students to stay in school.

The Florida Department of Education, for example, found a direct correlation between an active fine and performing arts program and increased student motivation and a lower dropout rate.[1] The Manchester Craftsmen's Guild in Pittsburgh, an organization that apprentices young at-risk, inner-city students in the arts while teaching them math, English, and other subjects, found a correlation between the arts and student academic performance. Some 75 to 80 percent of these students go on to a higher education in all fields, not just in the arts. At the Duke Ellington School for the Performing Arts in Washington, D.C., students graduate at an astonishing 99 percent rate, and 90 percent go on to higher education.

THE ARTS AND THE SAT

As part of the Student Descriptive Questionnaire, high school students who take the Scholastic Assessment Test (SAT) provide information on their participation in the arts. According to the College Board, the administrators of the SAT, those students who study the arts do substantially better on their verbal and math scores than do students who take no arts courses (Table 14.1)[2]

The College Entrance Examination Board reports that arts students

TABLE 14.1   *Correlation Between Study of the Arts and Scores on the SAT*

Arts Coursework	Verbal Mean Scores			Math Mean Scores		
	1993	1994	1995	1993	1994	1995
Music appreciation	455	456	461	501	504	508
Music performance	446	446	451	496	498	501
Acting/play production	463	463	469	501	503	507
Art history/appreciation	439	438	443	488	489	491
Dance	432	431	437	473	474	478
Drama appreciation	453	453	458	489	491	494
Photography/film	443	443	448	491	493	496
Studio art/design	443	444	449	494	498	501
No arts coursework	401	397	400	464	462	462
Mean for all students	424	423	428	478	479	482
Years of Arts Study		1994	1995		1994	1995
4 or more years		453	459		500	506
3 years		432	436		481	483
2 years		426	430		481	482
1 year		417	422		478	481
.5 year or less		408	411		470	470

* *Since the number of years spent studying a subject was calculated differently through 1993, scores for that year are not given.*

Source: Reprinted by permission from *Profile of SAT and Achievement Test Takers for 1993, 1994, and 1995.* Copyright © 1993, 1994, 1995 by the College Entrance Examination Board.

consistently and impressively outperform their nonarts peers, and that the longer they study the arts, the better their scores are. In 1993 those who studied the arts for more than four years scored fifty-three points higher on the verbal test and thirty-seven points higher on the math test than did students with no coursework in the arts (Figure 14.1).[3]

The question that has not yet been answered is the degree to which these arts students are self-selective. Do better students naturally gravitate to the arts, or does studying the arts truly improve academic performance? Obviously, there is a correlation between arts study and SAT scores, but is this a clear-cut case of cause and effect? Can the arts be credited?

1995 Mean SAT Verbal Scores

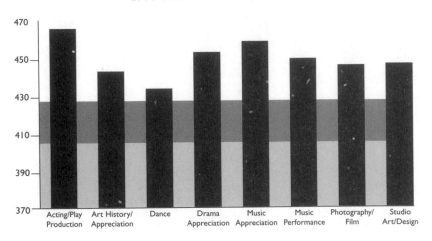

1995 Mean SAT Math Scores

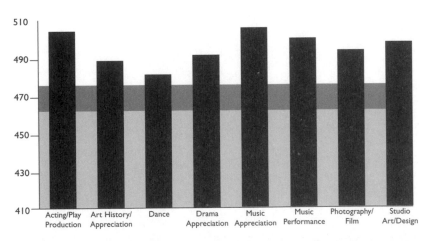

FIGURE 14.1. Ninety-five percent of the students registering for the SAT voluntarily complete the Student Descriptive Questionnaire, providing information on their backgrounds, academic performance, extracurricular activities, and college plans. Students who take arts courses score significantly higher on the test's verbal and math portions. The black vertical bars represent scores for students who have taken one or more courses in the listed subjects. Scores for students who reported no arts study and the mean for all students are shown in the shaded backgrounds. (Reprinted with permission from College Entrance Examination Board, *Profile of SAT and Achievement Tests Takers.*© 1995. This information was published in *Teaching Music*, December 1995.)

Participation in the arts can help students establish and maintain a high level of interest in school. For some, the arts become a commitment and a dedication that turns their lives around. For this reason, some people believe that the arts can be a factor in helping young people avoid crime. The federal crime bill calls for ways to support programs that help root out the causes of crime. One of the intentions is to give young people something constructive to do after school. Consequently, the bill refers to the arts as a counter to inner-city gang violence and other problems.

THE ARTS AND EDUCATIONAL EXCELLENCE

A 1991 study sponsored by the National Endowment for the Arts investigated how the arts contribute to excellent education and documented the relationship between instruction and experience in the arts and the students' overall educational performance.[4] The study tried to establish scientific evidence to support the belief that the arts can make positive contributions to academic performance, contributions that teachers, students, parents, and researchers have observed in practice.

Eight arts-focused schools were studied in depth to identify the ways that the arts contribute to educational excellence. These schools, selected from more than 500, represented a range of elementary, middle, and high schools. All had open admissions and multidisciplinary arts programs. The study found that changing from a traditional to an arts-based model both transformed and renewed these schools. In all of them, observers found links between strong arts programs and educational quality and accomplishment. A profile emerged from these schools that defined their educational approach in five themes, which, though consistent in all the schools, were present in different degrees.

Theme 1: The Arts Can Foster the Development
of Students Who Are Actively Engaged in Learning

These arts-infused schools did a better-than-average job of engaging students, teachers, and principals. Learning was fun and challenging. By offering varied modes of learning, the arts create greater opportunities for students and teachers to connect in productive ways.

Howard Gardner's theory of multiple intelligences (see Chapter 4) suggests that people differ in their specific intelligence profile. Some may be more linguistic and mathematical; others more musical, spatial, or kinesthetic. This helps suggest why the arts can play an important role in stimulating engagement. They provide a variety of ways for students to use their minds and learn. For example, the Karl H. Kellogg Elementary School in Chula Vista, California, involves all its students in "living history" explorations, in which activities of the performing arts—acting, dancing, singing, constructing, performing, writing, and researching—breathe life into history.

Each year the school selects a different civilization to study. When ancient Egypt was the focus, students constructed an Egyptian palace and a tomb; they produced a play with the music, costumes, and jewelry of that period; and they prepared an Egyptian feast. The principal, the classroom teachers, and the performing arts resource specialist found this approach to be much more effective than teaching strictly by the book. Their students, they explained, learn concepts because they think, feel, see, and are history.

Theme 2: The Arts Contribute to the Development of a Creative, Committed, and Exciting School Culture of Teachers, Students, and Parents

The arts gave these schools quality. Creativity, high standards, self-motivation, and presentation—all derived through artistic pursuits—marked the schools' culture. These schools were not merely exhibiting a curriculum that provided time and space for artwork; instead, they were using the arts as the core of a school culture of high standards.

The presentation of artistic work in these schools challenges students to create work that they are proud of. A student at the Roosevelt Middle School of the Arts in Milwaukee made the case: "Most of us want to look our best in front of others." In these exemplary, arts-focused schools, artwork can be found everywhere: in the classrooms and overflowing to the walls and ceilings in the hallways. At the Fine Arts Core Education (F.A.C.E.) program in Montreal, students in grades K through 11 developed a strong sense of themselves as creators and performers that carried over into all their activities. Because there is no one "right" answer in artistic creation, the students must determine for themselves what is right and good. They refine their ideas until their work conveys their meaning. The dance teacher at the Ashley River Creative Arts Elementary School in Charleston, South Carolina, discovered, that "my students could do 'C' level work to satisfy a teacher's requirement in any other course; if they only strive to do 'C' work in a dance production, however, they will be falling short of their peers' expectations of creating high quality on stage." Moreover, such performances invite parents to participate in the school's program.

The teaching in these schools is innovative. Teachers catch the creative urge themselves, and their teaching improves. A twenty-year veteran primary school teacher at the Kellogg Elementary School, who taught in the traditional way until the arts-infusion program was established, found that "teaching with the arts as a basis for thematic teaching is demanding, but I have enjoyed these last three years most out of my entire career." Teachers want to teach in these schools. There are waiting lists, and teacher's absence rates are relatively low and their retention rates are comparatively high.

Theme 3: The Arts Play a Role in Generating a Dynamic, Coordinated, and Cohesive Curriculum

Arts-infused schools stress the content, skill, and knowledge of individual disciplines at the same time that they use the arts to coordinate a multi- or interdisciplinary curriculum. Whereas traditional schools teach discretely defined classes such as math, science, and music, arts-focused schools look for connections across disciplines. The complementarity of the arts with other subjects such as social studies and history provides a mechanism to create thematic, cohesive curricula.

At the Elm Creative Arts School in Milwaukee, pupils study the usual array of academic subjects matter as well as the visual arts, music, movement, and creative writing. The principal claims that "it is not what the children learn but how they learn that makes Elm different from other elementary schools." Using the arts in all subject areas encourages students to use their senses in learning and helps them see the arts as a part of everyday life, not as separate isolated activities, even though they are taught as both discrete disciplines and interdisciplinary vehicles. Students studying the American Revolution, for example, sing songs dating from that period and attempt to understand their meaning. They analyze paintings, prints, and sketches from the 1700s; dramatize a particular battle; re-create a debate in the Continental Congress; and write their own bill of rights. They become involved in history through their own direct experience. The curricular theme changes every eight weeks, and it is used in all subject areas. Examples of these themes are Japan, medieval times, 100 years of Chicago architecture, the rainforest, black history month, Egypt, the weather, the American Revolution, and the sea.

Theme 4: The Arts Can Build Bridges, to the Larger Community, the Broader Culture, and Other Institutions

When schoolwork extends to life outside the school, the entire concept of learning is enlarged. Community and school resources join in mutually supportive educational initiatives. Students shift their attitudes toward learning's being limited to just school. The extended resources enrich learning and make it more relevant. Students see that their life outside school can contribute to their education.

A group of seventh graders at the Roosevelt Middle School, for example, combined their interests and abilities to create an environmental handbook. They researched scientific stories and neighborhood news to address concerns such as recycling, air and water pollution, and local attitudes toward these issues. One of the students explained how the collaboration worked: "I was the editor, since I was good at spelling and at putting ideas together. Mary was the poet, Yolanda was the science writer, and Jenny was the political writer. Alex was the artist, because he was really good at drawing, and Sondra was putting a bibliography together." Students in these schools regularly use community resources such as artists, museums, and theaters and tap the knowledge resources of citizens. One result is the establishment of a network of artists who demonstrate their skills, act as critics, and share their lives with the students.

During a week-long poet-in-residence program at the John Eliot Elementary School in Needham, Massachusetts, the students created and published a book of their own poetry inspired by the resident poet's work. Work with artists can inspire students and keep teachers fresh and excited.

Theme 5: The Arts Can Humanize the Learning Environment

In all the model schools, the arts helped "humanize" the learning environment. They were a key ingredient in encouraging students and teachers to examine their intuitive and emotive selves, to develop empathy and compassion, and to share and appreciate different cultures. Educators in the schools went to great lengths to stress that their goal was not to train artists or even to improve the students' test scores. Rather, the eight schools visited were dedicated to helping students learn and grow into well-rounded human beings. At all levels, the intent was to define education as more than the acquisition of skills and knowledge. Whereas the focus of the three Rs often stresses skills over personal development, the arts teach both.

In all these schools the arts serve as a catalyst for achieving educational quality. They improve the school environment and make sure that the students can relate to it. As she guided visitors past tables of sculptures, dioramas, puppets, murals, banners, and exhibits of student artwork, the principal at the Eliot School noted that the arts are the vehicle through which the students realize that "Eliot School is theirs to live in, to learn in, to grow in, and to show in." The arts do more. For the schools in this study, a return to the basics is not limited to the three Rs. Because the arts deal directly with the humanity of each student, they are considered to be more basic than other subjects. The St. Augustine School for the Arts in Bronx, New York, for kindergarten through grade 8, school, develops the intangible and intuitive side of its students, through music, painting, and sculpture. The school attempts to educate the whole student, not just those dimensions traditionally taught through the three Rs.

As they studied the history of South Carolina through the pottery of local Native Americans, the students at the Ashley River School investigated the technology, materials, and history of these people. They mixed clay with cow dung and fired their pieces in a pit, much as these American Indians had done. Re-creating the designs and colors of the pottery gave the students an understanding of and a respect for the aesthetic and cultural backgrounds that helped shape their local culture.

The arts can be the means for developing a sense of empathy and compassion. For a Vietnamese child who entered school in the middle of the year, art was her salvation. Initially her classmates teased her about her language inability and dress, but her meticulously drawn illustrations of her old and new homes won the hearts of those who had made fun of her. An appreciation and acceptance of diversity can be a significant outcome of arts study that encompasses different cultures.

PROOF OF EDUCATIONAL IMPACT

The observations of these schools suggest that there were indeed strong, though not well-articulated or researched, connections between the arts and educational excellence. Although these schools, quite independently of one another, set out to establish a reciprocal relationship between the arts and learning, they did so more on an intuitive hunch than according to a proven theory. The data assembled by these schools show, however, that the arts did have a positive effect.

Students who enter first grade at the Aiken Elementary School, a public school of 1,300 children in kindergarten through grade 6, one-third of whom are minorities, quickly overcome their apparent academic weaknesses. These students have consistently outpaced their district and state peers in both reading and mathematics achievement tests. Fourth-grade Aiken students rank almost twenty percentile points above district and state students in reading, language, and mathematics; and fifth grade students score sixteen to twenty-five points higher, even though they are far behind when they start. According to the state of South Carolina, Aiken Elementary is in the top 1 percent of that state's schools in its student's performance on standardized tests.

Unlike those at Aiken, 80 percent of first graders at the Ashley River School, an arts magnet school of 475 students, do meet readiness standards. More than 90 percent of students in grades 1 through 3 meet basic skills assessment standards in reading and math, and in recent years, more than 96 percent of the students have met those standards. Ashley River students score at least six and often as much as twenty percentile points higher on both country and state levels in each of the subjects tested.

Although one-third of the students at the Elm Elementary School are eligible for the free lunch program and, like the Ashley River School, Elm has no academic or arts performance requirements for student selection, Elm's students performed better than their peers in 1990 in basic academic skills as early as the second grade. More than 60 percent or more tested above national averages in reading, vocabulary, and mathematics. In comparison, only 38 percent of the other second graders in Milwaukee tested above national averages in vocabulary, 43 percent in reading, and 48 percent in mathematics. In 1990, Elm's fifth-grade students scored twenty-six percentage points higher than their citywide peers.

At the Kellogg Elementary School, where approximately 48 percent of the students are members of minorities, including 41 percent Latino, third graders have remained above state averages in reading, writing, and mathematics and have shown increases since the arts program started. Although their scores generally fell below national norms before the program was introduced, their average scores on both reading and mathematics were above the national norm in all grades by 1990. The Kellogg students' language scores, too, were above the national norm in grades 3 through 5; only grade 6 was below the fiftieth percentile. Considering that these students are not academically advantaged, this is generally impressive.

About 59 percent of the students at the Roosevelt Middle School are minorities, somewhat less than the 68 percent of minority students overall in Milwaukee's middle schools. Minority students at Roosevelt and in Milwaukee as a whole performed substantially below national norms on the Iowa Test of Basic Skills (ITBS), and so the introduction of an arts-focused curriculum has had a dramatic effect on school performance. The percentage of students meeting state reading competency standards rose from less than 30 percent two years before the program was started to more than 80 percent. Whereas less than 10 percent of Roosevelt's students met the competency standard in mathematics in 1982/1983, before the arts program, competency achievement levels in math rose and have remained at 50 percent since 1984/1985. By 1989/1990, 60 percent of the students had met the math competency standard. Average daily attendance has risen from 85 percent to about 92 percent. Whereas the percentage of students suspended in the year before the program was initiated exceeded 50 percent, since the start of the program the rate has fallen below 15 percent and was lower than 10 percent during the 1989/1990 school year.

Standardized test results at the F.A.C.E. Program, a kindergarten-through-grade 12 open-admissions alternative school for about 1,000 students, indicate that these students perform consistently and substantially better than do students throughout Montreal's education system. The students passing the 1990 ministry examinations exceeded averages in all but seven of sixty-three different courses.

Even though these schools do not pursue selective admissions policies, standardized test results indicate that the students compare favorably with students enrolled in more academically selective schools. Their performance results, however, are not always above average: Some students receive only low scores on standardized tests, and some are retained in grade. In other words, even though these findings overall are highly promising, the arts are clearly not a panacea for all educational ills. Although many arts teachers express misgivings about using the arts to improve performance in other subjects, they acknowledge the possible beneficial impact. But not enough is known yet to state with certainty that the arts are a primary factor.

— part four —

REFORM

Education always seems to be involved with some kind of reform. The current reform movement began with the publication in 1983 of *A Nation at Risk*, a report by the National Commission on Excellence in Education. It sounded an alarm about "a rising tide of mediocrity that threatens our very future as a Nation and a people," and it tied "our once unchallenged preeminence in commerce, industry, science, and technological innovation" directly to the schools, assuming that they were responsible for the country's economic well-being. To maintain our global competitive edge, a more rigorous curriculum consisting of "Five New Basics"—English, mathematics, science, social studies, and computer science—was emphasized. The arts were largely ignored.

It took a decade of effort for this flagrant neglect of the arts to be recognized and corrected. The Goals 2000: Educate America Act, passed by Congress in 1994, finally included the arts in national education goal 3 as one of the core content areas in which students should demonstrate competency. The arts are now part of the national effort to achieve high standards in the core academic disciplines.

The implications of this inclusion are far reaching. In extending to the arts the status of other core subjects, they place the arts on the school reform agenda. Until now, arts education has been viewed as slighted and misunderstood but as essentially competent in providing instruction, particularly in teaching production and performance. Now the arts, too, must improve their ways.

The role of reformer is not a natural one for arts educators, who tend to be habitual in their ways, not receptive to criticism or even subjected to it, and convinced that they know how to deliver excellent instruction. Now they must face the same pressure for change and prospects of revision that have constantly pervaded, and sometimes encumbered, other subject areas in the general education curriculum. Reform is no longer everybody else's problem. It has come home to the arts. While establishing new and improved ways to operate will cause a certain amount of anguish, the field should be better for rethinking itself.

States are examining every facet of their education systems and are considering comprehensive changes. What these changes should be has sparked nationwide debate. Administrative structures are under scrutiny, for example, school-based management, charter schools, multiage grouping at the elementary level, the length of the school day and year, more community participation, greater use of technology, and increased parental involvement.

Reform is being taken very seriously. Oregon and Kentucky, for example, have passed comprehensive education reform legislation to address the needs of students and future workers. These are not the fragmented reforms of the past but an attempt to revolutionize the educational system. Systemic reform is taking a comprehensive, long-term approach to changing the entire educational system. The goal is to improve student achievement in order to guarantee the nation's economic future. Since change of any kind is difficult, it is not surprising that such large-scale reforms are generating strong debate.

Many of these reforms attempt to restructure education on a broad scale, for example, the Copernican Plan to replace the Carnegie Unit of one course, one credit. Along these lines, Minnesota requires students to demonstrate learning outcomes rather than to compile a list of courses they have taken, based on clock hours. The Copernican Plan is a way to organize high schools using large-block scheduling. Students enroll in one class at a time for about four hours each day for a period of thirty days. Large-block scheduling has been very successful. The large block is supplemented by a block of time each day that permits teachers and students additional time for extra help, study, and planning. In the afternoon, students participate in seventy-minute seminars. Students need to learn complex and creative thinking skills and to be able to think critically in analyzing and solving new problems. Teachers, too, need to be more broadly educated. They need to change the way they teach.

Reform can take many shapes, and among them is the way the arts can be redesigned to relate directly to overall educational revisions, nationally, statewide, and locally.

In keeping with the need to reform, Part IV explores some new ways to think about an education in the arts. Teaching the value of the art, not just technical ability, is offered as a possible emphasis. If people leave schools without understanding the role and value of the arts in their lives, they will not support the study of the arts.

— chapter fifteen —

REDEFINING THE MISSION:
VALUE-CENTERED ARTS EDUCATION

Three issues must be addressed if the status of the arts in public education is to be improved. First, the bad news. What major obstacles reduce or compromise educational credibility?

PUBLIC PERCEPTIONS OF ARTS EDUCATION

Arts educators have generally not been successful at convincing the public of the educational importance of music and the other arts. Strong evidence of the public's unfavorable attitude toward education in music and art is presented in "The 22nd Annual Gallup Poll of the Public's Attitudes Toward the Public Schools."[1] When asked what subjects they would require every college-bound public high school student to take, the respondents rated music the lowest of fourteen subjects. When asked what subjects they would require of every non-college-bound public high school student, they again rated music lower than all other subjects, including health education, foreign languages, and art. When asked what subjects should be given more emphasis than they now receive, less emphasis, or the same emphasis, 39 percent of the public said that music should be given less emphasis. Only art rated lower, with 42 percent of the public calling for less emphasis (Table 15.1).

The public's preferences concerning curriculum content, however, have changed in emphasis over the years. "The 26th Annual Phi Delta Kappa/Gallup Poll," for example, shows remarkable gains for music and art since 1990 (Table 15.2).[2]

Nonetheless, the public does not consider the arts basic to the education of American youth, perhaps—and here I am speculating—because it associ-

TABLE 15.1 *1990 Results, Core Courses*

Should the subjects listed be given more emphasis, less emphasis, or the same emphasis, as they now receive in high school?

	More emphasis (%)	Less emphasis (%)	Same emphasis (%)	Don't know (%)
Mathematics	80	3	14	3
English	79	3	15	3
Science	68	11	18	3
History/U.S. government	65	9	23	3
Geography	53	18	25	4
Foreign language	37	34	25	4
Music	13	39	43	5
Art	12	42	40	6

Source: Stanley M. Elam, "The 22nd Annual Gallup Poll of the Public's Attitudes Toward the Public Schools," *Phi Delta Kappan*, September 1990, p. 49. Reprinted by permission.

TABLE 15.2 *1994 Results, Core Courses*

	More emphasis (%)	Less emphasis (%)	Same emphasis (%)	Don't know (%)
Mathematics	82	1	17	*
English	79	2	19	*
Science	75	3	22	*
History/U.S. government	62	6	31	1
Geography	61	7	31	1
Foreign language	52	16	32	*
Music	31	22	46	1
Art	29	24	46	1

*Less than one-half of one percent.

Source: Stanley M. Elam, Lowell C. Rose, and Alec M. Gallup, "The 26th Annual Gallup Poll of the Public's Attitudes Toward the Public Schools," *Phi Delta Kappan*, September 1994, p. 51. Reprinted by permission.

ates the arts with entertainment rather than edification, with doing rather than thinking, with preparation for leisure rather than preparation for work.

During the past three decades the educational credibility of the arts at all levels has seriously eroded. Many programs have been eliminated or reduced, and others are in jeopardy.[3] During the past thirty years, the time allotted to general music in small elementary schools has decreased by 25 percent; the time allotted to the arts, by 28 percent; and in large schools, more than 29 percent, from seventy-five minutes per week in 1962 to fifty-three minutes per week in 1989. In art, the drop was from seventy minutes a week in 1962 to sixty minutes in 1989. In grades 4 through 6, there was a 22 percent loss of time in music during the same period. Instrumental instruction has been severely cut back: 30 percent in wind and percussion and 40 percent in strings. Although more secondary schools now offer more art courses, they offer fewer music courses, other than chorus and band (Figure 15.1).[4]

If you read Louis Harris's latest survey of public opinion, you would think that the arts were flourishing in American schools. A 60 percent

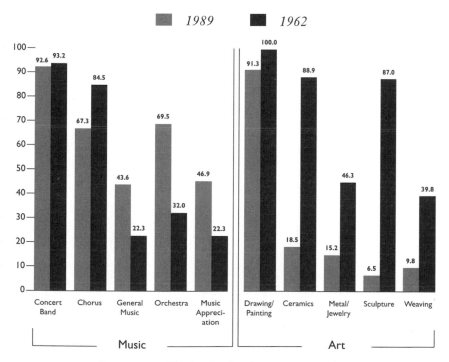

FIGURE 15.1. Percentage of high schools offering music and art. The black bars show figures from 1962; the gray bars, from 1989. (Extrapolated from Charles Leonhard, *Status of Arts Education in American Public Schools* [Urbana: University of Illinois Press, 1991], pp. 178, 179. Used with permission).

majority felt that school-based exposure to the arts for children was "very important"; 76 percent believed that the arts should be paid for "by the school system as part of the regular school budget"; and 60 percent considered the arts to be "as important as learning math and science."[5] But the rhetoric (wishful thinking?) does not match the reality. When tight budgets force the public to choose between the arts and other subjects, support for the arts almost always fades. We cannot escape the fact that in many schools, dance, the visual arts, music, theater, and even creative writing are given little attention or are absent altogether.

PUBLIC PERCEPTIONS OF THE ARTS

At the same time that they question the educational value of the arts, people wonder whether the arts are immoral and socially irresponsible. The decade-long uproar over grants by the National Endowment for the Arts is one more sign of the uncertainty with which the arts have been forced to contend. The cover of the April 1, 1991, issue of *Newsweek* asked, "Violence Goes Mainstream: Movies, Music, Books—Are There Any Limits Left?" An article in the *Washington Post* was entitled "The New Sound of Hate: In Europe, a Generation of Neo-Fascists Uses Music to Spread Its Message."[6] Obscenity charges were filed against 2 Live Crew's album, *As Nasty as They Wanna Be*; Ice-T's song "Cop Killer" and Tupac Shakur's album, *2Pacalypse Now* caused outrage, the latter because it was allegedly linked to the shooting death of a Texas state trooper.

Do not misread my message. I'm not advocating the suppression or censorship of such music. The point I'm trying to make is that the political and social criticisms lodged against music have invaded public perceptions. The climate of offensiveness and controversy has eroded the status of the arts themselves in American culture, causing them to lose respectability. Many people simply do not see the arts as necessary to their everyday lives. Indeed, some people perceive them to be harmful; an attitude that is reflected in a recent survey of the American public commissioned by the National Cultural Alliance, a coalition of forty-one arts and humanities organizations (Figure 15.2).

THE PERCEPTIONS OF ARTS TEACHERS

Arts educators generally like what they do and think that they do it fairly well. They often feel victimized by the system, by a public that does not understand their effort or its importance. If educators have failed, it is in not being able to convince enough people of the worth of arts study.[7]

Recently, I sat in on a meeting of school administrators and board members while they discussed arts education. Their statements were in stark

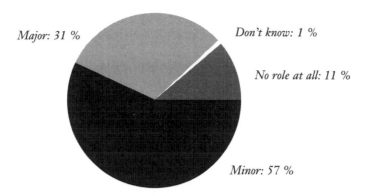

Major: 31 %

Don't know: 1 %

No role at all: 11 %

Minor: 57 %

FIGURE 15.2. The role that the arts and humanities play in our lives. (From National Cultural Alliance, *The Importance of the Arts and Humanities to American Society* ([Washington, D.C.: National Cultural Alliance, February 1993], p. 13)

contrast to the solicited testimonials heard at most arts conferences. They were in total agreement about the need for major changes if arts education is to improve its status in American schools. They saw the arts now as elitist, isolated from the realities of life and insulated from the purposes of education. These are strong indictments because they place the arts outside the values and priorities that lie at the core of basic education.

These people were particularly critical of arts frameworks and objectives because they do not relate to or address general education. Look, for example, at the objectives of arts education spelled out in the 1991 *National Arts Education Accord*, a joint effort of the American Alliance for Theater and Education, the National Art Education Association, and the Music Educators National Conference. My purpose is not to denigrate these arts organizations. Indeed, their objectives, like the national standards now being developed, reflect the prevailing thought of the field.

Although there is nothing inherently bad about these objectives, they do not connect what students should learn in the arts and the benefits that will accrue. Almost without exception, standards for the arts promote art for art's sake, but arts education would serve its own cause better if its relationship of objectives to general education were made explicit.

VALUE-CENTERED ARTS EDUCATION

A new paradigm promises to give arts education a tighter and more compelling focus. The idea is deceptively simple: that arts education in all its forms—whether discrete or interdisciplinary—should be based on human value so that its contributions to general education are clear and irrefutable.

National Arts Education Accord: Objectives of Arts Education

The arts education associations believe that K-12 arts programs should be designed to produce individuals who:

1. *Have a background in all of the arts and advanced knowledge and skill in at least one art form.*
2. *Are able to exercise their creative abilities through the arts.*
3. *Are able to use the vocabulary of the arts.*
4. *Are able to respond to the arts aesthetically, intellectually, and emotionally.*
5. *Are acquainted with a wide variety of art forms, including diverse styles and genres.*
6. *Understand the role the arts have played and continue to play in the lives of human beings.*
7. *Are able to make aesthetic judgments based on critical perception and analysis.*
8. *Have developed a commitment to the arts.*
9. *Support the artistic life of the community and encourage others to do so.*
10. *Are able to continue their learning in the arts independently.*

Source: American Alliance for Theatre and Education, Music Educators National Conference, and National Art Education Association, *National Arts Education Accord: A Statement on Arts Education to Governors and State Legislators* (Reston, Va.: Music Educators National Conference, 1991), p. 4. Reprinted by permission.

This is not a suggestion about integrating art with other subjects; rather, each art form must be presented as basic to the general education of all students. I call this new paradigm Value-Centered Arts Education (VCAE). If the arts are to improve their status in American schooling, the curriculum must focus on those aspects of each art that make it essential to our present and future well-being. Stated simply, the mission is to teach students the value of the arts.

The idea is not radical. Mathematics and science take pains to teach value to students. It is not a coincidence that the first of the five new standards or goals for students in mathematics is "Students should learn to value mathematics."[8] In 1989, the National Science Foundation put a priority on teaching appreciation for science.[9] Physicist Leon Lederman, who is reinventing science education, does not just want to train a new generation of scientists; he also wants voters and politicians to "understand the value of a well-spent science dollar."[10]

If a subject isn't valued by the students and the public, it will eventually lose its position and prestige in the core curriculum. Its status reflects its perceived value. If the intent is to secure a place for the arts in the core curriculum, then the credentials of the subject as essential to all people must be made clear.

According to Paul Lehman, "The unvarnished truth is that if music is not taught, the reason is simply that it is not valued highly enough.... Money is not the real problem. The question is simply one of priorities."[11] This question of value should be taken directly into arts classrooms; the value of the art should be taught. If the schools want to make sure that we educate a public that understands and values the arts, this is an important part of what should be taught.

As it is now, arts programs tend to put off the value question, hoping students who learn technique will acquire respect for the medium along the way. If this does not happen, the schools try to persuade people later through advocacy efforts. But telling people what they should value is rarely an effective substitute for persuasion through actual experience. A supportive public is secured by making certain that students leave school with a solid understanding of the role and importance of the arts in their lives.

To increase the stature of the arts in public schooling, I believe that the purposes and practices of arts education must be reconceptualized to emphasize value in everything done and taught. Arts teachers should never teach just technique, history, aesthetics, repertoire, theory, or criticism without also teaching why it is important. Let us rid the arts curriculum of all disembodied knowledge. We should never teach just the art; we should always teach its relationship to people, its purpose, and its meaning. These connections to value are the essence of arts education, the often forgotten other side of the coin.[12]

Elliot Eisner noted that "many of us have not been able to provide the kind of persuasive rationale for the importance of music in the general education of the general student, as contrasted with an education for specialization as a musician." This rationale would secure the "credibility that we need to have in justifying or legitimizing the kind of work we are doing in the field of [arts] education."[13]

In the process of teaching its value, the art itself will be taught, but instead of teaching technique, theory, history, creativity, criticism, and other aspects apart from their meaning, technique and information will be taught in the context of their connections with human needs. The opposite is not the case; that is, when the mission is simply to teach the subject, teaching its worth and function tends to be slighted or ignored.

I'm not suggesting that we teach spelling through band or that we emphasize performance less. I'm not referring to interdisciplinary approaches. Rather the arts should focus on the real contributions of the arts to human development and well-being.

TEACHING VALUE

We should go back to the art itself to determine its usefulness. What is it that people gain from the arts that justifies their learning about them? A strong arts program helps educate all students to be better and more productive human beings. What are the unique aspects of each art that make it essential to human life and to our present and future well-being? Why are creative writing, dance, music, theater, and the visual arts worth studying?

An education in the arts can help people break through the narrow, widely held, and incorrect belief that truth is dispensed primarily through science. No one symbol system can say everything. We need them all in order to explore the infinite facets of our human existence, which is why the development of multiple forms of literacy is so necessary. They permit us to achieve new levels of consciousness and understanding. Cultivating our senses so that they can work for us helps us react to and interpret the meaning of our experience.

One of the great attributes of all the arts is that they characterize their age, distinguishing our relationship to time by showing us as we were yesterday and as we are today. They can be an important adjunct to history and social studies, lending them a human dimension that cannot be obtained in any other way.

_ chapter sixteen _

THE ARTS AS CATALYSTS
FOR EDUCATIONAL REFORM

What is it about the arts that allows them to function as change agents in education? To act, to dance, to draw, and to make music may be compelling ways to learn and to experience ourselves and our world, but are they vehicles for substantive educational change? They can enhance and enliven education, to be sure, but probably not alter it fundamentally from the standard six-period day; grades segregated by age; twenty-five children per classroom; equal treatment of everyone; overreliance on lectures and memorization; and true–false, multiple-choice evaluations, among other arcane structures and practices that have dominated education for fifty years. The arts can add dimensions that improve the effectiveness of education, but *reform* might be too strong a term to characterize these contributions. A few examples of how the arts have been used as inducements for change follow.

AT-RISK STUDENTS

How do schools recapture the enthusiasm for learning that children exhibit almost universally? Somewhere along the way, at-risk students become soured on education. They do not see the relevance of what they are asked to learn and its usefulness in their lives. They lose their enthusiasm for school and for learning, and they disengage.

The Drew School in Arlington, Virginia, introduced an integrated art and language arts program for at-risk, first-grade children during the 1992 school year. The primary approach was to combine art (drawing, painting, crafts, and so on) with language arts teaching, with an emphasis on small-group, individualized instruction. Students kept journals and illustrated their own books, which helped them get excited about reading and writing.

Although this program was limited in magnitude, the arts were the key ingredient for improving achievement in the language arts.[1]

COMMUNITY INVOLVEMENT

The arts naturally relate to many community enterprises, and they can be a key to connecting the school with community resources. Every community has artists and performers, such as a theater group, a dance studio, and private music teachers. Unlike history, mathematics, and other subjects, the arts provide the means to bring community enterprises together to enhance and enrich education. In this way, they extend the curriculum, making it less isolated and far more relevant.

CULTURAL DIVERSITY

The arts provide "culturally vibrant modes of teaching and learning that celebrate and reflect the diversity that has always been our nation's greatest strength."[2] The arts can be readily used to promote multicultural understanding. As no other subjects can, the cultural aspects of the arts add a dimension to education that is beneficial to all students. But calling it *reform* may be an exaggeration.

SCHOOL-BASED MANAGEMENT

Although teachers usually have little to say about the administration of their school, site-based management gives them a voice in its daily operation. As a result, they assume more responsibility and gain more autonomy. They are permitted to participate in the governance of their schools and to make decisions about its educational program and management. For many years, teachers were the last to be consulted about educational policy but instead were expected to follow the principal's orders and not make waves.

Although most schools benefit when teachers assume more responsibility, they sometimes abuse their newly acquired power and authority. An elementary music teacher in Kentucky, whose name shall remain anonymous for obvious reasons, wrote me as follows:

> The arts are under attack by our own fellow teachers. The elementary faculties are voting out of their buildings both art and music, so the school can then use that money for other purposes. The devastation to music alone will be irretrievable, not only in textbooks and equipment but in the blow these actions have dealt the music teachers.[3]

This kind of action is irresponsible, but people motivated by their own selfish interests can be shortsighted. Fortunately, such actions are the exception, not the rule.

When principals, teachers, parents, and members of the community together decide on goals, curricula, discipline policies, budgets, and personnel, they have a greater sense of ownership and responsibility for the quality of their students' education. Reinventing education does not stop with changing the way schools are run; it also changes the way teachers learn to teach. "The role of the teacher now includes not only teaching, but also helping run the schools, integrating needed social services, learning new teaching and assessment methods, handling increasing school violence, incorporating community resources, and using current technology, among a growing number of other tasks."[4]

GROUP COLLABORATION

The arts provide many opportunities for learning to work collaboratively with others. Students work together to create a mural, a sculpture, or a collage. Through performances in dance, theater, and music, they learn how to mesh their own efforts with others to ensure a quality result. The arts can teach students to work together with a disparate group of individuals, something they will need to know when they join the workforce. But even though all these modes of operation—and there are others—are intrinsic to the arts, they do not add up to major educational reform.

A+ SCHOOLS

Ralph Burgard's A+ Project with the Kenon Institute in North Carolina is designed to show that a collaboration of interdisciplinary teaching and daily arts instruction can improve the classroom learning environment and academic performance. The program has now been instituted in fourteen schools, in six states, affecting 12,500 students every day. In September 1994, thirty-three school districts were selected to participate in an eight-month planning process that adapts the A+ program to meet local conditions. These A+ schools also establish strong partnerships with their area school of education to influence the way that teachers are educated and with community arts agencies to make greater use of the area's cultural resources.

Neither of the basic program elements—interdisciplinary teaching and arts instruction—is new to educators. But schools are using them to improve the classroom learning environment, raise test scores, increase parental participation, and establish strong school–community partnerships. For a minimum of four years, all students will take at least one full instructional period of arts daily and will cover at least four disciplines a week, including, when possible, media arts (film, photography, video, and computer graphics). Interdisciplinary study units, often themed, will be phased in over the first three years, with new units to be added as experience with the program is gained. In fifth grade, for example, the theme is atomic structures, with students assuming the movement of protons, neutrons, and electrons. In five minutes, they use a combination of science and improvisatory dance to absorb the materials. Although it is not a radical or revolutionary departure, the A+ program has improved education in these schools.

At Sunset Park Elementary School, an A+ School in Wilmington, North Carolina, which began the program in September 1993, the number of students suspended dropped from seventy the preceding year to only three in the first A+ year. Because the learning environment is stimulating and personal, violence and discipline are not a problem in A+ schools.

TED SIZER'S COALITION OF ESSENTIAL SCHOOLS

Many of the early "reforms" never asked the basic questions, such as how schools are organized. Yet the schools need fundamental reshaping in the way they are run. To remedy this, starting with five schools in 1984, Ted Sizer's Coalition of Essential Schools has grown to nearly 800 in all stages of development, mainly on the high school level. The coalition relies not on a formula that the school implements but on the support of and collaboration among teachers, students, and their families. Unfortunately, in most schools there is little consensus among teachers that fundamental changes in the school's structure or teaching practices are needed.

Coalition schools reduce the number of students assigned to each teacher, and so even if nothing else changes, this has an immediate effect. Students can no longer get away with anonymity. Such reductions do not necessarily cost more money but can be done by simplifying the program and creating teams of teachers. When paring down the curriculum to a more manageable size, the coalition is usually opposed by the committees that created the goals, standards, and assessments. But the program establishes its own credibility as the students discover its merits.

School choice is another reform that the coalition schools have widely adopted. If a school has a monopoly, it can become complacent. Choice provides an alternative that keeps everyone on his or her toes. Still another reform is performance or portfolio assessment, which, by using actual examples of work, keeps track of a student's progress. Teachers and students can then study his or her progress over time, instead of relying solely on the last quiz. What these schools don't want is more of the same. So such reforms should come not from a governor's commission but rather from local people who are familiar with local issues.

INTEGRATIVE LEARNING

Interdisciplinary learning can lead to a more cohesive curriculum. The arts, unlike other subjects, can cut across disciplines.

> They provide schools with a ready way to formulate relationships across and among traditional disciplines and to connect ideas and notice patterns. Works of art provide effective means for linking information in history and social studies, mathematics, science, and geography. A work of art can lead to many related areas of learning, opening lines of inquiry, revealing that arts, like life, is lived in a complex world not easily defined in discrete subjects.[5]

The concept of integrative learning transforms teaching and learning, by demonstrating the connections between subjects that are too often treated as independent. The result is a more integrated curriculum that encourages students to see the relationships of knowledge and information across subjects. Students and teachers engage in productive and creative activities that call their imaginations into play.

SCHOOL RESTRUCTURING

There is a dramatic shift under way in the way that the arts are related to, or seen as essential to, education reform.[6] School reforms of the past did not succeed in improving students' achievement. Unlike the modest, though desirable, contributions just outlined, the arts can totally transform teaching and learning. By applying the thought processes, imagination and creativity, and ordered relationships that are indigenous to the arts, community participation, curriculum construction, scheduling, assessment, relationships with parents, and other fundamental changes are possible. In response to low student achievement, Oregon, Kentucky, Kansas, South Carolina, Tennessee, and Washington recently adopted comprehensive educational reform legislation, although the plans have not yet been fully implemented.

> School restructuring is difficult because it involves systemwide reform. Systemic reform means taking a comprehensive, coordinated, and long-term approach to changing the entire educational system. . . .
> Systemic change involves fundamentally changing the way schools are run, the way teachers are trained, the way teachers teach,

and the way students learn. It also includes integrated services, community partnerships, and lifelong learning.[7]

Reform has taken various forms during the 1980s and 1990s. The first wave, stimulated mainly by *A Nation at Risk*, was intensification, doing more of what is already being done. Reading, math, and science were made more demanding, rigorous, and challenging. Structural reform followed, which involved bringing decision making closer to the school and the classroom and building more flexibility into the school day and year. Schools are now considering substituting nongraded schools for the customary age–grade organization. Rather than being grouped according to their chronological age, students will be grouped according to their level of achievement in the task at hand. "Time on task" can be adjusted to suit the learner's needs. Not all children learn at the same rate, with some requiring more time than others. Calls to keep schools open longer are growing louder.[8] A longer school day would cut the amount of time that "latchkey" children spend alone and unsupervised. It might also provide alternatives for teenagers who now spend over twenty hours per week watching television.

This more global approach to reform was the dominant approach from 1985 or so through 1989. Now this movement has been labeled *systemic reform*, which, as the name implies, alters basic structure and content. It refers to such new ways of thinking and operating as the theory of multiple intelligences, what we have come to understand about knowing and learning, new and more sophisticated methods of assessment, and improved uses of time. These systemic reforms are transforming the curriculum, teaching, and learning. The CAPE Project in Chicago and the Galef Program in Los Angeles are two examples of how the arts can be used in systemic reform.

THE CHICAGO ARTS PARTNERSHIPS IN EDUCATION

One example of how the arts can be catalysts for systemic reform is the Chicago Arts Partnerships in Education (CAPE), an ambitious six-year, city-wide curriculum reform initiative involving thirteen neighborhood-based partnerships made up of fifty-three professional arts organizations, forty-three Chicago public schools, and twenty-seven community organizations. The Marshall Fields Department Store initiated the program. The plan for CAPE is to infuse the arts into teaching, like mortar between bricks.

Typically, each partnership has four arts organizations, three schools, and two community organizations, with one organization serving as the coordinator or "anchor." The neighborhoods are located throughout the city; the student populations are culturally diverse; and the arts organizations range from small grassroots operations to large regional institutions. The focus is on developing innovative approaches to teaching and learning by integrating the arts into the curriculum and by joining in-school arts programs with after-school and community-based learning experiences. The plan is to create a range of exemplary, self-determined models of school improvement through the arts, not only as a way of serving the students and communities of the pioneering schools, but also as a way of leveraging new public understanding, policies, and actions concerning the arts. The schools and the arts organizations are reexamining the role and function of the arts in general school improvement, moving from an enrichment/exposure model to an integrated curriculum model that entails learner-centered instruction and student self-assessment.

CAPE attempts to make arts experiences available to all students by confronting and overcoming the isolation and marginalization of the arts that place them on the fringes of the educational experience. The initiative has broken down the usual isolation between students in the classroom, between teachers and their colleagues, between teachers and their principals, between principals in neighboring schools, between parents and educators, and between artists and art teachers of all disciplines across the city. Arts educators view the outside practicing artists as allies, validating the specialists' importance in their own schools.

CAPE is built on the belief that the integration of substantive arts programming across the curriculum is one of the primary pathways for schoolwide change. By their very nature, the arts combine thought, feeling, and action, creating both a demilitarized zone that allows schools to reflect on their learning climate and an exotic terrain that encourages student initiative, cooperative learning, creative problem solving, self-critique, inquiry-based learning, attention to culturally diverse contexts, a sense of action and impact, and all the best practices of the school-restructuring movement.[9]

THE GALEF INSTITUTE

The mission of the Galef Institute is to collaborate with teachers and administrators in the creation, testing, and implementation of approaches that help children develop positive attitudes toward learning, school, and themselves, thereby increasing the likelihood of their becoming contributing members of society. The program, designed by Linda Adelman, is called "Different Ways of Knowing." It is an interdisciplinary kindergarten-through-grade-6 program that joins history and social studies themes with the visual and performing arts, literature, writing, math, and science. Early assessment reveals success in motivating and improving the performance of both teachers and students in classrooms across the country, from Massachusetts to Mississippi and from the inner city of Los Angeles to Salinas, California.

Mechanisms for extensively documenting and evaluating children's attitudes and academic progress, as well as for refining teaching approaches and curricula materials on the basis of student performance and teacher input from the field, are built into the program. From the outset it was evident that to accomplish its mission, the institute had to provide, at least initially, both professional development and appropriate curricular materials.

"Different Ways of Knowing" is a multifaceted intervention for effecting positive change in schools by helping educators manage diversity, focus restructuring efforts, and reinvigorate experienced teachers. Because it models ways for teachers to enrich and interrelate the different disciplines, it is a tool for restructuring the entire school curriculum. It places curricular change and teacher development at the center of school restructuring. Organizational changes are designed to shift power, authority for decision making, and resources from the district to the school level. This is systemic change. Teacher training and curricular activities encourage assessment of prior knowledge and demonstrations of learning through diverse media: writing, oral language, artistic works, dramas, and movement. The assessment of student work portfolios is ongoing.

Systemic change is a complex set of problems. It is stressful, but if properly managed, diversity and conflict can lead to breakthroughs. And even the best changes need to be reassessed, as systems like to stay the way they are. Individuals thus must work together differently and make real applications on the job.[10]

chapter seventeen

OVERHAULING TEACHER EDUCATION: CAN IT BE DONE?

We all have had both terrible and great teachers, and these experiences confirm the obvious: Quality education depends on quality teaching. Increasingly, those who are determined to reform education are looking at how to better prepare teachers.

Today, arts specialists face more demanding conditions: a transcultural curriculum, increasing competition from other academic areas for finite school time and limited resources, and skepticism about the educational value of the arts among some educators, administrators, school-board members, and parents. If they are going to serve as cultural coordinators, organize comprehensive programs, incorporate community arts resources, apply the potential of today's technology, develop curricula to meet new graduation requirements, supervise arts programs taught by classroom teachers, and provide teachers with instruction and direct advocacy efforts to win broader support, these new and expanded responsibilities will require extensive changes in their preservice education. Like every other subject in the public school curriculum, the demands of teaching and learning in the arts are growing.

THE CONDITIONS OF TEACHING

Teaching today, by all accounts, is more challenging, largely because the conditions of teaching are changing. One in five children in this nation now live below the poverty level, and the same number live in homes with no father. Increasing numbers of "latchkey" children go home from school to houses without parents. Five times as many children are born out of wedlock today as in 1970. Children from such problem situations consistently fail to achieve in school at the level of children from nonproblem situations. Yet all teachers, including those who teach the arts, face children from problem situations as a matter of routine.[1]

In 1990, more than 30 percent of the total school-age population in the United States were minorities. I was in an elementary school in New York City recently in which more than fifty languages are spoken. Clearly, communication alone requires extraordinary efforts. As if the changing population of students doesn't present enough new difficulties, teachers of every kind are being asked to demand more of their students and to motivate and maintain higher standards of achievement.

These conditions are compounded by controversies over such matters as abortion rights, affirmative action, political correctness, sexual harassment, euthanasia, AIDS, cultural diversity, family values, gay rights, declining moral values, ethnic and religious tension and intolerance, and freedom of expression. As James Davison Hunter, a professor of sociology at the University of Virginia, reminds us, "The disputes amount to a fundamental struggle over the 'first principles' of how we will order our life together."[2] What kind of learning and society will we have, and will the arts be part of them?

PRESERVICE EDUCATION

Arts Specialists

The education of arts teachers needs substantial, perhaps radical, revision. The fact that many arts teachers are not adequately covering such matters as history and the role of the arts in contemporary culture raises questions about their preservice preparation. If the arts are to be taught more comprehensively, then arts teachers must be educated more broadly. A college degree by itself does not guarantee that new teachers know their art or how to teach it.

Classroom Teachers

There is nothing that makes elementary teachers more insecure than having to teach something they know little or nothing about. Even teachers who are not expert at math have years of study to steady them and keep them well ahead of their students. But this is rarely the case in the arts, as art teachers' own education has often failed to give them much background. The discomfort of having to teach what one does not know leads to timidity, avoidance, and, ultimately, ineptitude.

There is considerable ambivalence regarding the matter of classroom teachers teaching the arts. Should they or shouldn't they be expected to teach the arts and, if so, to what extent? Some educators believe that elementary teachers should extend the programs (where they exist) taught by arts specialists. Others feel that teachers should be expected only to integrate or infuse the arts into their general subject-matter teaching, with the assistance of arts specialists. Still other classroom teachers resist taking any responsibility at all for teaching the arts, as they already feel overburdened by new standards and curricula and view the arts as frivolous distractions in a curriculum devoted to learning basic skills.

Perhaps the enlistment of classroom teachers is not the main issue. Their college education in the arts frequently is inadequate, limited to one—at most two—and sometimes no courses or requirements in arts education. This problem is compounded by the lack of arts in public schooling. Seldom can classroom teachers and school administrators fall back on the knowledge and skills acquired through their own study of the arts in their elementary and secondary education. Without these, classroom teachers can provide few substantive experiences in the arts, and school administrators— most of whom started out as classroom or physical education teachers—lack the background to value the arts and understand their educational importance. This is a self-generating cycle. They did not get it, and therefore they cannot give it. Yet the trend in many elementary schools is to reduce the number of arts teachers and hand the responsibility for teaching the arts to classroom teachers. But if a school system requires its classroom teachers to teach the arts, then it should require them to have adequate arts background and expertise.

How, then, should the preparation of classroom teachers be altered? In regard to the arts curriculum for prospective elementary teachers, the college and university system does not work. The arts will continue to get short shrift unless teacher education requirements are changed. One course in college cannot make up for years of neglect. If classroom teachers are to help students in the arts, they will need skills and experience in developing an integrated approach that incorporates the arts. Prospective teachers must be better prepared in the first place.

Given the blatant disregard for the arts in the education of classroom teachers, logic suggests that if we want classroom teachers to incorporate the arts, the number of college credits and courses in the arts should be increased. Sound simple? It's not. The turf wars at institutions of higher education are fierce. Schools or departments of education guard requirements in their area with the tenacity of a lioness guarding her cubs. Moving credits from, say, the School of Education to the School of Fine Arts reduces faculty "load" in one department and increases it in the other. The funding of departments, based on the numbers of students enrolled in the

They should have

1. A thorough grounding in their major art form, including in-depth experience in production performance, creativity, history, theory, aesthetics, and criticism.

2. Knowledge of their art form not as a narrow specialization but in the context of all the arts, a vast subject matter encompassing creative writing, dance, music, theater, and the visual arts, including the media. People who teach the arts need literacy in all of these, not the tunnel vision that is the rule. When they are blinded by their specialism and suffocated by their isolation, arts teachers sacrifice their impact.

3. A view of their major art form in the context of general education, fortified with a substantive curriculum that clearly makes the arts basic. Today's arts teachers need to know what makes an education in the arts necessary for every student. They need to know how to create a value-centered curriculum, one that transcends the teaching of technique. Advocacy and the development of public support should be part of every arts classroom every day.

4. Experience with and an understanding of the arts of different cultures, particularly those of immigrant populations. The focus should be on learning the characteristics and influence of the arts of Asian, African, European, Latino, and Native Americans. One simply cannot teach relevantly in today's classrooms without that knowledge. The emphasis should be on techniques for teaching in the cities, including the development of broad intracultural understanding and the recruitment of more minority teachers.

5. The ability to develop and teach a broad curriculum that offers opportunities for arts study to every student, kindergarten through grade 12. In music, for example, performing groups, though essential, do not comprise a comprehensive curriculum with choices for all. Schools should offer more options for learning about all the arts, and prospective arts teachers should learn how to teach such courses.

6. Background and experience in teaching, preferably as an apprentice or a master teacher. Those who major in an art, not just those in arts education, should be encouraged

or required to take a methods course in teaching their art form, since most end up teaching at least part of the time. As it is now, the curriculum for applied majors is based on the precarious promise that there are adequate career opportunities for musicians, artists, dancers, and actors.

7. Expanded knowledge of and experience with electronic technology, its potential and limitations, and how it can be applied to enrich and extend the arts curriculum, enhance expression and communication through an art form, and improve learning.

8. Experience working with and coordinating the use of community arts resources, particularly how to integrate them into the curriculum-based program.

9. Background and experience in knowing how to provide in-service education to classroom teachers so that they can infuse the arts into the general education curriculum. This means being able to serve as a resource expert who can relate music to general learning.

10. Background and experience in assessment and evaluation, including the use of portfolios and other techniques.

department's courses, tends to reduce curricular discussions to economic issues. Change does not come easily to departments vying for the credits that will sustain them. These vested interests do not operate on the basis of what courses make good sense for the prospective teacher. Rather, they operate protectively and politically to preserve the department. College and/or departmental prestige is also a factor. These intense power conflicts make changing requirements very difficult, in fact, almost impossible.

At best, changing preservice education is a long-term solution. Although strengthening the arts requirements for prospective classroom teachers is viewed as a necessary step, the effects of such a change would not be felt at the school level for many years. Any change in arts requirements adopted, say, in 1995 would not affect graduates until 1999, and it would take until 2015 before a critical mass of teachers would be reached that would make a difference. In this view, in-service education—teaching teachers on the job—appears to be the most productive route for improving the ability of classroom teachers to teach the arts. Kathryn Martin, dean of fine arts at the University of Illinois at Urbana, maintains that "the quality of teaching is improving because of in-service education, *not* because of what we are doing in colleges and universities."

IN-SERVICE EDUCATION

One of the most effective and efficient ways to improve the teaching force is through in-service education. Even if preservice education in the arts is adequate, which it seldom is, additional education makes it more likely that teachers will incorporate the arts and use interdisciplinary approaches. Given the difficulties in changing college course requirements for classroom teachers, providing educational opportunities in the arts through in-service education makes sense.

Those who voice concerns about the ability of most classroom teachers to assume responsibility for arts education at the elementary level do not consider this route to be a legitimate substitute for classes taught by arts specialists. Still, classroom teachers who incorporate the arts can make a substantial contribution to their students' general education, and some do this very well.

What should elementary classroom teachers know about the arts? Ideally, classroom teachers should understand the educational potential of at least one major art form and be able to introduce the arts into their subject-matter teaching. To teach the arts, classroom teachers need to be familiar with the basic techniques, the aims and methodology of teaching them, and interdisciplinary applications.

One of the problems with in-service programs in the arts is persuading elementary teachers to take advantage of them. Elementary teachers are constantly being told that they need to be retooled, and they are not always responsive to these "opportunities" to correct their insufficiencies. The first attempts at in-service education in the arts for classroom teachers in Mississippi, for example, were disastrous. Nobody showed up. The program was accepted only after the University of Mississippi offered credit to the participating teachers, and the program was taught by arts specialists who were brought in from the highly successful arts-in-education program in the Jefferson County (Colorado) schools.

The Tennessee Arts Academy in Nashville, like a number of other institutes across the country, offers classroom teachers hands-on workshops in theater, music, and the visual arts taught by outstanding artists and educators. From its inception in 1987, more than 2,000 teachers across the state have participated in this intense two-week residential summer arts program. The academy has attracted educators from 120 of the state's 138 school systems. Participants concentrate on making art and learning the techniques and skills needed to sing, conduct, write a play, act, create a print, and so forth. These experiences are deepened by discussions and performances that help build a descriptive and discerning vocabulary. To make certain that these educators have sufficient support in their home schools to implement what they learn, the academy encourages the participation of a balance of classroom teachers and arts specialists from the district. One isolated teacher cannot institute major change; teachers need the support and encouragement of their peers.

In-service education is often more effective than preservice education. Experienced teachers know their needs and have a good idea of what will work. As in-school programs of arts instruction have been cut back, the role of artists in education has become even more important. In Oklahoma, where the elementary schools have no arts specialists, the schools rely on a statewide program of artists-in-schools and a massive in-service program that encourages teachers to extend what the artists do. Compas, a creative writing program in St. Paul, stresses workshops for teachers. Each visiting writer spends one day working with the faculty. Performing arts centers and museums throughout the country are giving higher priority to their educational programs, based on the conviction that only cooperative efforts with the schools today will ensure their audiences tomorrow. The Kentucky Center for the Arts sponsors about fifty in-service workshops for teachers each year. The Lincoln Center Institute (New York City) serves upward of 800 teachers a year in some thirty school districts. Many schools send teams of as many as ten teachers. Schools must agree to provide administrative support and make time for the arts in their ongoing programs. In this way, the program achieves maximum impact. The Lincoln Center Institute has spin-offs, among them Outward Bound Nebraska at the Joslyn Art Museum, which brings teachers to Omaha for ten days to formulate a curriculum unit using the museum's collections. The museum follows through by sending a staff member to observe each of the participating teachers teach the unit they develop.

These efforts are proliferating. The Kennedy Center's Imagination Celebrations (Washington, D.C.) that take place in about ten states contain a teacher training component. Both the Los Angeles County Museum and the Museum of Fine Arts in Houston have well-established teacher education programs, as do many performing arts centers, symphony orchestras, and opera companies. Unfortunately, in-service programs in the arts face considerable competition from other subject areas, but schools encourage classroom teachers to participate in these programs by providing release time.

CERTIFICATION

In order to teach in the public schools, teachers must be licensed or "certified." The states have different certification requirements. Some states grant provisional certification to prospective teachers upon completion of a bachelor's degree. Others require prospective teachers to pass a teacher's examination. Permanent certification usually requires a master's degree or its equivalent.

One of the stumbling blocks to changing the preparation of arts teachers is state certification. Several states automatically grant certification to teach art or music upon completion of a bachelor's degree, but states differ widely in their regulations for distributing semester credits among courses in the arts, methodology, and practice teaching and courses in the liberal arts. Some states first offer provisional certification, with permanent certification granted after the teacher attains the equivalent of a master's degree and completes a required number of years of teaching experience. Obviously, such state certification standards as now applied can affect the adequacy of academic preparation. Enforcing these standards by testing the prospective teacher is becoming increasingly common. More than forty states now require a test for initial certification, and the other states seem to be moving in this direction.

Even though state certification in art and music is well established, only thirteen states certify professional specialists in dance, and only eleven certify professional specialists in theater. Such certification practices discourage the teaching of these art forms, prevent the arts curriculum from being viewed in its broad outlines, and blur the relationship between these disciplines and teaching.

Nearly half the states now certify classroom teachers without any courses in the arts, tantamount to making their teaching of the arts legally ineffective. Other states require only modest credentials in the arts, in effect, vitiating arts education. Changing the states' certification requirements is very difficult, having the effect of raising the ineptness of the status quo to a policy in perpetuity. In dance, for example, teachers are certified as physical education teachers, because most states have no provision for certifying teachers as dance teachers. The same situation prevails in many states in the field of theater. One way the states have circumvented this obstacle is through the Artists in Education program of the National Endowment for the Arts. In Michigan, for example, the main purpose of the Dancers in Schools program is the in-service education of elementary teachers in movement.

Many school administrators would benefit from further arts education. Those who now champion the arts admit that it was a hands-on experience that provided the breakthrough. Administrators and classroom teachers need more studio work if they are going to excel at any aspect of arts education. At the same time, arts specialists need to learn how to provide such in-service education and hands-on experience.

SOME POSSIBLE SOLUTIONS

Considering the changing conditions of teaching, the ramifications of the educational reform movement, the new demands being placed on arts specialists, and the inadequacy of arts education for classroom teachers, what solutions are being recommended? General recommendations have come from the National Education Association and the Carnegie Foundation and also arts education organizations.

The National Education Association recommends four practical steps to encourage outstanding teaching.[3] Prospective teachers should first complete a basic liberal arts curriculum and maintain at least a 2.5 grade-point average before being admitted to a teacher education program. Once accepted into such a program, the teacher candidates would master the professional knowledge of teacher education and apply this to "progressively more demanding student teaching experiences." They would then complete a teaching internship with experienced teachers. After this, as professional teachers, they would be evaluated annually and given in-service educational opportunities.

This proposal is less radical than many. The Carnegie Foundation proposed the standardizing of certification requirements throughout the country and administering a national test to assess teaching over a period of time, including provisions to correct inadequacies. The reactions to testing teachers have been mixed. Generally, teachers do not believe that such tests can measure their ability to teach. Perhaps some form of group observation and evaluation of teaching practice like that instituted in Georgia, Florida, and other states can provide a basis for certification. The Carnegie Foundation recommends that the undergraduate program concentrate on general and specific subjects followed by a master's degree program in professional education and an internship program guided by a master teacher.[4]

Generally, reformers call for more emphasis on subject matter and less on methodology. Some advise learning teaching skills and knowledge after acquiring a liberal arts degree. Many suggest a period of internship working with a master teacher. Most make some provision for continued study, recognizing that everything cannot be accomplished in a four- or five-year college program.

Professional organizations representing arts educators (the Music Educators National Conference, for one) recommend that at least 50 percent of the teacher preparation curriculum for arts specialists be studies in the art form, and in addition, prospective teachers must master the pedagogy of their discipline.

A teacher of the arts needs to master a great deal more than just artistic and pedagogical technique, however. Some educators believe that teaching music as both a discipline and a high art will fail if tainted by popular connections with leisure and entertainment. They disdain popular culture, preferring an exclusive emphasis on European-based, classical music—an atypical, though important, part of American culture. Funny, I think I could learn a great deal from Lionel Richie, Billy Joel, Quincy Jones, Elton John, and other popular artists.

The recommendations of the Task Force on Music Teacher Education for the Nineties of the Music Educators National Conference recognize the urgent need for change in the preparation of music teachers.[5] In the main, it is the only organization to suggest a partnership between college and public school music teachers in educating teachers. This "new sense of community" acknowledges that the responsibilities for music teacher preparation must be shared among music education professors, cooperating elementary and secondary school music educators, and all college music-teaching faculty. The task force's Professional Development Plan promises the right mix of the ideal and the real, the theoretical knowledge and the practical experience that are necessary to produce an excellent teacher. The plan and the suggestions are fully applicable to the other arts.

Will the push and pull between competing interests and viewpoints create the change that is needed? If the need for change and improvement is as great as I believe it is, bold and imaginative new initiatives are called for. Will the leadership rise to answer the call?

chapter eighteen

AN AGENDA:
WHAT SHOULD WE EXPECT?

The potential of the arts to transform and improve education has been
documented sufficiently to establish them as credible and effective
learning strategies. In numerous ways in school systems throughout the
country, the educational value of the arts has been demonstrated. According
to R. Craig Sautter, a poet and writer at the School for New Learning at
DePaul University,

> Years of experience among arts educators and classroom teachers
> who use the arts to motivate and instruct students, thousands of suc-
> cessful artist-in-residence programs over the last 25 years, and a
> growing body of research in arts education all strongly suggest that
> education in and through the arts can play a significant role in
> changing the agenda, environment, methods, and effectiveness of
> ordinary elementary and secondary schools.[1]

Sautter believes that reformers and schools have overlooked this favorable
track record, and he objects to the arts continuing to be treated as "merely
pleasant diversions from the core academic basics of schools." He wants to
know what would happen "if we spread the arts across the curriculum of the
middle school years, when many students so dramatically lose interest in
classroom activities."

To come to terms with what a school district's arts program ought to be
is a matter of choosing among a number of alternatives. No two school systems or communities are alike. Cultural resources that are plentiful in one
community may be nonexistent in another. State and local regulations differ
from locale to locale. Probably no one established curriculum in the arts can
be borrowed and adopted wholly, and even national standards are only

179

guideposts. Therefore, every community must figure out its own best solution within certain parameters. With this in mind, what should we expect of an arts education program?

VISION

First and foremost, every program of arts instruction should be grounded in a set of goals or standards. There should be broad agreement on these goals, and they should be accepted by the school board, school administrators, and parents. The standards, goals, and frameworks (labels often used interchangeably) for the arts should reflect the focus of the program and the general content of the curriculum.

Fundamental to any credible arts education program is a thoughtfully crafted statement of purpose, a vision of what the program stands for and is trying to accomplish, including an overview of the curriculum in the various arts. As an example, the Evanston (Illinois) Township High School offers a four-year comprehensive curriculum consisting of approximately 275 courses, of which about fifty are in the fine arts. The high school serves the multiracial cities of Evanston and nearby Skokie. The community is situated on Lake Michigan, immediately north of Chicago. The student body is 45.4 percent white, 44.3 percent black, 6 percent Latino, 3.3 percent Asian or Pacific Islander, and 1 percent multiracial. During the 1994/1995 school year there were 15.3 teachers in the fine arts department. Those students who took the Scholastic Assessment Test (SAT) in 1993/1994 did better than the national average. The Evanston students scored a mean of 464 (the national mean is 423) on the verbal test and a mean of 525 (the national mean is 479) on the math test.

The Evanston school offers plays, musical concerts, dance recitals, art exhibitions, and full-length movies throughout the school year. Each year the students are invited to subscribe to a theater and a music series. These events include a multicultural film series, dance, and a writers' showcase, among many other events. Since 1988, the Evanston high school has sponsored Bravo Arts, a biennial festival of the arts that offers master classes in an array of arts, including mask making, mobiles, African dance, beginning ballet, and improvisation, in addition to the more traditional arts.

The total number of students enrolled in all classes in the fine arts department for the 1994/1995 school year was 1,675. The school serves a total of 2,705 students. Its facilities are extraordinary and include fifteen gyms, a dance studio, and a computerized lab for the electronic music students. The school's performance facilities are used by dozens of vocal and instrumental music groups, theater and dance companies, for at least one public performance a month. The school has a 1,500-seat auditorium, two other theaters, and a cable-television studio. Students produce a semiweekly newspaper, a yearbook, and scripts for at least two theater productions. Among the many academic contests is one for creative writing. The school maintains a fine arts requirement for graduation, consisting of a total of three credits in fine and applied arts. Among the offerings are cartooning and commercial illustration, ceramics, computers in art, jewelry, and photography.

The goal of Evanston's fine arts department is to offer to as many students as possible an opportunity to become involved in an arts experience through presentation or performance. The department attempts to advance the artistic development of every participant. The intention is to instill a lifelong involvement in and appreciation of the arts.

THE ARTS AS GENERAL EDUCATION

The arts curriculum should be based on educational objectives that establish the arts as an educational priority, and there is no better way to accomplish this than to form a relationship with basic education. One of the first priorities is to focus the arts on how they intersect with and serve the educational needs of every student. Once presented as a partner in the educational enterprise, the arts can help contribute to a more appealing, meaningful, cohesive, comprehensive, and integrated curriculum. The arts, then, can become a factor, perhaps even a central factor, in making positive educational change,[2] a recognized force in creating educational excellence.[3]

ADEQUATE AND SENSIBLE EVALUATION

One way of improving arts curricula is to recognize that political and economic issues drive educational agendas. The Council of Chief State School Officers' *Arts Education Assessment Framework* sets the parameters for the National Assessment of Educational Progress (NAEP) in dance, music, theater, and the visual arts that will take place periodically. Nonetheless, any single plan to assess the arts faces difficulties:

> The task of designing an arts assessment is complicated by the fact that currently the arts are often a marginal experience for students at the elementary and middle school level, and an elective subject in high school. In addition, many schools have cut arts education to the bone: it is occasional, rarely involves dance and theater, and seldom combines in-school and out-of-school arts experiences. In some cases—arts magnet schools or schools that have elected to use the arts to motivate learning—arts education is abundant. Given this

disparity of opportunity, how is it possible to design a national assessment for all students?[4]

Among the assessment methods suggested are portfolios (a collection of samples of the student's art that are assessed by the student, the teacher, and a jury), performances, written responses, interviews, and observations, but these are more costly and labor intensive than multiple-choice and short-answer questions. Arts educators worry about assessments of those aspects of the arts that cannot be unquantified—inspiration, imagination, and creativity. It is reassuring to see that other subject areas are now adopting the long-standing arts assessment techniques of performance and portfolio evaluation. These assessments go well beyond the old paper-and-pencil machine-scorable tests. In theater, for example, students might participate in a production exercise that asks them to assume characters and act out a scene from a story. Then they might analyze what they did and how they might do it better and also respond to some multiple-choice items identifying elements of the scene. The variety of responses ensures a fair overview of what students know and are able to do. Judging interdisciplinary programs poses its own set of problems because of the difficulty in constructing an assessment that accurately appraises students' achievements.

The NAEP should be supplemented by state and local assessments. Arts teachers are always evaluating what students are learning, particularly in their performance classes, and students are taught to evaluate themselves and correct their performance. Such procedures should lead to high standards and a quality program. In addition, a strong arts program should have a plan for regular student assessment of every aspect of the program.

ACQUIRING BOTH SKILL AND UNDERSTANDING

What parents see are arts programs that stress playing in the band and creating holiday art. They tend not to be aware of the mental processes and the constant reevaluation and decision making that are required. Developing technique is not seen as mentally demanding; on the contrary, it is viewed as play and physical activity. In schools that are largely devoted to the development of mentation, such activities are viewed as having marginal importance.

In recent years, the conflict between making and appreciating art has intensified. The traditional emphasis is on skill development, and this is reinforced in the national standards for arts education. Indeed, this ingrained national educational penchant for developing artistic skills ("doing" art) at the expense of attaining understanding of it ("learning about" art) may well account for the segregation of the arts from the academic curriculum.

BALANCE

Doing art is still the best way of knowing it. By using the artist as the model, we fashion the educational program around making art and studying and analyzing its technical, historical, theoretical, and critical aspects in relationship to performance and creation. The simple sense of this approach is that it keeps students thoroughly engaged. But there is a problem with this. Often, the public's perception is that certain subjects address the head and others the hand. Schools favor cultivating the former. John I. Goodlad pointed out that "headedness" is more highly valued than "handedness," that is, the academic over the manual:

> Teachers in elementary schools and of academic subjects are rein-
> forced in many ways in the belief that their job is to develop minds
> and that this is best done through the academic subjects and an aca-
> demic mode of learning. Like other citizens, they tend not to see
> manual activity as both intimately connected with the mind and an
> alternative mode of learning. Arts and crafts tend to become supple-
> mental, a relaxed, undemanding relief from the reading, writing, and
> arithmetic that really count, but of little value in themselves.
> Learning becomes a one-lane street.[5]

One consequence of this blindness is that students who have propensities toward and preferences for manual modes of learning are often judged to be poor and slow learners. The most prestigious subjects are the academics; the least so are the nonacademics. Unfortunately, Goodlad tells us, handedness "frequently becomes an end in itself, not a means to some broader under-standing."[6]

In the visual arts, creating and making art—assuming the role of the artist—remains at the center while the students, at the same time, explore the expressive styles of great artists throughout history and develop their ability to analyze, interpret, and critique visual forms. This means that production and creativity are the impetus for developing curiosity, knowledge, and understanding, not just a repertory of techniques.

AN INTERDISCIPLINARY DIMENSION

The arts can relate to just about any subject matter, no doubt because the subject matter of the arts concerns many aspects of life. Why try to relate? Why not be satisfied with a discrete arts program that like other subjects, is separate and distinct and unrelated to the rest of the curriculum? There are many examples of programs that are insular and self-contained, and this may well be the prevailing and conventional operating mode. But the best programs create a web of relationships that reach outward into the larger curriculum.

This kind of integrative learning brings new dimensions to all subject areas, including the arts. By relating the arts to, and making them part of, the basic curriculum, they become the motivating energy of learning. Even though interdisciplinary approaches that rely on the arts are well documented and notably successful, schools and teachers are often reluctant to adopt them because they are uncomfortable and unfamiliar with the arts. This technique requires teachers to change their mode of operation, but once they do, none would choose to return to the self-contained, single-subject approach.

A CURRICULUM THAT IS SEQUENTIAL AND SPIRAL

The arts, like the other basic subjects, represent a huge accumulation of knowledge. Thus children need to study the arts throughout their schooling, just as they study language arts, history, science, and mathematics on a long-term basis. Students move from the simple to the complex. For example, they learn first to draw what they see; later they learn and apply the rules of perspective.

Although there is an ordered sequence to much learning (we learn addition before multiplication, algebra before calculus), it also has a built-in redundancy. Students of the arts are doing basically the same things at every level, but with increasing understanding, perception, and adeptness. In dance, they explore movement and rhythm from the first day onward; in the beginning they learn the art of performance and expression in very basic ways and then with increasingly greater finesse. This is the concept of the "spiral" curriculum, that learning in the arts is repeated at ever more sophisticated levels. This spiral curriculum overlays the sequential organization, spinning the students toward acquiring more detailed and discerning understanding.

EQUAL ACCESS

Students cannot reap the benefits of the arts if they are not given opportunities to study them. The study of the arts is not vocational education; it is general education in best sense of what general education means. Majoring in English does not mean that the student has to become an author. Nor does the study of music and art imply that the student has to become a musician or artist. Rather, the arts benefit everyone in fundamental ways. All students should have the opportunity to study the arts.

One of the critical issues of education today is equality of access to knowledge and learning. In many school districts only privileged children can aspire to an education in the arts. Only the well-to-do who can afford private instruction for their children can hope to understand the arts and to have the pleasure and edification that the arts provide. All children can use the arts in their lives, not just those who exhibit unusual talent.

QUALITY TEACHING

Quality programs of arts instruction depend on the quality of the teaching and the adequacy of the teaching staff. Our greatest educational resource is excellent teaching. We all can remember our best teachers. They inspired, encouraged, and instilled a desire in us to learn and succeed. They had high expectations and helped us reach for them. They instructed our minds but with a good deal of understanding and caring. Expert arts teachers know how to get the best from their students. They use imagination and invention; they make their students think, figure out possible solutions, and weigh their options.

ADEQUATE TIME ON TASK

Students cannot excel without spending adequate time studying the subject. But devoting time to the arts seems to evoke fears that the "important" subjects will be compromised. Along with a number of other educators, Elliot W. Eisner believes that including the arts in the curriculum at the elementary and middle school levels does not detract from reading, writing, and arithmetic but, rather, enhances and reinforces them. Eisner thinks that

> by broadening our conception of literacy ... the skills of reading, writing, and computing will themselves improve.... To write requires the ability to see, to hear, and to feel the world so that the writer will have a content to express and a desire to share it with others. Such achievements are not educationally marginal. Attention to the development of multiple forms of literacy should not be regarded as a diversion from what is important in schools; rather, it is at the very heart of what education requires.[7]

As you might expect, there are marked differences in children's opportunities to acquire knowledge of all kinds, from none or very few to many and exemplary. For instance, in the equivalent of our grades 9 through 12, French, German, and Japanese students spend more than twice as much time on core academic subjects as do their American counterparts.[8]

John I. Goodlad asks "Why do we spend so much time debating ... over which school subjects are basic and must be taught when we can have all of the major ones without sacrificing anybody's definition of basics?" He believes the reason is that school policy and decisions regarding the use of school time are made without sufficient data. Decisions, he says, are frivolous and based on opinion, not information.[9]

Goodlad proposed a plan for the distribution of time in the three upper elementary grades, based on 23.5 hours available each week, just thirteen minutes more a day than the average:

Subject	Hours a week	
Language arts	7.5	(an average of 1.5 hours a day)
Mathematics	5.0	(1 hour a day)
Social studies	2.5	
Science	2.5	
Health/physical education	2.5	
Total	20.0	hours

This still leaves 3.5 hours free each week, plenty of time to accommodate the arts, and this is based on average instructional time. Some schools have the luxury of an instructional week of twenty-five hours or more.

Inherent in this framework is the efficient use of time, something many classroom teachers are not particularly adept at. Goodlad says:

> To those legislators, school board members, and others who often sound as though they would deprive children of access in school to social studies, science, health education, and the arts in order to assure attention to reading, writing, spelling, and mathematics, let me simply say that the sacrifice is unnecessary. If the schools of our sample are representative, it will just be necessary for the principal and teachers of some elementary schools—perhaps most—to become more efficient in the allocation and use of school time.[10]

Goodlad observed that at the junior high level, schools strive for curricular balance, with an average 11 percent of teachers allocated to the arts. At the high school level, this figure dropped to 8 percent of the total teaching staff, probably because of college entrance requirements and state mandates for high school graduation.[11]

In terms of time and resources, what is a reasonable goal for the arts? At an invitational symposium in 1987, 150 leaders in the arts, education, and government recommended that "approximately 15 percent of the instructional program of every student at all levels, K–12, be devoted to the arts" and that "every high school should require at least two units of study in music, art, theater, dance, and creative writing for graduation." This study also advised that "every secondary school have at least seven periods a day, a length sufficient to permit study of the arts."[12]

GRADUATION REQUIREMENTS

State departments of education govern the schools by mandate, and the schools are required to comply with these regulations. The state specifies the number of credits required in English, math, science, social studies, and other subjects. In order to establish and maintain a presence for the arts amid all these other requirements, some states have moved to require study of the arts for high school graduation (Table 18.1).

TABLE 18.1   *State High School Graduation Requirements in the Arts*

State	Carnegie Units	Subjects
Alabama	Local Control	The University of Alabama requires one Carnegie unit of fine arts for admission to the freshman class. One school system in Alabama currently requires one credit of fine arts for graduation
Alaska	Local control	
Arizona*	One-half unit	Music, visual arts, drama, or a survey of the fine arts
Arkansas*	One-half unit	Drama, music, visual arts
California	One unit (one full year)	Fine arts (dance, drama, music, or visual arts) or vocational education. California requires two units for college-bound students
Colorado	Local control	
Connecticut	One unit	Arts or vocational education (25 percent of local districts specify one arts credit)
Delaware	Local control	
District of Columbia	None	

State	Carnegie Units	Subjects
Florida	One or one-half unit in each	Fine and practical arts (speech, debate, and vocational courses in practical arts)
Georgia	None, but students are required to take one elective unit in fine arts (dance, drama, music, visual arts), computer technology, vocational education, or ROTC	
Hawaii	One unit	For academic honors only (art or music)
Idaho	Four units	Fine arts (creative writing, dance, drama, music, visual, foreign language, or humanities)
Illinois	One year	Art, music, foreign language, or vocational education
Indiana	Two units	Fine arts for academic honors diploma
Iowa	None	
Kansas	None	
Kentucky	None	
Louisiana	One-half unit	For students in the Regents Program
Maine	One unit	Music, art, dance, drama, forensics, interior design, photography, or integrated studies if approved by the state
Maryland*	One credit	Fine arts (dance, drama, music, visual arts)
Massachusetts	None	
Michigan	None	
Minnesota	None, but two art courses and two music courses must be offered	May change in May 1995 to a state requirement of two fine arts courses. However, this would not become effective until between 2001 and 2004

State	Carnegie Units	Subjects
Mississippi	One unit	Chosen from art, instrumental music, choral music, drama, dance, debate, speech, or public speaking
Missouri*	One unit	Fine arts (visual arts, music, dance, theater)
Montana*	One unit	Visual arts, performing arts, literary arts, or instruction that incorporates the history of fine arts, criticism, production, performance, and aesthetics
Nebraska	None	
Nevada	One unit	Fine arts, literature, or humanities
New Hampshire*	One-half unit	Visual art, music, dance, drama, or communication arts
New Jersey	One year	Fine arts, practical arts, or performing arts
New Mexico	One-half unit	Fine arts (visual arts, music, dance, drama), practical arts, or vocational education
New York*	One unit	Dance, drama, music, or visual art
North Carolina	One unit	For students enrolled in the Scholars Program
North Dakota	None	
Ohio	None	
Oklahoma	Two units, one in each	Visual arts and general music, effective in 1993/1994 school year
Oregon	One unit	Fine arts, applied arts, foreign language, or vocational education
Pennsylvania	Two units	Arts or humanities or both (arts include music, visual arts, dance, theater, film studies, practical arts; humanities include additional English, literature, language, or social science elected beyond mandated courses in these areas)

State	Carnegie Units	Subjects
Rhode Island	One-half unit	Art, music, dance theater for college-bound students
South Carolina	None	
South Dakota*	One-half unit	Fine arts (music, art, drama, or debate)
Tennessee	One unit	Music, art, theater, or dance for students who choose the university path. There is no arts requirement for graduation in the vocational path. All state colleges and universities require one unit in the arts for entrance.
Texas	One unit	Either fine arts or speech for advanced academic students (drama, music, or visual arts). No fine arts requirement in the regular program
Utah*	One and one-half units	Dance, drama, music, or visual arts
Vermont*	1 year	General arts, dance, drama, music, or visual art
Virginia*	One unit	Fine arts (art, music, dance, theater) or practical arts
Washington	None	
West Virginia	One unit	Music, visual arts, or applied arts
Wisconsin	None	No state graduation requirements
Wyoming	None	No state graduation requirements

* *States that require all students to study the arts.*

Note: This list was compiled with the help of Gail Crum, information service manager, Music Educators National Conference, and Danielle Jones, graduate student at American University.

One important consequence of these requirements is the necessary foundation for this study that must be provided in the elementary and junior high schools. These requirements, then, could have an effect on the total program, kindergarten through grade 12. But they will mean nothing if arts teachers choose to ignore them. I'm reminded of the response of a Texas band director to the new high school graduation requirement in the arts. He said, "Let them take it in art." And students evidently are.

PARTNERSHIPS WITH COMMUNITY-BASED RESOURCES

Part of the strength of an outstanding in-school arts program is its relationship with community-based arts resources. In some cases, alternative arts education programs and structures outside the schools—in museums, theaters, symphony orchestras, opera or dance companies, performing arts centers, libraries, and so forth—compensate for the lack of arts in schools. Community artists are invited into the school to present programs and work with students. These linkages broaden the scope of the school-based arts curriculum, provide quality arts instruction, bring wider access to the arts for all children, and, most important, offer real examples of the adult enterprises of the arts and how they function. At their best, these cultural agencies and resources become collaborators—an "ecology of resources" that includes the home, television, newspapers, religious institutions, colleges, businesses, as well as artists and arts organizations.

There is a reciprocity between in-school and out-of-school arts education programs. The community arts enterprises have a vested interest in developing new audiences and ensuring their own survival. In-school programs are often inadequate and incomplete, and community arts assets extend the curricular range and provide professional credence. Artists-in-schools—poets, storytellers, dancers, filmmakers, artists, sculptors, composers, performers—give students experiences that the in-school program alone could not provide. Where these community resources work well, the arts program is enriched and students are the beneficiaries.

THE CHARACTERISTICS
OF OUTSTANDING ARTS PROGRAMS

The Blue Ribbon Schools Program of the U.S. Department of Education identified forty-two schools for their exemplary programs in the arts during the 1989/1990 and 1990/1991 school years. These schools share the following characteristics:

:: The conviction that an arts education is a basic and necessary component of a balanced educational program for pre-kindergarten through grade 12 students.

:: A broad understanding of arts curricula and pedagogy matched with the highest-quality instructors available, arts specialists, artists/teachers, and highly trained classroom teachers.

:: A balance of art forms, including music, dance, drama, poetry, creative writing, and the visual and media arts. Music, the visual arts, and drama were offered most frequently.

:: A realization that the arts need time, space, and financial and administrative support. The time spent in direct arts instruction ranged from two to seven hours per week. The ratio of arts teacher to students ranged from one to eighty to one to 250.

:: An understanding of the instructional power that comes from using the arts as part of an integrated approach to teaching. Every school infused the arts into other parts of the curriculum.

:: A commitment that all students will have access to instruction in the basic art areas and also differentiated levels of instruction based on student motivation and talent.

:: Parent involvement as volunteers, program designers, and fundraisers.

:: A strong connection to the local arts community and an awareness that successful arts programs lead to wider community support for education in general.[13]

_ chapter nineteen _

PROSPECTS:
HOW DO WE GET THERE?

Just who is responsible for educating the next generation in the arts —the
schools, other agencies, or a combination of both? Each community is
responsible for providing opportunities to its youth to ensure that they will
be adequately educated in the arts. How those responsibilities are carried
out differs from one community to the next. In those communities with few
cultural resources, the schools must assume the primary responsibility. In
urban and suburban communities that have access to museums, arts centers,
and living artists of all kinds, the responsibility can and should be shared
between the schools and the community.

CHANGING SCHOOLS

Change requires several agencies working together on a common plan of
reform. Professional arts education organizations can intercede and become
highly persuasive, leading their members in new directions. Unfortunately,
these organizations are generally not proactive and seldom urge specific
improvements. Institutions of higher learning, local and community arts
organizations, artists, and district and state arts administrators therefore need
to assert their leadership. Strong in-service and staff development programs
for teachers in the field sponsored by the Lincoln Center Institute and the
Tennessee Arts Academy, among others, are developing a leadership that will
empower people to become local leaders for arts education reform. Working
with education agencies such as the Association for Supervision and Curriculum Development (ASCD), the Parent Teachers Association (PTA), and
national administration organizations such as the National Association of

Secondary School Principals (NASSP) and the National Association of Elementary School Principals (NAESP) can activate these constituencies and help them become informed advocates for the arts. These agencies have generally not been used well.

The arts, like other subjects, must address the impact of such current reforms as multi-age grouping, year-round schools, the effect of technology on arts instruction, site-based management, and other proposed educational reforms. Add to this the fact that the absorption of any significant change takes, at best, several years, and you will begin to see the patience and persistence that such change requires.

Schools are large, conservative, bureaucratic institutions that usually do not react favorably to calls for change that emanate from outside. In size alone, the American school system is intimidating. The United States contains more than 15,000 school districts, enrolling more than 40 million students.[1] The largest of these systems employs more than 60,000 teachers and has a yearly budget exceeding $4.5 billion. In addition, 6.4 million students or 14 percent, in nursery through secondary schools are enrolled in private schools. During the 1982/1983 school year, there were a total of 2,138,572 classroom teachers in this country's elementary and secondary schools.[2]

Improving an arts program is not a matter of simply adding more courses or requiring courses or credits in the arts. Although mandated changes can be an important step toward making certain that all students acquire a background in and an understanding of the arts, more important is investing the arts with greater substance, making certain that courses in the arts bring students both knowledge and understanding at the same time, and extending the program to provide experience in all the arts and to make certain that the arts are available to all.

PLANNING

In order to effect change, school systems generally set up a planning committee in the arts. Since educational change is not easily imposed from outside the schools, it is wise to work within the system. A fine arts committee for the school should thus consist of persons representing the community, particularly a concerned and respected parent, but also a school administrator, arts educator, and classroom teacher.

Any change in education usually sets off a chain reaction, like toppling dominoes. Given a fixed, six-period day, for example, any increase in high school graduation requirements in math or science could cause a de-emphasis of the arts by crowding the school day. When planning educational change, then, it is important to anticipate any possible detrimental ramifications. To succeed in increasing requirements in the arts for high school graduation, for example, it might be necessary simultaneously to lengthen the school day to seven periods in order to eliminate any negative effect on—and resistance from—other subjects.

When attempting to make improvements in arts education programs, differences in the arts must be taken into account. Many programs, for example, are not truly comprehensive, often lacking a dance, theater, and creative writing component. These arts may require special attention. Likewise, at the urging of the J. Paul Getty Foundation, visual arts programs are moving *beyond* creativity to encompass the history, aesthetics, and criticism of art—a "discipline-based" approach. In contrast, music programs that have generally been strong in performance, history, and aesthetics, may be moving *toward* creativity. Visual art lessons can require longer periods of time than other subjects do. Because they may not fit the breaktime pattern for classroom teachers, they may suffer scheduling bias and union problems.

TESTING AND EVALUATION

As concerns for educational standards become more pressing and schools move to put greater emphasis on academic pursuits, arts proponents face more urgent demands to prove the arts' educational credibility. Evaluation could help, as it provides a means to improve programs, teaching, and materials as well as a way to establish the validity of arts programs, thereby qualifying them to obtain private and public funding and to gain educational equity. But many arts teachers are wary of evaluation. They are concerned that the subjective, personal, and qualitative aspects of the arts curriculum will be ignored by objective measurements or that these aspects will be slighted in favor of areas that can be evaluated more easily.

It is well known that schools test what they believe is important and that teachers teach and students learn what is tested. Teachers know that schools put a high value on being able to measure progress and determine worth. Help for them is already on the way. As of 1997, the National Assessment of Educational Progress (NAEP) will again, as it did in 1972 and 1978 in art and music, assess the condition and progress of student achievement in dance, music, theater, and visual arts. (Creative writing will be assessed as part of English.) These assessments are planned for grades 4, 8, and 12. A national consensus process has set appropriate achievement goals and determined testing specifications, which are designed to tell what students have learned and are able to do. NAEP assessments are congressionally mandated.[3]

FACILITIES AND MATERIALS

Effective fine arts programs require special facilities for dance, drama, music, and the visual arts, with attention to factors such as sound, light, floors, and safety. The architects should be advised by experts who understand the environmental needs of these arts education activities. But currently, facilities for dance and theater are practically nonexistent, particularly in elementary and junior high/middle schools. Even in most secondary schools, educators call the theater facilities "ludicrous." School systems need help developing theater facilities inexpensively.

PAYING THE BILL

Who should pay the bill for America's schools? Many Americans believe that the federal government pays more than half of the nation's costs for elementary and secondary education. That's not so. The federal government actually pays less than 10 percent. Of every dollar spent to educate our children, only a little more than six cents comes from the federal sector. Of the remaining bill, 50 cents comes from state governments and 43 cents from the local level. During the 1980s, the federal share dropped by more than 30 percent. It used to be about 10 percent.

According to the Department of Education's own report, *A Nation at Risk*, which sparked the education reform movement in 1983, "The federal government has *the primary responsibility* to identify the national interest in education. It should also help fund and support efforts to protect and promote that interest." The report adds that "excellence costs. But in the long run mediocrity costs far more."[4]

Contrary to what most people think, money is quite often not the primary resource necessary to improve education. Admittedly, small grants, wisely directed and administered, can be enormously effective. Far more important than funding, however, are knowledge of the educational system and how schools operate and leadership—the ability to envision, articulate goals, organize and plan, identify strategies, communicate effectively, and inspire others to work tenaciously.

CERTIFICATION

One of the reasons there are few dance and theater programs in the public schools is the lack of established state certification requirements in these subjects. Certification establishes standards for minimum teacher preparation in the arts and other subjects. Without certification, teachers can't teach. The differences among the arts in their battle to establish certification is as follows:

Almost every state now certifies teachers in music, with the exception of Alaska, which has no music teachers, and the states of California and Hawaii, which lack certification in music and art on the elementary level.

In the visual arts, eight states (Alaska, Colorado, Maine, New Jersey,

South Carolina, South Dakota, Washington, and Wyoming) do not yet certify teachers for either elementary or secondary schools; one state, Utah, doesn't certify elementary visual arts teachers at all.

In contrast, just twelve states and Puerto Rico certify teachers in drama in the elementary schools, and twenty-three states and Puerto Rico certify teachers in drama in the high school. The situation for dance is even less encouraging. Only nine states certify dance teachers in both elementary and secondary schools, and four other states, just on the secondary level. When it is taught at all, dance is usually taught by physical education teachers.

Surprisingly, elementary and secondary teachers of creative writing are certified in only three states—Delaware, Florida, and Pennsylvania—and on only the secondary level in Arizona and California.

There is a relationship, though not an absolute one, between certification and both the quality and the amount of teaching in a particular art. It stands to reason that if school systems could hire certified drama and dance teachers, they might opt for these programs. Those states that have no established certification in a particular art form also do not have college and university teacher education programs in that subject. The exception to this has been in the field of dance, which generally used to be, and still is in some institutions of higher education, organized as a part of the physical education program. Prospective physical education teachers can major in movement, but are still certified as teachers of physical education. Although this system has produced several dance teachers for the public schools, it is less and less the case today.

During the past decade and a half, many institutions of higher education have established schools of fine arts with a separate dance department and program for dance majors. Graduates of these departments see themselves as performers, not teachers. But this change in college structure is harming the delivery of dance in public schools: As physical education departments in these institutions relinquish their responsibilities to provide a curriculum in dance, physical education majors in these institutions take fewer dance courses. Consequently, fewer physical education teachers are graduating with a background in movement, and so there are fewer teachers who can teach dance in the schools.

How can this situation be improved? College and university dance departments must recognize the need for establishing teaching programs in dance. Physical education departments could encourage their majors to take dance through a cooperative arrangement with these new dance departments. State certification in dance could be instituted to encourage dance departments to develop programs in dance education. Sometimes this can backfire, however. When states certify dance specialists, physical education teachers may no longer qualify to teach dance. So efforts must be made simultaneously to encourage the state departments of education to hire specialists in dance.

ADVOCACY

Arts programs do not exist in public schools because of good will. Almost anyone connected with education thinks the arts are important and generally has a good word to say. Although the arts seem to have no enemies, translating that "support" (albeit passive) into increased budgets for the arts, more arts teachers, or new comprehensive programs of instruction is very difficult.

Support for the arts is the foundation of any outstanding arts education program, and parents are the best arts advocates of all, as they can have considerable influence over what the public schools teach their children. If parents are convinced that the educational potential of the arts has been largely underestimated and that the arts should be made basic in American education, they will also have to understand that they must win others to this viewpoint—state and local authorities who have the power to alter the present status of the arts in the schools—if they are going to improve educational opportunities in the arts.

Advocacy is a strategy to persuade, to make a convincing case for the educational value of the arts, to convert school officials, and to organize community support. The stronger the regular in-school arts programs are, the better the pool of talent that it will train. But talent usually takes care of itself. What cannot be taken for granted is the nurturing of all students in the arts, and this requires public support.

Arts teachers are usually not convincing advocates, perhaps because they are too close to their problems and appear as partisan. Furthermore, when programs are threatened, they do not always know how to respond effectively. Many school administrators, school-board members, and parents do not see how the arts, as they are now taught, relate to the purposes of basic education. Consequently, they view the arts as tangential to American schooling. To persuade them of the educational value of the arts, we need a more convincing, informative approach.

Advocacy itself needs to be redefined. It has to be more substantial and substantive, with clear examples of what students derive from studying the arts. Arts teachers must learn how to translate their values into reasoning that wins over school boards. For example, if we talk about the need for aesthetic education in today's depressed educational marketplace, school boards will say, "Oh, that's all very nice, but we really can't afford that kind of thing anymore."[5] Arts teachers need to know how to repackage the concept of aesthetic education as an educational necessity.

Why do we need more effective advocacy? Because the arts are competing for limited and diminishing funds. The American public and the arts education profession will have to be much tougher if arts education is going to resist being pushed further to the periphery. When we go before school boards and congressional committees, as we do periodically, we need to present a strong case for how the arts contribute to the prevailing priorities, whether they be competitiveness, our economic future, our workforce, or school reform. And we need to compound our voice by inviting professional arts organizations and enterprises to join us in this crusade.

And let's use the courts if we have to. Suits filed by the American Civil Liberties Union and twenty-six local Louisiana school districts charged that the state failed to provide an adequate education for its children, in part because of attempts to save money by further slashing arts education.

These suits were modeled on a successful 1989 suit brought against Kentucky, whose state supreme court ordered "sufficient grounding in the arts to enable each student to appreciate his or her cultural and historical heritage."[6] We need stronger advocacy efforts and action on all fronts—local, state, and national—and we need to provide training for our teachers in these techniques.

The Kentucky Education Reform Act of 1990

The new public school system is to allow and assist all students in the acquisition of the following capacities:

:: *Communication skills necessary to function in a complex and changing civilization.*

:: *Knowledge to make economic, social, and political choices.*

:: *Understanding of governmental processes as they affect the community, the state, and the nation.*

:: *Sufficient self-knowledge and knowledge of one's mental and physical wellness.*

:: *Sufficient grounding in the arts to enable each student to appreciate his or her cultural and historical heritage.*

:: *Sufficient preparation to choose and pursue one's life work intelligently.*

:: *Skills to enable one to compete favorably with students in other states.*

LEADERSHIP

Sometimes it takes a coalition of agencies, organizations, and individuals to bring about change. Many agencies and organizations can assist parents in their advocacy efforts. The Music Educators National Conference, the National Academy of Recording Arts and Sciences, and the National Association of Music Merchants have joined together to conduct a grassroots campaign throughout the nation to help parents, local business people, and educators strengthen music and the other arts in the schools.[7] Besides the professional arts education associations, the professional education organizations must become involved, organizations such as the Association for Supervision and Curriculum Development (ASCD), the National Association of Elementary School Principals (NAESP), the National Association of Secondary School Principals (NASSP), the education program of the National Endowment for the Arts, the Getty Center for Education in the Arts, the Parent Teachers Association, institutions of higher learning, local community arts organizations, state departments of education, and state arts agencies.

Reform in arts education requires leadership to pull together the resources of organizations and people and to develop a common agenda to reform arts education and its delivery.

Convincing School Administrators

Vern Bennett, superintendent of the Fargo (North Dakota) public schools, is often asked how he, a former coach without even a minor in the arts, was transformed into an advocate for the arts. He explained, "We had some experienced, well-informed art advocates in Fargo in the early seventies who found the time over several months to persuade and prove to me that the arts are essential." They took him to arts meetings and gave him some hand-on experience. "This is the secret: Pick out your community power brokers—the decision makers—and accept the challenge of making them arts advocates. You can do it. It happened to me." He advised arts proponents: "Stop preaching to the converted. Instead, reach out and share your insights with influential leaders who haven't seen the light. Help from school principals, superintendents, and school board members is crucial to the success of art education in every community. They hold the keys to the curriculum."

Bennett also suggested some practical ways to influence administrators: Clip articles on the arts and send them to the power brokers; send them copies of minutes of your arts meetings; invite them to arts events and conferences; and never argue, just persuade.

The commitment of principals is crucial. Their interest can mean the difference between a program's being accepted or not. Principals establish the budget and control resources. One principal can create an oasis of success in the arts that will be envied—and replicated—by others.

Often it's a hands-on experience that wins over people. "We need to involve people to let them see what the arts are all about," says Eleanor Chow, a former president of the board of education in the Montebello (California) Unified School District. Personal involvement can convert. Taking one's shoes off and actually dancing is the kind of personal involvement that can immediately clarify why studying the art has educational value. Knowing this, the Southeast Center for Education in the Arts in Chattanooga, Tennessee, insisted that classroom teachers and arts specialists participating in their staff-development program be accompanied by their principal, to ensure that administrative support and resources be made available.

The experience of Arnold Rael, former assistant superintendent of instruction for the Bernalillo (New Mexico) public schools is relevant. When Rael was the principal of an elementary school in 1975, the state education department cited his school district for its lack of arts programs. In response, Rael took a course in art education. From then on, the superintendent of schools looked to him. "If you can help me solve this problem," he said in so many words, "I'll make you director of instruction." "That felt good," Rael admitted, and he attended some arts meetings where he got involved with dance. He was hooked. "I went back and immediately announced a dance program in high school for the following year," Rael says. "I needed $2,500. The principal of the school said 'What?!' And it was difficult to convince the staff, especially the coaches whose reaction was incredulity. 'You're going to spend $2,500 on dance?' I said, 'We have citations to get rid of.' Well, the program was well received."

The next year Rael got $20,000 for the program: $10,000 from the New Mexico Arts Commission, which was matched by the school district. The program has prospered. During the 1981/1982 school year the district allocated $45,000 for the program. As a result, these schools now have arts specialists who work directly with the students, as well as classroom teachers who follow through. The program is a model for the state in such areas as poets-in-the-schools, folk arts, dance, drama, and the visual arts. And all this happened because someone managed to get a principal to stand up and dance.

Winning the School Board

Decision making in schools is hierarchical. Those who wish to improve the lot of the arts in schools must reach the board of education and the superintendent. One school-board member advises arts people to "call a board member or take them to lunch, but don't smother them with any more stuff to read." One-on-one meetings are far more effective than written documents.

Once a nucleus of arts supporters is established in the community, few boards of education will be able to resist the pressure. Paul Flower, a parent and past member of the school board in Oskaloosa, Kansas, explained how it works:

> A small nucleus in the community—eight of us—wanted significant changes in the school program. We wanted a speech and drama and an art program, of which we had none. This nucleus had talked with individual school board members numerous times with no success. We have a seven-member board, and in Kansas you operate on a simple plurality of four votes. So a concerted effort was made to replace a plurality of the school board. That was accomplished, and the desired changes in the school program were made within two years.

The schools in Oskaloosa now have an arts program for the visual arts, music, poetry, and dance.

The president of one school board thinks that one of the best ways to approach the board is to show rather than tell. A slide presentation, for example, can capture their interest. Exhibits and performances are other means. Or talk about some success story—the scholarships that their students have won in the arts. In Louisville, both the Chamber of Commerce and the Junior League meet regularly with the school board and have been instrumental in bringing the community and the schools together.

Selling the Community

Turning around communities to favor the arts is a matter of changing attitudes. Ervin Kimball, principal of the Village Elementary School in Gorham, Maine, counsels proponents of the arts to know their community: "Have vision about what could happen, and believe you can make it work." He doesn't think they need the support of a hundred people in the state; three or four is often enough. Arts education programs can't be created at the top and handed down. They have to come up from the community level.

Michael Pool, an English teacher at Sandy Creek High School in Fairfield, Nebraska, credits the community's support for its outstanding arts education program. Originally, he recalled, he found three advocates in the community. He got the Nebraska Arts Council to help promote the program, and succeeded in getting a drama teacher. He now has 300 people in the community who are active advocates. The school has four visiting artists each year, and classroom teachers continue the program when the artists leave. Fairfield now has a county arts council that enables it to share artist residencies with other communities. The artist residencies have transformed the way these teachers view their subject.

Committed principals and teachers persuade other principals and teachers. When they assume ownership of the arts program, educators give the program added legitimacy and presence. Ownership is commitment of a high order, one that means the difference between programs that languish and those that prosper.

The role of parents in providing support for arts programs can be decisive. Parents are often the missing link, not just in the arts, but in all segments of education. In Columbus, Ohio, all 118 units of the Parent Teachers Association support the arts. That support can be translated into both dollars and volunteers. For the annual school arts festivals, Columbus's PTA provides 1,500 volunteers. Parents also serve on an advisory committee working with the arts programs. They are determined to establish equality of opportunity in the arts and will not rest until their own in-school arts program is as good as the one they have heard about across town.

Poor parents and minority parents can be just as supportive. The difference between affluent and impoverished parents is that minority or low-income people need extra help. One expert suggests: "Bring them in. Get them involved. Win them, and they will fight for the arts because they see the importance of these subjects for their children."

What is clear is the growing need for political action on behalf of the arts in American education and the growing capability of arts proponents in the political arena. No longer can those who care about the arts afford to ignore politics, for political action has become central to improving education programs in the arts.

Ours is, indeed, a nation at risk. Our culture is an invaluable heritage, a birthright, and an educational obligation of the schools. That obligation has been set aside too long. It is time that the arts were rescued from years of neglect and permitted to realize their potential significance in the education of every American citizen.

NOTES

___ chapter one ___

1. Richard L. Luftig, *The Schooled Mind: Do the Arts Make a Difference? An Empirical Evaluation of the Hamilton Fairfield SPECTRA Program, 1992–93* (Oxford, Ohio: Miami University, 1994).

2. Charles Fowler, *Can We Rescue the Arts for America's Children?* (New York: American Council for the Arts, 1988), p. 14.

3. National Commission on Music Education, *Growing Up Complete: The Imperative for Music Education* (Reston, Va.: 1991), p. xiii.

4. National Endowment for the Arts, *Toward Civilization: A Report on Arts Education* (Washington, D.C.: Government Printing Office, 1988), p. 13.

5. See Getty Center for Education in the Arts, *Beyond Creating: The Place for Art in America's Schools* (Los Angeles: Getty Center for Education in the Arts, 1985), pp. 2–6.

6. Mary Futrell, a former president of the National Education Association, made this point at Conference on Artistic Intelligences, University of South Carolina, April 22, 1989.

7. National Commission on Excellence in Education, *A Nation at Risk: The Imperative for Educational Reform* (Washington, D.C.: Government Printing Office, 1983).

8. National Endowment for the Arts, *Toward Civilization*, pp. 13, 18, and 19.

9. Maxine Greene, "Esthetic Education: Towards Wide-Awakeness" (speech delivered at the Conference on Artistic Intelligences, University of South Carolina, April 22, 1989).

10. Jonathan Baron and Rex V. Brown made this point in "Why Americans Can't Think Straight," *Washington Post*, August 7, 1988, p. B3.

11. See Elliot W. Eisner, *Cognition and Curriculum: A Basis for Deciding What to Teach* (New York: Longman, 1982), pp. 73, 74.

12. A number of reports on education from American business tell us this. For example, see Committee for Economic Development, *Investing in Our Children: Business and the Public Schools* (New York: Committee for Economic Development, 1985), pp. 2, 17; and Task Force on Education for Economic Growth, *Action for Excellence:*

A Comprehensive Plan to Improve Our Nation's Schools (Denver: Education Commission of the States, 1983), pp. 13, 18.

13. See College Entrance Examination Board, *Academic Preparation in the Arts: Teaching for Transition from High School to College* (New York: College Entrance Examination Board, 1985), p. 54.

14. Eisner, *Cognition and Curriculum*, p. 55.

15. As quoted in William Raspberry, "Math Isn't for Everyone," *Washington Post*, March 15, 1989, p. A23.

＿ chapter two ＿

1. Harry Hillman Chartrand, "The American Arts Industry: Size & Significance," unpublished study, Research Division, National Endowment for the Arts, 1992, pp. 1, 2.

2. David Rieff, "A Global Culture?" *World Policy Journal* 10 (Winter 1993–1994): 78.

3. Ibid., p. 77.

4. Orlando Patterson, "Ecumenical America: Global Culture and the American Cosmos," *World Policy Journal* 11 (Summer 1994): 103, 105.

5. Peter Manuel, *Popular Music of the Non-Western World* (New York: Oxford University Press, 1988), p. 20.

6. Rieff, "Global Culture?" pp. 78, 80.

7. Chartrand, "American Arts Industry," p. 3.

8. Ibid., p. 1.

9. Ibid.

10. Boyce Rensberger, "Scientist Shortfall a Myth," *Washington Post*, April 9, 1992, p. 1.

11. Chartrand, "American Arts Industry," p. 3.

12. Ibid.," p. 4.

13. Bruce Seaman, *A Perspective on the Arts Industry and the Economy* (Washington, D.C.: Research Division, National Endowment for the Arts, October 1993), pp. 18, 19.

14. National Commission on Excellence in Education, *A Nation at Risk: The Imperative for Educational Reform* (Washington, D.C.: Government Printing Office, 1983), p. 5.

15. National Endowment for the Arts, *Toward Civilization: A Report on Arts Education* (Washington, D.C.: Government Printing Office, 1988, p. 7.

16. Committee for Economic Development, *Investing in Our Children: Business and the Public Schools* (New York: Committee for Economic Development, 1985), pp. 2, 17, 21, 22.

17. U.S. Department of Labor, *What Work Requires of Schools: A Letter to Parents, Employers, and Educators* (Washington, D.C.: Department of Labor, 1991), pp. 1–5.

18. Ira Shor, *Culture Wars: School and Society in the Conservative Restoration, 1969–1984* (Chicago: University of Chicago Press, 1992), pp. 27, 53.

19. Northeast–Midwest Institute, *Literacy at Work: Developing Adult Basic Skills for Employment* (Washington, D.C.: Northeast–Midwest Institute, 1985), p. 2.

20. Task Force on Education for Economic Growth, *Action for Excellence: A Comprehensive Plan to Improve Our Nation's Schools* (Denver: Education Commission of the States, 1983), pp. 13, 17.

21. Committe for Economic Development, *Investing in Our Children*, pp. 21, 22.

22. Ibid. Emphasis added.

___ chapter three ___

1. National Endowment for the Arts, "Audiences—Overview: 1987–1991 Planning Document" (unpublished document, National Endowment for the Arts, 1985), p. 5.

2. Henry E. Putsch, "AICA Survey of Current Trends in Art Education," in *Art Education in the Schools: Strategies for Action* (Washington, D.C.: Alliance of Independent Colleges of Arts, 1984), pp. 29–30.

3. John I. Goodlad, *A Place Called School: Prospects for the Future* (New York: McGraw-Hill, 1984), p. 119.

4. Association for Classical Music, "Survey of Students' Attitudes Toward Classical Music" (New York: Association for Classical Music).

5. National Center for Education Statistics, *Course Offerings and Enrollments in the Arts and the Humanities at the Secondary School Level* (Washington, D.C.: Government Printing Office, 1984).

6. Harry S. Broudy, "How Basic Is Aesthetic Education? Or Is Rt the Fourth R?" *Educational Leadership* 35 (November 1977): 139.

7. National Center for Education Statistics, *Course Offerings*, pp. 44, xvi.

___ chapter four ___

1. Howard Gardner, *Frames of Mind: The Theory of Multiple Intelligences* (New York: Basic Books, 1983).

2. Much of the information conveyed here is from presentations at the Conference on Artistic Intelligences held at the School of Music at the University of South Carolina, Columbia, in April 1989. The papers presented there were published in William J. Moody, ed., *Artistic Intelligences: Implications for Education* (New York: Teachers College Press, 1990).

3. Howard Gardner, *Multiple Intelligences: The Theory in Practice* (New York: Basic Books, 1983), p. 141.

4. Ibid., pp. 141, 142.

5. Ibid., pp. 142, 143.

6. Ibid., p. 148.

7. Ibid., p. 149.

8. Ibid., p. 153.

9. Gardner, *Frames of Mind*, p. 71.

— chapter six —

1. Charles Taylor, *Multiculturalism* (Princeton, NJ: Princeton University Press, 1994), p. 30.

2. Ibid., pp. 32, 33.

3. Nelson Goodman, "The Way the World Is," in E. Credo and W. Feinberg, eds., *Knowledge and Values in Social and Educational Research* (Philadelphia: Temple University Press, 1982), pp. 129–36.

4. Irwin Edman, *Arts and the Man: An Introduction to Aesthetics* (New York: New American Library, 1949), p. 53.

5. Clifford Geertz, *The Interpretation of Cultures* (London: Hutchinson, 1975), p. 448.

6. Taylor, *Multiculturalism*, p. 78.

7. Brice Marden, quoted in Taylor McNeil, "Talent in the Air," *Arts*, Summer–Fall 1994, p. 4.

8. Mary J. Reiching, "On the Question of Values in Music Education," *Philosophy of Music Education Review* 1 (Fall 1993): 120.

— chapter seven —

1. Ron Berger, "Building a School Culture of High Standards" (unpublished paper).

— chapter eight —

1. These statistics are from the 1992/1993 Professional Opera Survey conducted by OPERA America and published in *Outlook*, October 1994, p. 13.

2. See James Davison Hunter, *Culture Wars: The Struggle to Define America* (New York: Basic Books, 1991), particularly the chapters on education and media and the arts.

3. Malcolm Gladwell, "Downbeat in Funding Sounds Sour Note for Small-City Arts," *Washington Post*, September 6, 1994, p. A3.

4. National Endowment for the Arts, "Audiences—Overview: 1987–1991 Planning Document" (unpublished document, National Endowment for the Arts, 1985), p. 4.

5. This survey, conducted by the now-defunct Association for Classical Music, polled almost 900 students in nine cities.

6. National Endowment for the Arts, "Survey of Public Participation in the Arts" cited in National Endowment for the Arts, *Toward Civilization: A Report on Arts Education* (Washington, D.C.: Government Printing Office, 1988), p. 33.

﹍ chapter nine ﹍

1. Charles Leonhard, Council for Research in Music Education, *The Status of Arts Education in American Public Schools* (Urbana: University of Illinois, 1991), pp. 14, 174, and 176.

2. Ibid., 16–21.

3. Judith M. Burton, "Art Education and the Plight of the Culture: A Status Report," *Aesthetic Education in the USA*, p. 18.

4. National Center for Education Statistics, *Course Offerings and Enrollments in the Arts and the Humanities at the Secondary School Level* (Washington, D.C.: Government Printing Office, 1984).

5. These and the following statistics are from ibid.

6. Jacqueline Trescott, "NEA Chief Endorses Artistic Freedom," *Washington Post*, October 12, 1994, p. C2.

7. Phillip Lopate, "Time as an Ally: Homage to Aunt Forgie," *Teachers & Writers Magazine* 8 (Winter 1977): 3.

8. See Music Educators National Conference, *The School Music Program: A New Vision* (Reston, Va.: Music Educators National Conference, 1994).

9. Lawrence Kramer, in a letter in response to Charles Rosen's, "Music a La Mode," *New York Review of Books*, September 22, 1994, p. 74.

10. Nellie McCaslin, *Creative Drama in the Classroom*, 4th ed. (New York: Longman, 1984), p. 11.

11. Barbara Salisbury Wills, letter to the author, August 18, 1994. Also, see her *Theatre Arts in the Elementary Classroom* (New Orleans: Anchorage Press, 1986).

12. Getty Center for Education in the Arts, *Beyond Creating: The Place for Art in America's Schools* (Los Angeles: Getty Center for Education in the Arts, 1985), preface.

13. Ibid., p. 3.

14. The term *discipline based*, originally used to denote a broader and more academic approach to education in art, is now being applied across the arts.

15. Jean Johnson and John Immerwahr, *First Things First: What Americans Expect from the Public Schools* (New York: Public Agenda Foundation, 1994), p. 19.

16. Robin Longman, "Creating Art: Your Rx for Health, Part II, *American Artist*, June 1994, p. 68.

17. For more detailed information, contact Very Special Arts, Education Office, John F. Kennedy Center for the Performing Arts, Washington, D.C. 20566; (202) 628–2800.

18. Federal Bureau of Investigation, *Crime in the U.S., 1991: Juveniles and Violence 1965–1990* (Washington, D.C.: Government Printing Office, 1991).

19. Ibid., p. 10. See also the "Phi Delta Kappa/Gallup Survey of the Public's Attitudes Toward Public Schools," a phone survey of 1,326 adults, September 1994.

20. Steve L. Dash, "Rosa Lee & Me," *Washington Post*, October 2, 1994, p. C1.

21. Ibid., p. C3.

22. Ibid.

23. Robert Winter, *Igor Stravinsky's "Rite of Spring,"* [interactive multimedia compact disk] (Los Angeles: Voyager, 1993).

24. See *The Imagination Machines* [video] (Los Angeles: Getty Center for Education in the Arts, 1991).

⎯ chapter ten ⎯

1. John I. Goodlad, *A Place Called School: Prospects for the Future* (New York: Mc-Graw-Hill, 1984), p. 67.

2. Thomas Ewens, "Beyond Getty: An Analysis of *Beyond Creating: The Place for Arts in American Schools,"* in Thomas Ewens, ed., *Discipline in Art Education: An Interdisciplinary Symposium* (Providence: Rhode Island School of Design), pp. 40, 41, 49.

3. Ibid., p. 3.

4. Maxine Greene, "Creating, Experiencing, and Sense-Making: The Art World in the Schools" paper presented at a Columbia University symposium, Arts Curricula in Transition, July 1986), p. 5.

5. College Board, *Academic Preparation in the Arts: Teaching for Transition from High School to College* (New York: College Board 1985), p. 62.

6. National Endowment for the Arts, *Toward Civilization: A Report on Arts Education* (Washington, D.C.: Government Printing Office, 1988), p. 13.

7. Ernest L. Boyer, *High School: A Report on Secondary Education in America* (New York: Harper & Row, 1983), p. 95.

8. Broudy's statements are from Charles Fowler, ed., *The Crane Symposium: Toward an Understanding of the Teaching and Learning of Musical Performance* (Potsdam, N.Y.: State University College of Arts and Science, 1987), chaps. 11, 12.

9. Judith Hanna, ed., *Dropout Prevention: Literacy and the Performing and Visual Arts* (Washington, D.C.: Department of Education, Office of Research and Improvement, 1991).

10. Elliot W. Eisner, *Cognition and Curriculum: A Basis for Deciding What to Teach* (New York: Longman, 1982), p. 55.

11. Harry S. Broudy, "Praise May Not Be Enough," in Fowler, ed., *Crane Symposium,* p. 39.

12. Goodlad, *Place Called School,* p. 350.

13. Boyer, *High School,* pp. 305–6.

14. Goodlad, *Place Called School, p.* 353.

15. Junius Eddy, "Beyond Enrichment: Developing a Comprehensive Community-School Arts Program," in Jerome J. Hausman, ed., *Arts and the Schools,* (New York: McGraw-Hill, 1980), p. 164.

⎯ chapter eleven ⎯

1. Fred Inglis, "The Narratives of Culture and the Education of the Citizen," in *Media Theory: An Introduction* (Cambridge, Mass.: Blackwell 1990), p. 175.

2. David Rieff, "A Global Culture?" *World Policy Journal* 10 (Winter 1993–1994): p. 80.

3. Ibid.

4. Arts, Education and American Panel, *Coming to Our Senses: The Significance of the Arts for American Education* (New York: McGraw-Hill, 1977), p. 255.

5. Ibid., p. 189.

6. E. D. Hirsch Jr., *Cultural Literacy: What Every American Needs to Know* (Boston: Houghton Mifflin, 1987), p. 96.

7. Ibid., p. 98.

8. Barbara Jordan, "The Arts: A Necessity for Our Economy and Our Souls" [1993 Nancy Hanks Lecture], *Washington Post*, March 21, 1993, p. G11.

9. Arthur M. Schlesinger, Jr., *The Disuniting of America: Reflections on a Multicultural Society* (Knoxville, Tenn.: Whittle Books, 1991), p. 79, 80.

10. Jacques Barzun, *The Use and Abuse of Art*, Bollingen Series 35, vol. 22 (Princeton, N.J.: Princeton University Press, 1974).

11. For an exploration of the complexities of multicultural education, see David J. Elliott, "Music as Culture: Toward a Multicultural Concept of Arts Education," *Journal of Aesthetic Education* 24 (Spring 1990): pp. 147–66.

12. Schlesinger, *Disuniting of America*, p. 80.

13. Lynne V. Cheney, *American Memory: A Report on the Humanities in the Nation's Public Schools* (Washington, D.C.: National Endowment for the Humanities, 1987), p. 11.

ᐟ chapter twelve ᐠ

1. Judith M. Burton, "Art Education and the Plight of the Culture: A Status Report," *Aesthetic Education in the USA*, pp. 24–25.

2. John I. Goodlad, *A Place Called School: Prospects for the Future* (New York: McGraw-Hill, 1984), p. 220.

3. Burton, "Art Education," p. 25.

4. This account is from Linda Palazzola, fifth-grade teacher, P.S. 116, CSD 2, in Manhattan.

5. Burton, "Art Education."

6. J. W. Getzels and P. W. Jackson, "The Highly Intelligent and the Highly Creative Adolescent," in C. W. Taylor and F. Benson, eds., *Scientific Creativity: Its Recognition and Development* (Huntington, N.Y.: Krieger, 1975), p. 169.

7. *Share the Music* (New York: Macmillan/McGraw-Hill, 1995), book 6, pp. 41, 85, 131, 183, 231.

8. OPERA America, *Adventures in Music and Words: The Opera Experience* (Washington, D.C.: OPERA America, 1990).

ᐟ chapter thirteen ᐠ

1. Charles Leonhard, *The Status of Arts Education in American Public Schools* (Urbana: Council for Research in Music Education, University of Illinois, 1991), p. 195.

2. Jack E. Schaeffer, "More Music for More Students: Broadening the Base of Involvement," in *NASSP Bulletin* (Reston, Va.: National Association of Secondary School Principals, 1975), p. 19.

3. Music Educators National Conference, *National Standards for Arts Education: What Every Young American Should Know and Be Able to Do in the Arts* (Reston, Va.: Music Educators National Conference, 1994).

4. Ibid., pp. 15, 16.

5. Ibid, p. 59.

6. Ibid., p. 61.

7. Elliot Eisner (speech delivered at the Young Audiences 1993 National Conference, Atlanta, April 1993), p. 10.

8. Ibid., p. 11.

9. Ibid., p. 13.

10. Mathematical Association of America, *Professional Standards for Teaching Mathematics, Executive Summary* (Reston, Va.: Mathematical Association of America, 1991), p. 4.

11. Elliot W. Eisner, "The Federal Reform of Schools: Looking for the Silver Bullet," in NAEA *Advisory* (Reston, Va.: National Art Education Association 1992), p. 2.

12. Council of Chief State School Officers, with the College Board and the Council for Basic Education, *Arts Education Assessment Framework* [prepublication edition] (Washington, D.C.: Council of Chief State School Officers, 1994).

13. Joy E. Lawrence, "New Ideas for the High School 'Music Appreciation' Class," *General Music*, Spring 1989, p. 19.

14. Edith Borroff, "A New Look at Teaching Music History," *Music Educators Journal* 79 (December 1992): 41.

━ chapter fourteen ━

1. Florida Department of Education, 1990.

2. College Board, *Profile of SAT and Achievement Test Takers for 1990, 1991, 1992, and 1993* (New York: College Board, 1994).

3. Ibid.

4. Gertrude J. Spilka, with Charles Fowler and Bernard J. McMullan, *Understanding How the Arts Contribute to Excellent Education* (Philadelphia: Organization and Management Group, 1991).

━ chapter fifteen ━

1. Stanley M. Elam, "The 22nd Annual Gallup Poll of the Public's Attitudes Toward the Public Schools," *Phi Delta Kappan*, September 1990, p. 49.

2. Stanley M. Elam, Lowell C. Rose, and Alec M. Gallup, "The 26th Annual Phi Delta Kappa/Gallup Poll of the Public's Attitudes Toward the Public Schools," *Phi Delta Kappan*, September 1994, p. 51.

3. Enrollments in music education in institutions of higher education have been declining since 1971—almost 27 percent in the ten years from 1971 to 1981. See Henry E. Putsch, "AICA Survey of Current Trends in Art Education," in *Art Education in the Schools: Strategies for Action* (Washington, D.C.: Alliance of Independent

Colleges of Arts, 1984), p. 22. See also Daniel V. Steinel comp., *Music and Music Education: Data and Information* (Reston, Va.: Music Educators National Conference, 1984), p. 27, chart 2.3.

4. Charles Leonhard, *The Status of Arts Education in American Public Schools* (Urbana: Council for Research in Music Education, University of Illinois, 1991), pp. 174, 175, 178, 179.

5. American Council for the Arts, "Americans Speak out on the Place of the Arts in the Education of Their Children," in *Americans and the Arts VI* (New York: American Council for the Arts, 1992), pp. 16–19.

6. "The New Sound of Hate," *Washington Post*, July 12, 1992, p. G1.

7. For a list of recommendations for outward and for inward change, see Charles Fowler, "Finding the Way to Be Basic," in Richard J. Colwell, ed., *Basic Concepts in Music Education, II* (Boulder: University of Colorado Press, 1991), pp. 24, 25.

8. National Council of Teachers of Mathematics, *Executive Summary: Curriculum and Evaluation Standards for School Mathematics* (Reston, Va.: National Council of Teachers of Mathematics, 1989), p. 6.

9. Teaching appreciation for science is considered so important by the National Science Foundation that half its educational funds are now spent on elementary and middle school education.

10. See Richard Wolkomir, "Putting a New Spin on Pitching Science to Kids," *Smithsonian*, April 1993, p. 108.

11. Paul Lehman, *Music in Today's Schools: Rationale and Commentary*, Reston, Va.: Music Educators National Conference, 1987), pp. 7, 8.

12. See Charles Fowler, "Redefining the Mission of Music Education: Teaching the Value of Music" (speech delivered at the University of Maryland's symposium "Winds of Change," April 1993).

13. Elliot W. Eisner, "Music in the Active Nature of Learning," in Charles B. Fowler, ed., *Symposium '85 Report: Music Is Essential to Quality Education* (Austin: Texas Music Educators Association, 1986), p. 19.

— chapter sixteen —

1. Constance J. Usova and George M. Usova, "Integrating Art and Language Arts for First Grade At-Risk Children," *Reading Improvement* 3 (Summer 1993): 117–21.

2. Ramon C. Cortines, *The Arts: Partnerships as a Catalyst for Educational Reform* (Sacramento: California Department of Education, 1994), p. 9.

3. Letter to author, November 8, 1994.

4. Jana Zinser, *Reinventing Education* (Denver: National Conference of State Legislatures, 1994), p. 8.

5. Arts Education Partnership Working Group, *The Power of the Arts to Transform Education: An Agenda for Action* (Washington, D.C.: Arts Education Partnership Working Group, 1993), p. 7.

6. Much of this information is from a letter February 20, 1995, and other materials assembled by David O'Fallon.

7. Zinser, *Reinventing Education*, p. 4.

8. Much of this information is from Ceryl M. Kane, *Prisoners of Time* (report of the National Education Commission on Time and Learning, Washington, D.C.: Government Printing Office, 1994).

9. This information is from a description of the program circulated by the Chicago Arts Partnerships in Education.

10. Michael Fullan, "Harnessing the Forces of Educational Reform," in *Teacher-to-Teacher* (Los Angeles: Galef Institute, 1995), vol. 3, no. 2.

▬ chapter seventeen ▬

1. These statistics are from C. Emily Feistritzer, *Cheating Our Children: Why We Need School Reform* (Washington, D.C.: National Center for Education Information, 1985).

2. James Davison Hunter, "America at War with Itself," *Washington Post*, September 13, 1992, p. C1. See also his *Culture Wars: The Struggle to Define America* (New York: Basic Books, 1991).

3. National Education Association, *An Excellent Teacher in Every Classroom* (Washington, D.C.: National Education Association, 1985).

4. Carnegie Forum on Education and the Economy, *A Nation Prepared: Teachers for the 21st Century* (Hyattsville, Md.: Carnegie Foundation, 1986).

5. Music Educators National Conference, *Music Teacher Education: Partnership and Process* (Reston, Va.: Music Educators National Conference, 1986).

▬ chapter eighteen ▬

1. R. Craig Sautter, "An Arts Education School Reform Strategy," *Phi Delta Kappan*, February 1994, p. 433.

2. See National Endowment for the Arts, "Arts and Education: A Partnership Agenda," report of a conference, March 25–27, 1992.

3. See Gerri Spilka, with Charles Fowler and Bernard J. McMullan, *Understanding How the Arts Contribute to Excellent Education* (Philadelphia: Organization and Management Group, 1991).

4. Council of Chief State School Officers, with the College Board and the Council for Basic Education, *Arts Education Assessment Framework* [prepublication edition] (Washington, D.C.: Council of Chief State School Officers, 1994), p. 10.

5. John I. Goodlad, *A Place Called School: Prospects for the Future* (New York: McGraw-Hill, 1984), p. 142.

6. Ibid., p. 143.

7. Elliot W. Eisner, *Cognition and Curriculum: A Basis for Deciding What to Teach* (New York: Longman, 1982), p. 81.

8. Cheryl M. Kane, *Prisoners of Time Research* [report of the National Education Commission on Time and Learning] (Washington, D.C.: Government Printing Office, 1994), p. 18.

9. Goodlad, *Place Called School*, p. 134.

10. Ibid., pp. 134–36.

11. Ibid., pp. 136–37.

12. Ibid., p. 121.

13. *Blue Ribbon Schools: Outstanding Practices in the Arts, 1989–90 and 1990–91,* (Washington, D.C.: Department of Education, 1992), pp. 1, 2.

⎯ chapter nineteen ⎯

1. According to the *Digest of Educational Statistics 1983-84* (Washington, D.C.: Government Printing Office, 1985).

2. C. Emily Feistritzer, ed., *The American Teacher* (Washington, D.C.: Feistritzer Publications, 1983), p. 1.

3. Council of Chief State School Officers, with the College Board and the Council for Basic Education, *Arts Education Assessment Framework* [prepublication edition] (Washington, D.C.: Council of Chief State School Officers, 1994).

4. National Commission on Excellence in Education, *A Nation at Risk: The Imperative for Educational Reform* (Washington, D.C.: Government Printing Office, 1983), p. 33.

5. Kenneth H. Phillips, "Utilitarian vs. Aesthetic," *Music Educators Journal,* March 1983, p. 30.

6. "Looking for a Renaissance: The Campaign to Revive Education in the Arts," *U.S. News & World Report,* March 30, 1992, pp. 52, 53.

7. Music Educators National Conference, *Growing up Complete: The Imperative for Music Education* (Reston, Va.: Music Educators National Conference, 1991), p. xii.

INDEX

References to figures are indicated by an *f* after the page number. References to illustrations are indicated by an *i* after the page number. References to tables are indicated by a *t* after the page number. Headings not otherwise identified refer to arts education; for example, Academic content refers to the academic content of arts education programs.